LANGUAGE BROKERS

ARTICULATIONS STUDIES IN RACE, IMMIGRATION, AND CAPITALISM

EDITORS
Cedric de Leon
Pawan Dhingra

LANGUAGE BROKERS

Children of Immigrants Translating Inequality and Belonging for Their Families

HYEYOUNG KWON

STANFORD UNIVERSITY PRESS
Stanford, California

Stanford University Press
Stanford, California

Printed in the United States of America on acid-free, archival-quality paper.

Library of Congress Cataloging-in-Publication Data
Names: Kwon, Hyeyoung, author.
Title: Language brokers : children of immigrants translating inequality and belonging for their families / Hyeyoung Kwon.
Other titles: Articulations (Stanford, Calif.)
Description: Stanford, California : Stanford University Press, 2024. | Series: Articulations : studies in race, immigration, and capitalism | Includes bibliographical references and index.
Identifiers: LCCN 2023050351 (print) | LCCN 2023050352 (ebook) | ISBN 9781503638686 (cloth) | ISBN 9781503639461 (paperback) | ISBN 9781503639478 (ebook)
Subjects: LCSH: Children of immigrants—California, Southern—Language. | Mexican American children—California, Southern—Language. | Korean American children—California, Southern—Language. | Immigrant families—California, Southern. | Immigrants—California, Southern—Social conditions. | Parent and child—California, Southern. | Translating and interpreting—Social aspects—California, Southern.
Classification: LCC JV6920 .K76 2024 (print) | LCC JV6920 (ebook) | DDC 305.9/06912097949—dc23/eng/20231221
LC record available at https://lccn.loc.gov/2023050351
LC ebook record available at https://lccn.loc.gov/2023050352

Cover design: Lindy Kasler
Cover mural: *Ascendancy*, San Miguel, Chile

CONTENTS

PREFACE

When I was fourteen years old, my friends showed up to the airport in Seoul, to say goodbye to me. Some of them began sobbing as I waved goodbye before entering the security screening area. But I was excited. After all, my family was moving to Los Angeles, the city that was full of Hollywood's glitz and glamour. I did not sleep for the duration of the fourteen-hour flight. Nothing could change how I felt, even though my mom spent most of the time weeping next to me. Perhaps she knew what kind of challenges were awaiting us, but I was too excited to ask many questions.

My maternal aunt had been the first person in my family to immigrate to the United States, in 1975. After graduating from a university that was well known for nurse training in Seoul, a provision in the 1965 Immigration Act—designed to recruit professionals trained in high-demand occupations from overseas—enabled my aunt to become a nurse in Los Angeles. She gained permanent resident status through employment sponsorship and became a US citizen several years later, at which point family reunification policies in the United States allowed her to sponsor my grandmother, my uncles, and my family's visas.

There was a clear difference between my aunt's migration path and my family's journey to the United States, however. While my aunt had the skills that the United States desired, my parents lacked training to seek employment in occupations that pay decent incomes. They were also without the economic means to start a small business in the United States, as many other Korean immigrants do. We didn't even have enough savings to rent an apartment on our own. Instead, my parents, my younger sister, and I stayed with my grandmother, in her one-bedroom apartment in Koreatown.

The neighborhood where we lived in Koreatown was not the America that I dreamt of. The first school I attended, where almost 90 percent of students qualified for free or reduced-priced lunches and the majority of students were Latinx, was deprived of resources. Security guards positioned at the school entrance checked for weapons and drugs. In my ESL classes, I competed with other students for used textbooks, which were covered with doodles from previous students. I began learning Spanish before English while waiting in long free-lunch lines that snaked around the cafeteria. Several years later, however, I experienced culture shock for a second time. When my family moved to an upper-middle-class suburb, where the majority of students were White or Asian American, less than 10 percent of students qualified for free or reduced-price lunches. In this neighborhood, million-dollar homes with lush green lawns were commonplace. Students carried SAT books and violins into the school without being subjected to pat downs and searches.

Unlike my family, who rented a small apartment, those around me lived in sprawling two-story houses complete with swimming pools. As my classmates changed into cheerleading outfits and soccer uniforms, I could be found in the restroom, putting on my waitress outfit for my after-school job. My Korean-monolingual mother—now a single parent who worked until 11:00 p.m.—always told me that I should go to college, but she did not know how to navigate the college application process. Instead, I sought help from my classmates, who—upon discovering how little I knew about college—began laughing about how different my family was in comparison to other "Asians" at the school.

When I was not doing my homework or supplementing my parents' meager wages by working as a server at a restaurant, I translated for monolingual family members. My parents and extended family often relied on my bilingual skills to speak with doctors, teachers, social workers, landlords, and other English-speaking adults. Just like the children of immigrants whose perspectives are highlighted in this book, I did not think twice about whether I should offer to help—even when translating interfered with my ability to study for tests or complete homework assignments on time.

One time, I accompanied my uncle, who was a taxi driver, to the emergency room. Like many working-class immigrants, he did not have health insurance or paid time off from work. Instead, he lived with pain and postponed treatment until he began coughing up blood. When my sister and I arrived at the crowded hospital, the doctor told us that he suspected that my uncle had tuberculosis and would need to be placed in quarantine. Another doctor reassured us that our uncle would be okay and encouraged us to leave. My uncle died of heart attack shortly after I left for work. He was only forty-four years old.

I spent the next several years wondering whether my uncle would still be alive if I had stayed at the hospital that day. Although the ER was in a low-income neighborhood where the majority spoke a language other than English, I hadn't observed any doctors or nurses communicating with other patients in Korean. Had my uncle been able to communicate any pain he might have felt to the doctor in the moments leading up to his heart attack? What if the hospital staff neglected him and left him in an isolated room because the ER had been so busy? Did the doctor encourage us to leave because he assumed the ER wasn't a safe place for "kids" like us? I never found out the answers to these questions, but the anger and confusion I felt as working-class daughter of immigrants left me with an intense curiosity to understand how multiple forms of inequality shape the lives of working-class children of immigrants. It was for this reason that I entered the field of sociology.

Although I was determined to study the lives of young people like me, I felt frustrated by the initial literature reviews I conducted in graduate school. I quickly discovered that sociological studies on immigration often overlook children's contributions to their families and the larger society. Because children's work is largely assumed to be a hallmark of America's past, most existing scholarship on children of immigrants explicitly or implicitly focused on determining whether they are absorbing American values and assimilating into the mainstream. If children's contributions to their families are mentioned at all, the research mostly focuses on the number of "chores" that immigrant youth—especially daughters—are expected to complete. And yet, over time, I began to find frameworks that more fully accounted for the multiple forms of inequality working-class children of immigrants encounter in the United States. While reading work by scholars such as Patricia Hill Collins, W. E. B Du Bois, and bell hooks, for example, I began to see the intersecting forms of inequalities shaping language brokers' lives. Rather than being only a site of oppression, these scholars helped me identify ways that the margin is also a social location that enables resistance. When paired with childhood studies, theories of symbolic interactionalism, and sociology of culture, I was able to more fully identify ways that young people creatively use their social position and culture to achieve specific ends during translation encounters.

By bridging these different subfields, *Language Brokers* shows how children of immigrants navigate systematic and intersecting forms of inequality to ensure their families' access to social provisions in the US. And considering that many youth I spoke with were eager to be "heard," it is my hope that, in writing this book, I can serve as their public "language broker." By translating the lives of working-class immigrant youth of color to the broader public, this book identifies, in vivid detail, the incredible resilience young people cultivate when attempting to broker belonging on behalf of their families.

ACKNOWLEDGMENTS

The time has finally arrived for me to acknowledge the individuals who have made this book possible, a moment that I've been eagerly anticipating for quite some time. My heart is brimming with gratitude and a profound sense of humility for the invaluable wisdom, unwavering support, and encouragement that they have generously bestowed upon me throughout this endeavor.

My heartfelt gratitude extends to the children of immigrants who graciously took part in this study and shared their poignant narratives. These remarkable young people, despite their busy lives filled with multiple responsibilities and challenges posed by flawed institutions, generously devoted their time and, in many cases, encouraged me to see this book through to completion. Their resilience and poignant stories truly served as a source of motivation.

I extend my deepest gratitude to my graduate committee. To Leland Saito, who has been an unwavering cheerleader throughout many years, offering his critical insights while consistently encouraging me to prioritize my well-being and health. It was through his humanity and generous spirit that I not only survived graduate school but also thrived. To Sharon Hays who provided incisive comments, profound empathy, and encouragement that I needed to complete this book. I continue to eagerly look forward to our phone dates, text messages filled with hearts and photos, and "therapeutic sessions," where I find solace to talk about my struggles. To Pierrette Hondagneu-Sotelo, who taught me the art of conducting qualitative research. The project born from her class later evolved into my first publication, and Pierrette remained a guiding light throughout the journey of this book, many years after her initial class. To Veronica Terriquez for teaching me the intricacies of writing for academic journals. It was through our collaboration on a paper—and later writing an early version of this work under her guidance—that I truly honed my skills in crafting literature reviews, conducting critical analyses, and presenting findings persuasively. And to George Sanchez, who provided me with razor-sharp feedback on my work despite his demanding schedule.

I express sincere thanks to my mentors and colleagues within the Department of Sociology, the Center for Research on Race and Ethnicity in Society, and the Asian American Studies Center at Indiana University (IU). Special thanks to Dina Okamoto, who guided me through the complex process of publication, and provided unwavering encouragement as I navigated my postdoctoral fellowship and later my very first tenure-track position amid personal crises. I could not have asked for a more exceptional mentor and friend, and her steadfast belief in my scholarship has consistently empowered me to rise resiliently, even during the most vulnerable moments in my life. Brian Powell has been a constant pillar of support from my very first day at IU. Brian's strong commitment to pushing for excellence, providing guidance at every critical turn, and his unshakable belief in recognizing the potential within this book—long before I could envision its completion—have been a constant wellspring of inspiration. Tim Hallett's helping hand, genuine mentorship, and invaluable advice came precisely when I needed them the most. I cannot overstate my appreciation for his insightful comments on my drafts over coffee, the generous emails checking up on me, and his guidance during the often-anxious journey of junior faculty life in academia. Jennifer Lee, a superstar mentor and teacher, provided unceasing support, strong advocacy, and invaluable guidance. Her caring heart, thoughtful advice, and strong spirit have been a source of strength. I extend my heartfelt appreciation to Youngjoo Cha, who provided an empathetic ear during moments when I felt like I could not carry on. Her warm emails, sincere conversations, and unyielding advocacy felt like a lifeline during times of vulnerability. To Patricia McManus, Jane McLeod, Fabio Rojas, Art Alderson, and Eliza Pavalko for their exceptional leadership that played an essential role in propelling me forward. To Anna Mueller, Keera Allendorf, Peggy Thoits, Pamela Jackson, Jennifer

Barber, Brea Perry, and Ethan Michelson for essential support as I navigated the formidable challenges of academia. Finally, to my junior colleagues at IU. They sustained and nourished my spirit with laughter, shared happy hours, coffee chats, and uplifting camaraderie. To BK Lee (and his partner Jisun), Koji Chavez (and his partner Ashley), Elaine Hernandez, Mike Schultz, and Celene Raynolds; your friendship has been invaluable.

In the intricate tapestry of my academic journey, there were other mentors who played pivotal roles in my growth. I can never thank Jessica Calarco enough for the countless ways in which she has supported me, starting from my early days as a postdoctoral fellow at IU. Jess's incredible generosity, deep empathy, vibrant spirit, and her unbridled passion for research, mentoring, and teaching have been a humbling source of inspiration. Rhacel Parreñas appeared miraculously at the crucial moments, offering much-needed mentorship. Her guidance in navigating academia along with her enduring belief in the value of my scholarship have been vital. It was through Marjorie Faulstich Orellana's graduate seminar at UCLA that I delved into the world of language brokers, and her pioneering scholarship and mentorship served as the springboard for the development of my project. William Corsaro, a trailblazer in the sociology of childhood shared his wisdom and strong encouragement throughout my academic journey. I am profoundly grateful to Min Zhou, Jody Vallejo, Pawan Dhingra, Anthony Ocampo, Kyeyoung Park, Don Nakanishi, and Michelle Moyd for their mentorship at various stages of my academic career.

I had the privilege of presenting the initial version of this book to audiences at Dartmouth, the University of Toronto, the University of Arizona, Northwestern, UCLA, University of Louisville, and University of Pennsylvania. I am grateful for the critical feedback I received from those audiences. I'm particularly thankful to Hae Yeon Choo for her insights and encouragement during my visit. Portions of this book also appeared in *Social Problems* and *American Journal of Sociology*.

Wholehearted thanks to my exceptional editor, Marcela Maxfield, for her steady belief in this project from the very moment that we first discussed it. Marcela has been a constant presence, persistently and gently pushing this book forward while offering crucial advice and expertise. Marcela, a million thanks for your enthusiasm and guidance and for finding reviewers who have provided invaluable feedback on this book. I also appreciate the meticulous work of the entire production team at Stanford University Press in preparing this manuscript for production.

I am forever thankful to my friends who have provided solace and companionship over the years. To Minwoo Jung, Carolyn Choi, Mai Thai, Emir Estrada, Jess Butler, May Lin, Phi Su, Jennifer Candipan, Robert Chlala, Kushan Dasgupta, Radheeka Jayasundera, Tristan Ivory, Cara Caddoo, Edson Rodriguez, Denia Garcia, Glenda Flores, Jazmin Muro, Dorainne Green, Evren Savci, Susan Yoon, Tracy Quach, Betty Song, Max Greenberg, and Jeff Sacha, I extend my heartfelt gratitude for their support on this academic journey. To Kelly Woo, Jessica Suh, Yoonjoo Lee, Jaeeun Kim, and Katie Lee, who shared my childhood and teenage years in the United States. I cannot imagine a life without their love and friendship.

With deep appreciation, I acknowledge my family, including my aunts, uncles, cousins, and the Lin family, for their steadfast love and strength. I am especially thankful for Ma, Mei Lin, for raising a compassionate son and for her firm support throughout the years. Cathy Kim, my cousin, deserves special recognition. She not only provided me with much-needed sanity throughout my academic journey through countless drink nights, trips, and chats, but she also facilitated my access to healthcare providers for this project. My parents, Seoock Kim and Sangik Kwon, hold a special place of honor in my acknowledgments. Despite my mother's demanding work schedule that often had her returning home late at night, her selflessness displayed no bounds, and it is through her trust in me and her sacrifices that I stand here today. Thank you, umma, for raising me to be a resilient woman. I am also grateful for my dad, for his life, and for his indomitable spirit. He has remained strong (at least in front of his daughters), even when at times the odds seemed stacked against him. I cherish every moment I get to spend with him. My parents' immense pride in me serves as a constant source of motivation.

My deepest gratitude is reserved for my dear friend Michela Musto. Michela's extraordinary optimism, unwavering resilience, discerning gaze, and infectious sense of humor have sustained me since the day we first crossed paths in graduate school. Whenever I felt adrift, exhausted, and on the verge of giving up, she offered me desperately needed support. She played a pivotal role in helping me refine my writing, from my earliest draft born out of unfinished fieldwork and job applications to numerous journal articles, ultimately culminating in this very book. Together, we forged a writing group that has persisted since our graduate school days. I am elated about the exceptional book that she is currently crafting and immensely proud of her remarkable accomplishments over the years. Without her, our enduring writing group, and the countless drafts that we collaboratively penned for "my" book, I would not be here. Michela, this book is dedicated to you for being the broker of belonging for me in academia. Thank you, friend.

I also wish to dedicate this book to my younger sister, Shinyoung Kwon. Within our family, my sister carries the weight of being the language broker, a role she has shouldered entirely on her own since I left California to pursue my career in Indiana. Many of the young people that I had the privilege of speaking with reminded me of my sister—resilient souls like her, who my mom often describes as the "happy virus." I cannot fathom my life without her presence, and I am immensely grateful for everything she does for our family and for the countless sacrifices that she makes to ensure our family remains joyful, stable, and not lost in this bewildering world. Thank you, sista!

Lastly, but certainly not least, I wish to dedicate this book to my partner, Winston Lin. It is difficult to express my appreciation for him without becoming emotional. We crossed paths when I embarked on my Ph.D. program, and as if all the support he gave me during my graduate career was not enough, he made the life-altering decision to relocate to Indiana for my job, leaving behind his family and friends. Still, I often channeled all my anxiety, fear, stress, and frustration onto him. I must acknowledge that our division of labor is unequal, and that when I am with him, the world seems to revolve around me. I cannot thank him enough for the countless sacrifices that he makes for my career and our relationship. I eagerly anticipate our future together and the memories we will create as we grow older. To my dear friend, life partner, and counselor, thank you for placing our relationship above all else. I love you.

LANGUAGE BROKERS

ONE BROKERING BELONGING

"Thanks for coming on. What's on your mind, Maggie?" asked Mina Kim, the host of KQED radio *Forum*, a live call-in show that broadcasts in the San Francisco Bay Area. It was the summer of 2022. The show, titled "Coronavirus Disproportionately Hits Latinos in California," focused on conditions children like Maggie were facing.

"Me están preguntando qué está en mi cabeza." Maggie promptly translated the host's question into Spanish for her mom before saying, "I'm worried that my mom and dad will get the coronavirus again."

Maggie was ten years old. By the time Maggie reached out to KQED, she and everyone else in her family had already contracted COVID-19. Her mother, who worked at McDonalds, was the first to get sick. Since Maggie's mother was about to return to work, she wanted to know whether it was possible to get COVID again. But since her mother primarily spoke Spanish, Maggie, who was bilingual, translated her mom's question into English in hopes of receiving information from the show's guest expert, a doctor. After the doctor assured Maggie that the chances of reinfection were low, the child translated this information into Spanish for her mother and hung up the phone.[1]

This exchange lasted less than three minutes, but many listeners heard their own experiences reflected within it. Adrianna Morga, a Mexican American and a KQED contributor, was among them. The tweet she posted on social media received over 29,000 likes and hundreds of responses in just a few days. It said, "As I heard Maggie asking her question about whether her parents could get COVID-19 more than once and telling Kim she was just ten years old, I unconsciously placed my hands on my chest and started to tear up."

"This was literally my whole childhood," one person who wrote in a reply. "I don't know if non-immigrants realise this but it's a pretty universal experience of basically all immigrant kids whose parents don't speak English confidently. We really were out here aged seven educating ourselves about government processes to translate and explain."

In a follow-up segment, KQED asked listeners directly whether Maggie's story resonated with them. Had they, too, found themselves "standing up" for their parents? The children of parents who had migrated to the US from Middle East, Latin America, Africa, and Asia flooded KQED's inbox to share their own experiences.

Although children of immigrants translated for their parents long before COVID-19, it was not a coincidence that Maggie's story gained traction as a global pandemic swept across the US. As hospitalizations and death rates skyrocketed, systematic inequality embedded in virtually every institution—including the welfare state, healthcare, workplaces, education, and housing—left communities of color most vulnerable to the crisis. While mostly middle-class White professionals set up home offices and gyms, the media began to highlight low-wage "essential" workers like Maggie's mother—those who were risking their lives to work in grocery stores, meatpacking factories, restaurants, warehouses, and hospitals. In this moment, many people appeared to realize for the first time that low-wage workers, most of whom are immigrants and people of color, help ensure the nation's survival.

Though COVID-19 brought the failures of American institutions into the spotlight, many working-class immigrants of color were already experiencing health crises, financial precarity, and under- or unemployment long before the pandemic. In a nation where the state has historically failed to provide all citizens with sufficient forms of support and resources, low-wage "essential" workers often lack access to adequate healthcare, safe and affordable housing, and paid family and medical leave. Many also struggle to meet the educational expectations required of their children's schools. It is for this reason that many children of immigrants, including those who flooded KQED's inbox, vividly describe "standing up" for their parents as a "universal experience."

Indeed, years before Maggie called into KQED, I spoke with Jungmi, a seventeen-year-old Korean American who immigrated to the US with her family when she was eight. When I asked her to list all the places that she translated for her parents, Jungmi didn't even know where to start.

"Oh, my gosh, are you serious? Like, everywhere you can think of. Let's see . . ." Jungmi momentarily trailed off before listing the DMV, the doctor's office, school, the police station, the immigration office, the emergency room, the bank, the Social Security office, and Macy's. Sometimes, she recalled, she'd spoken on the phone with their landlord, as well as representatives from car insurance, credit card, and cable companies. Just the other day, Jungmi had phoned the unemployment agency after her mother had been laid off. She translated her parents' mail and helped them fill out forms. Recently, Jungmi had filed a police report after someone had stolen her father's identity and began using his credit card and Social Security number.

"I wanted to do everything I could do," she said of shouldering these obligations.

As Jungmi continued, it became clear that translating extended far beyond simple verbal communication. She also spent a considerable amount of time making important decisions and anticipating her family's needs. For example, whereas at first she had sat down with her parents to translate their bills and letters into English, several years ago she had started to simply "take care" of the mail herself. This was easier than attempting to work around her parents' busy and unpredictable work schedules. It was clear that Jungmi's multitasking, planning, and organizational skills helped keep her family afloat. When her father had been a victim of identity theft, for example, she had assembled evidence that showed that her father had been working at the time the transactions occurred. Although she was frustrated that no one took her or her Korean monolingual dad and his young daughter seriously, she maintained control of her emotions to avoid saying the wrong thing to the credit card company. Instead of growing upset, she tried to be "firm" and "let them know that I know what I am talking about." Jungmi exhibited deep conviction as well as charisma and calm when describing her attempts at proving her father hadn't authorized the fraudulent charges on his credit card. "I don't take no as an answer. I am known as the fighter in the family because I have to get what I want, especially when I call the credit card companies. It's money issues," she said.

Five blocks away from Jungmi's home, I interviewed Eduardo, a fourteen-year-old Mexican American. The son of garment worker, his family was experiencing more financial precarity than most other youth who spoke with me. Despite working long hours, Eduardo's parents could not always pay for electricity and food, and the boy's perceived "family responsibility" seemed exceptionally difficult. During his interview, Eduardo recalled a time he accompanied his mother—who spent upwards of ten hours a day, six days a week hunched over a sewing machine—to a local emergency room after "serious back pain" prevented her from standing up. With Eduardo's assistance, she told the ER doctor that concerns about costly medical bills had prevented her from seeking treatment for the near constant headaches, eye strain, neck stiffness, and shoulder and back pain she had suffered for years. Eduardo did his best to temper his frustration when the doctor began mapping out suggestions for his mother's care. Since her employer didn't offer workers paid time off, Eduardo knew it would be impossible for his mother to attend—let alone afford—the doctor's recommended biweekly physical therapy appointments.

Similar to Jungmi, Eduardo's descriptions of translating revealed the multiple forms of inequality his family encountered. Several weeks prior to her hospital visit, Eduardo's mother had asked him to inquire about the unexpected fees in their bank statement. After speaking with the bank, he learned that she had incurred overdraft fees; a quick glance at her deposit history also revealed how little money his mother was earning.

"I could not believe that my mom did not have any money in her bank account," he said. "But I never asked her why." He knew asking such a question would humiliate her. So instead of telling his mother how much he worried about her, Eduardo pretended her financial situation was not a big deal. "I lowered my voice and politely asked them to reduce the fees," he said.

These were not the only times Eduardo's bilingual skills had given him a glimpse into the hardship his parents faced—nor the degree to which his skills were crucial for them. A few weeks earlier, Eduardo had translated an eviction notice his parents received. Shortly thereafter, the reason for their eviction became obvious. A developer had purchased their building and was going to demolish it. Every tenant in his apartment complex found a relocation notice tacked to their door. Because of his reputation as a smart bilingual kid, other tenants began knocking on his door and asking questions about the notice.

Despite their differences, both Jungmi and Eduardo told me it was often difficult balancing their family and school responsibilities during crisis situations, which required them to "drop everything" to help their parents navigate issues as varied and weighty as medical emergencies, legal problems, and housing instability. Jungmi, for example, could not complete her homework when her father's identity was stolen. Instead, she spent many hours at a crowded police station with her "panicking" father. Eduardo also missed school to take his injured mother to the emergency room. Navigating the bureaucratic hurdles of adult-centric, English-speaking institutions left both Jungmi and Eduardo feeling "overwhelmed" and "drained." And yet, this did not mean they would ever consider declining their parents' requests.

Indeed, when I asked Jungmi if she had ever considered telling her parents no, she looked at me like I was from a different planet. "Because they are my parents!" she exclaimed. Her voice rose as she said, "I love them. Plus, if I don't go with them, people are going to think that my parents are dumb."

Eduardo echoed Jungmi's reply when I asked him the same question. "Of course not!" he scoffed. "I feel that people look down on my mom because she can't speak English. I feel bad. I get angry."

Eduardo and Jungmi are smart, capable, resilient—and much like many other children living in the US. Today, nearly a quarter of US children have at least one immigrant parent,[2] and nearly two-thirds of these children's parents aren't fluent in English.[3] Among Korean and Mexican immigrant parents— such as those whose children I interviewed for this book—the numbers are even higher. Seventy-six and 81 percent, respectively, have limited English proficiency.[4] Even in US cities where non-English-speaking immigrant neighborhoods and communities help attract billions of dollars in tourism revenue annually, institutions routinely fail to offer immigrants adequate translation services. As a result, children, who often learn English faster than their parents, regularly serve as language brokers or communication liaisons between their parents and English-speaking adults in a variety of situations.[5]

Although a lack of translation services compels young people like Jungmi and Eduardo to serve as translators for their parents, their language brokering encompasses far more than verbal exchanges. After language brokers Jungmi and Eduardo stepped in to translate, they quickly learned that their family lacked access to affordable housing, high-quality healthcare, and jobs that paid a living wage with flexible work schedules. Language brokers keenly understand that gender, race, age, and class all intersect to shape the way

English-speaking agents perceived them and their parents. Jungmi, a Korean American girl, did not want to appear passive. Instead, she wanted to be a "fighter" and be "firm" with the institutional agents in order to be taken seriously when speaking for her father. Eduardo, a Mexican American boy, tried to sound "polite"—rather than appearing aggressive—when representing his mother.

Casting light on the invisible realities of working-class immigrant families, this book takes readers inside the daily lives of Mexican and Korean American immigrant families as youth use their bilingual skills to serve as their parents' language brokers. Through extensive interviews, including with youth and healthcare workers, and ethnographic observations within a police station, I show how, for children of immigrants, language brokering becomes a way to solve the structural problems their families face in a variety of encounters. In these ways, bilingual youth whose lives are structured by inequality come to understand how important their assistance is and strive to ensure their families' survival. The language brokers I met wanted to "do everything" to make sure their parents could access vital social provisions: they filled out unemployment benefits forms and police reports, spoke with landlords, reversed bank overdraft fees, negotiated for lower credit card payments, and spent hours in crowded emergency rooms. In doing so, these young people also blurred the boundary between "adulthood" and "childhood" as they attempted to present their immigrant parents—who were stereotyped as inassimilable and undeserving free riders of social welfare systems—as Americans who deserved full social membership.

CONSTRUCTING IMMIGRANTS OF COLOR AS A SOCIAL PROBLEM

Children's translation work has received considerable attention within mainstream discourses. These narratives, however, look very different from the outpouring support that ten-year-old Maggie received from other children of immigrants when she called into KQED. As Marjorie Orellana demonstrated,[6] most magazines and newspapers, including prominent newspapers like the *New York Times, Los Angeles Times,* and the *Chicago Sun-Times,* have highlighted the detrimental effects language brokering has on children.[7]

These stories typically follow a simple narrative: Skyrocketing numbers of adult immigrants from Asia and Latin America are moving to the United States. With their limited English proficiency, adult immigrants rely on their young, bilingual children to translate for them. The "experts" quoted in these stories—ranging from family therapists to social workers and educators— often criticize immigrant parents for allowing their children to perform this work. Not only do experts frequently argue that young people are inherently incompetent for this task due to their age (that is, they lack the ability to correctly interpret adult conversations, especially sophisticated medical or legal terminology), they also claim that language brokering forces "innocent" children to grow up too fast. Drawing on rhetoric that is designed to spark a moral panic, journalists report that children performing this task are exposed to "adult" topics such as family finances and, hypothetically, their parents' sexual practices and histories of sexual violence. These reports, in turn, fret that such exposure must naturally cause language brokers to long for "normal" childhoods.

Because language brokers learn about their parents' personal lives, journalists also express concern that their translating work upends the "normal" parent-child dynamic. Inevitably, translation is blamed not only for increasing conflict between children and their parents but also for diminishing parents' authority. Some of these articles cite examples of children who start reprimanding their parents for having insufficient English-speaking capabilities and parents who resent this role reversal. If parents try to regain the authority they have lost, one educator claimed, children look for "other avenues where they can again exercise authority." An article in the *New York Times* even reported that translating for his parents drove a child to join a gang.[8]

Fictional depictions of juvenile language brokers generally follow a similar narrative arc. An episode of the wildly successful medical drama television show *ER* (1994–2009) depicted both a young language broker and her immigrant Spanish-speaking mother as unintelligent and incompetent.[9] While translating medication dosing instructions that her Spanish-speaking mother received from her English-speaking doctor, the episode depicts a child who accidentally misinterprets the English word *one* as the Spanish word *once* (eleven). Although counting to ten is one of the first things people learn when speaking a new language and most people would probably think twice before consuming eleven pills, the mother unquestioningly follows her child's instructions. Shortly thereafter, she dies of an overdose. However preposterous the story, the message is clear: it is dangerous for children to shoulder important "adult" responsibilities they lack the capabilities to perform.

Sensationalized depictions of language brokering engender strong reactions from the broader public, but these narratives decontextualize language brokers' lives. These accounts overlook the structural conditions and systemic inequalities that prompt young people to begin serving as language brokers in the first place. Instead, these accounts focus primarily on individuals' supposed wrongdoings. Indeed, lacking important contextual information, readers often criticize immigrant parents for not speaking English. People often leave comments on stories about child language brokers that say things like "This all could be avoided by the parents not being lazy and learning how to speak the English language" and "If you want to come here and live a life in America, become an American. That means knowing English."

Similar narratives about the importance of learning English routinely crop up when I share findings about my work. One of the first times I spoke about language brokering in an undergraduate course, for example, a student raised his hand several minutes into my talk. "Is there a way to penalize the parents? Like, tax them?" he asked.

I asked the student to clarify his question. He explained that immigrant parents were putting their children in "harmful" situations, so he thought they should be penalized with a fine.

Although this student's views were extreme, audience members often pose similar questions and comments that more subtly blame immigrant parents for primarily speaking a language other than English. Even those who claim to understand how difficult it is to learn a new language often express a sense of pity toward children who are language brokers and think children would be better off if they were relieved of translating responsibilities. Mirroring popular discourse, they worry about the way language brokering might shape children's eventual well-being. One of the most common phrases I've heard is "Children shouldn't have such a difficult childhood."

These accounts, however, ignore the perspectives of children who actually serve as language brokers for their families. Indeed, when the aforementioned White student raised his hand and suggested that immigrant parents who relied on their children for language support should be penalized with tax, a group of immigrant students of color in the class appeared to be irritated. One Latinx student closed his eyes and loudly sighed. Another Latinx student shook her head. And when class was over, an Asian American student who translated for her parents told me that White students were often quick to criticize her parents if they learned about her childhood. Children of immigrants I interviewed for this project also recalled feeling frustrated by the way other Americans perceived them. Early on, they learned that society often takes a deficit perspective toward their families and childhood experiences.

For the most part, scholars studying immigrants and their children recognize that popular stories and newspaper articles covering the so-called problem of immigrant families are sensationalized and incomplete. Yet, surprisingly little research has examined the actual *work* that children of immigrants shoulder when navigating structural inequality in the US. Instead, when children are the focus of immigration literature, scholars tend to examine whether and how youth "assimilate" into US society. This body of literature—which initially emerged in the early twentieth century in the US[10]—has developed different insights and ways of measuring assimilation outcome over the years.[11] Nonetheless, the core focus of assimilation theory has remained largely the same.[12] Theorists have concentrated on understanding how children of immigrants fare in relation to "native-born" groups. While doing so, they regularly identify circumstances that prompt immigrant youth to retain or lose their ethnic culture, as well as the ways "American" culture changes their behaviors, family relationships, identity, and educational outcomes.

Assimilation theory, however, risks perpetuating some of the same value judgments that reporters and the broader public make. However unintentional it may be, asking whether immigrant families are similar to or different from the "mainstream" implies that immigrant families of color are fundamentally different from the "typical"—or White and middle-class—American family.[13] Furthermore, because this body of literature often overlooks important distinctions between the historical trajectories of European and non-European immigrants, existing research often pushes notions of resistance and racism into the background.

How, then, do we study the lives of children of immigrants, especially those who are living at the intersection of multiple and intersecting forms of inequality, beyond the scope of assimilation theory? To extend our understandings of immigrant youth's lives, I highlight the ways that the lives of children of immigrants are shaped and constrained by state-sanctioned forms of exclusion by drawing on literature on citizenship, intersectionality, and critical youth studies. As I show throughout this book, the youth I interviewed regularly encountered multiple and intersecting forms of inequality while serving as their parents' translators (and while living in the US in general). In contrast to mainstream depiction of language brokers' lives,[14] however, these youth rarely saw their familial roles as being reversed. Nor did they criticize their immigrant parents for "failing" to learn English and assimilate in the mainstream. In a nation where the state constantly fails to offer support, bilingual children of immigrants have developed creative solutions to problems including, but not limited to, inadequate translation assistance.

By bringing youth's perspectives into the conversation, this book will demonstrate that the moralistic, ethnocentric, and classed assumptions about a "proper" childhood, a "normal" family, or a deserving "American" help to obfuscate systematic forms of inequality. These ideals—which are deeply embedded in various institutions that working-class immigrant families navigate—shape how English-speaking adults perceive and interact with children of immigrants and their parents. They also inform young people's understandings of their families and goals for their futures. Ultimately, language brokering is a way for children of immigrants to present their families as deserving Americans in a society that regularly depicts immigrants of color as "undeserving" foreigners.

FAMILY STRATEGIES IN THE FACE OF LACK OF CITIZENSHIP: WHERE ARE THE CHILDREN?

People's lives are shaped and constrained by state-sanctioned forms of exclusion and inclusion, which I refer to as "citizenship" throughout this book. Two widely discussed aspects of citizenship are *civil citizenship*, or the right to own property and exercise individual freedom and justice, and *political citizenship*, which is the right to participate in governance and vote.[15] These rights are largely reserved for people who are born in the United States but can also be conferred to those who meet certain residency and immigration criteria.

Citizenship, however, encompasses far more than a person's legal right to own property, work, vote, or reside in a country. Less tangible dimensions of citizenship also shape and constrain all aspects of people's lives. Often referred as *social citizenship*, these rights help ensure everyone obtains what sociologist Evelyn Nakano Glenn refers to as "belonging"—or full inclusion in society.[16] Although the concept of social citizenship is rarely talked about in the US., a common set of institutions and resources can help ensure everyone's humanity, safety, dignity, and respect.[17] For example, people should be able to call the police or visit a hospital and receive care and protection when their safety or health are jeopardized. They should also earn a minimum wage and have easy access to public resources such as unemployment benefits, subsidized housing, student loans, and supplemental nutrition assistance programs to meet their basic necessities.[18]

Living in the United Sates, however, doesn't automatically afford all individuals equal access to the rights, services, and opportunities that ensure their belonging in society. Historically, full citizenship rights in the US were reserved for the "civilized," or landowning, heterosexual White men with origins in Western European countries.[19] In contrast, White women, people of color, and children were regarded as "uncivilized," "irrational," "dependent," and "unfit" to rule themselves.[20] Consequently, they found themselves relegated to the fringes of citizenship, with access to far fewer social rights and privileges.[21]

This legacy continues to shape people's ability to secure social citizenship.[22] Due to their privileged position in society and the ways that privilege accrues generationally, White men have continued to enjoy more of the benefits of social citizenship, as evidenced by their greater access to education, higher-paying jobs, and positions of power.[23] They have also faced far less discrimination and bias in the criminal justice and medical systems.[24] Welfare programs like Social Security, unemployment insurance, and veterans' benefits have even been designed to ensure their economic security and well-being during times of need.[25] While these resources and privileges may be able to help White men weather any number of crises, women, people of color, and immigrants continuously face obstacles in accessing social rights, services, and opportunities that would otherwise ensure their well-being.

In the absence of state-sanctioned support and assistance, people in the US are often left searching for private solutions to social problems. Indeed, the US context is notorious for its lack of a comprehensive safety net. In addition to lacking affordable universal healthcare and a universal basic income, the United States does not offer citizens paid family or medical leave, publicly funded childcare, publicly funded eldercare, or nationwide rent control.[26] Consequently, parents and adult children often spend significant time and resources caring for those who are considered "dependents," such as their children or aging parents.[27] Relatives can also help individuals cope with economic hardship and social vulnerabilities by offering temporary financial assistance, housing, or employment opportunities until other forms of support are obtained, but this safety net is limited to the exhaustible resources of kin and community.

Further, although family members often willingly serve as one another's safety net, balancing family and work commitment can create strain and ambivalence among such caregivers.[28] This is especially the case for women, who provide a disproportionate amount of support and care when family members are in need. Focusing primarily on the invisible forms of household labor that White heterosexual women perform on behalf of their husbands and children, numerous studies have demonstrated that employed women in the US often feel exhausted, overstretched, and inadequate because their inability to complete a "second shift" of domestic work at home in addition to paid full-time work.[29] Indeed, as White middle-class women's labor force participation increased in the second half of the twentieth century, the absence of social provisions—such as federally funded childcare programs and family-friendly work policies—has intensified demand for commercialized care work. This has led to the emergence of global care chains, wherein caregivers from the Global South migrate and provide care for wealthier families in the US who have turned to private markets to help fulfill caregiving obligations.[30]

Although White middle-class women often balance work and family commitments by outsourcing some household tasks, the lack of social provisions in the US can place people of color in a different type of bind. Partially because they are excluded from jobs and occupations where English fluency is required, immigrants of color—especially women—often perform "back-room" labor such as cleaning houses, hospitals, hotel rooms, and office buildings. They serve and cook food in cafeterias and restaurants and care for children and the elderly in homes, daycare centers, and retirement homes.[31] Because this type of service work often occurs in private spaces like people's homes or outside standard business hours, these physically demanding and emotionally exhausting forms of work are often devalued and invisible to most Americans. Since these jobs also require manual labor, irregular work schedules, and take place in hazardous conditions, it can become more difficult for women in caregiving fields—especially those who incur injuries or chronic health conditions—to complete child-rearing or household tasks in their own homes. Nonetheless, people of color have long searched for and continue to develop creative solutions to ensure their well-being and dignity in society.[32] Some of the strategies that families marginalized by race and nationality draw on to ensure their family members are cared for include extended family co-residence,[33] split households,[34] a "patchwork" process of bringing different resources together,[35] and the "protective care work" of shielding their children from institutional racism.[36]

Scholars have long written about how adults attempt to balance work and family commitments, but less research has examined children's efforts to access resources and care for their family members. As noted by sociologist Allison Pugh, even studies that highlight the interdependent nature of care work tend to treat children and youth as passive recipients of adult care.[37] And yet, adults are not the only ones who actively work to fill gaps in the US's social safety net. In working-class and immigrant households, children, especially girls, often care for younger siblings and perform household chores while their parents are working outside the home.[38] As an emerging body of literature on the children of Latinx immigrants has demonstrated, young people routinely help their families settle in the United States by, for example, using their English-speaking skills to connect their immigrant families to a wide range of institutional resources and information.[39] Furthermore, because it is significantly cheaper than hiring an adult, immigrant parents often rely on their children—who work for free or for a small stipend—to sustain small businesses and other ethnic enterprises in the informal economy.[40] In short, when families are marginalized by race, class, and nationality, children's labor may be crucial to ensuring their family's survival.

Extending this body of work, I argue that the lack of citizenship rights afforded to immigrant families of color sets the context for language brokers to creatively use their in-between status to secure belonging for their families. In a society where English fluency is a sign of one's willingness to "assimilate" into an American way of life, immigrants of color—in this case, parents—who do not speak English often become walking targets of racialized nativism. Their alleged "failure" to learn English serves as a readily identifiable symbol of their outsider status and serves to justify their exclusion from their basic citizenship rights, including access to institutional resources as well as the right to security, dignity, and belonging. That is, language becomes an important mechanism through which racialized English-speaking institutions exclude and discipline immigrant families of color, especially those who are poor. Consequently, the importance placed on speaking English not only limits racialized working-class immigrants' ability to access social provisions, especially in crucial and life-threatening situations where one's physical safety or health is at risk, but it also compels their children to develop individual-level solutions to the structural problems. As a result of the multiple forms of inequality their families encounter in society, children's language brokering has become a way to secure their family's belonging or their full membership in society.

DIFFERENT CONTROLLING IMAGES

Racialization—the recursive process of ascribing racial meanings to human bodies and group practices—profoundly shapes the distribution of and access to citizenship rights in the United States.[41] One mechanism through which racialization occurs is through the production of "controlling images," a practice by which the dominant group portrays people of color in negative ways.[42] Embedded within the discourses of politicians, social commentators, and popular media, these racialized images—created and reproduced by the dominant group—legitimize broader patterns of inequality by constructing people of color as undeserving of full citizenship rights.

Although the concept of controlling images was originally developed to understand the gendered racism that Black Americans face in the United States, a growing body of research has also examined the ideological justifications that legitimize the structural forms of racism Asian Americans and Latinx people encounter in the US.[43] For example, politicians and anti-immigrant activists often exclude immigrants of color from receiving full citizenship rights by racializing them as perpetual foreigners.[44] In recent years, immigrants of color—including Asian Americans and Latinx people—have been depicted as a threat to public resources and a drain on the system that "true" Americans fund through taxes.[45] As Kitty Calavita has shown, dominant rhetoric depicts immigrants—especially those who are poor—as "undeserving parasites" who abuse welfare benefits.[46] Politicians and media outlets also characterize immigrants as an "invasion" or "flooding waves" ready to deluge the US and steal jobs reserved for "hardworking" Americans.[47] Because these images justify anti-immigrant hostility, they help politicians and anti-immigrant activists deny immigrants of color full citizenship rights while deflecting attention away from the fact that White men accumulate far more benefits and advantages through government-initiated social policies. In this context, systemic forms of inequality continue to prevent immigrants of color from accessing many of the civil and social dimensions of citizenship that are necessary for ensuring full access to safe, secure, and dignified lives.

Controlling images depict all immigrants of color as "foreigners," yet Asian American and Latinx people encounter different forms of racialized nativism. During the height of the civil rights movement in the US, controlling images elevated East Asian Americans to the position of "model minorities," or those who ostensibly achieved upward mobility by enacting the values of hard work and family solidarity.[48] Public officials and pundits deployed the model minority stereotype, evidenced by presumably high educational and occupational outcomes,[49] not to praise one group but to reinforce the "culture of poverty" thesis that depicted Black Americans as undeserving of full citizenship rights.[50] Numerous studies have debunked the model minority myth, but it persists today. Elected officials and conservative leaders routinely deploy this rhetoric to dismantle affirmative action policies by pitting Asian Americans against other people of color and advocate a return to "traditional" family structures.[51] At the same time, however, Asian Americans continue to be racialized as threats, with their financial and occupational success being signs that they are jeopardizing "true" Americans' economic opportunities.[52] In addition to deflecting attention from racial inequalities and socioeconomic differences within the Asian American population, this imagery helps obfuscate the ways in which Asian Americans lack full citizenship rights in the US, including the forms of racism they encounter when seeking employment, education, and housing.[53]

Although Mexican Americans were depicted as a group that was more "assimilable" than Asian Americans until the Great Depression, racialized imagery also constructs Mexican Americans as lacking the values and characteristics necessary to become "real" Americans.[54] Today, Mexican Americans are racialized as a problematic underclass that threatens the security of the nation.[55] Politicians and popular news outlets often reference Mexican "cultural values" as the drivers of their low educational attainment and high poverty rates, as well as Mexican women's "out of control" fertility rates.[56] At other times, Mexican Americans are depicted as "illegal" immigrants who drain government resources or are criminally "dangerous."[57] In addition to fueling anti-immigrant hostility, these controlling images can induce fear in Latinx communities, forcing immigrants to endure demoralizing conditions in workplaces.[58] And because these images can shape others' perceptions about Latinx people, they limit Latinx immigrants' ability to access basic rights, such as educational opportunities, affordable housing, and healthcare.[59]

Language Brokers systematically compares the experiences of Korean Americans and Mexican Americans, who are differently racialized in the United States. Although existing research has examined the impact of racialization processes on the lives of immigrant youth of color, qualitative research has largely focused on the experiences of either Asian American or Latinx immigrants. Focusing on only one group, however, provides only a partial understanding of how different racialization processes operate in relation to one another.[60] Furthermore, existing studies examining the lives of Asian American people largely center on the experiences of middle-class immigrant families, while research on Latinx people generally focuses on immigrant families who are poor or working-class.[61] Without comparing immigrants from similar socioeconomic backgrounds, it is difficult to fully theorize how race intersects with class to shape people's experiences of inclusion and exclusion in the US. Indeed, by examining the family lives of working-class Korean and Mexican Americans, this book reveals how young people's group positions in the contemporary racial hierarchy set the parameters through which language brokers attempt to present their families as deserving of full citizenship.

THEORIZING THE MARGIN: INTERSECTIONAL UNDERSTANDINGS OF CHILDREN'S POSITIONALITY

Citizenship is not only a site of exclusion. It is also a site of contestation where marginalized people develop creative responses to challenge systemic forms of inequality.

Intersectionality theorists, generally focusing on adults, have long argued that living at the intersection of multiple systems of inequality can enable people to produce new and often subjugated viewpoints on the world. For example, by taking into account the unequal power relationship between White and Black Americans, sociologist W. E. B. Du Bois argued that Black Americans experience a *double consciousness*, through which they can see racism that is often invisible to White Americans.[62] Similarly, in her intersectional analysis of gender, class, and race, bell hooks argued that the margin is "more than a site of deprivation."[63] Because the margin enables people from subordinated groups to look "both from the outside in and from the inside out," they often develop "a mode of seeing unknown to the oppressors."[64] In this way, the social location inhabited by young people in this study can simultaneously act as a site of oppression and resistance where they can use their "outsider-within" status to make "creative use of their marginality."[65]

Scholars of intersectionality have made significant strides in theorizing resistance at the margin, though existing accounts have largely overlooked how age intersects with other forms of inequality to shape people's ability to contest and resist exclusion in everyday life. In the US, young people are often viewed as lacking the capabilities to make rational and fully formed decisions on their own. As a result, laws are written in ways that are designed to shield young people from the realities and responsibilities of the adult world. For instance, people are not allowed to vote until they are eighteen years old. Most states require people to be at least sixteen years old before they can drive a motorized vehicle. It is also illegal for anyone under the age of twenty-one to consume alcohol. Many parents and schools use firewalls and internet monitoring programs to restrict or limit the forms of information and content that young people access and consume, and people under the age of eighteen need permission from their parents or legal guardians to live on their own, own property, open a bank account, or have a credit card. There are also legal restrictions preventing young people from earning an income. In most cases, children under the age of fourteen are prohibited from obtaining paid employment, and there are restrictions on the number of hours people between the ages of fourteen and eighteen can work. Instead, states expect young people to be full-time students through at least age sixteen.

Rather than assuming that children are inherently inferior to adults, however, sociologists often interrogate biologically deterministic understandings of age.[66] Since the 1980s, scholars within the sociology of childhood subfield have repeatedly demonstrated that children and youth are reflective and knowledgeable actors who strategize within their constraints and make a profound difference in their surroundings and in their families' lives.[67] Not only is "social age" shaped by the circumstances one encounters, but children's capabilities can also expand with sufficient social support.[68] In short, children are not just proto-people or embodiments of the future who must be safeguarded from the dangers of the adult world.[69] Instead, children's agency, experiences, and perspectives must be taken seriously in order to fully understand how children respond to and shape the world around them.

In fact, the assumption that children are largely dependent on adults for protection and guidance is a relatively recent invention. Until the end of nineteenth century, people in the US embraced the notion of a "useful childhood" and primarily perceived young people as "economic assets."[70] For example, parents often provided young children in urban areas with work responsibilities and apprenticeships to speed the process of "growing up."[71] Children in rural areas worked on farms at an early age and helped harvest crops.[72] As the industrial revolution made large families less necessary for survival, however, expectations around the "ideal" childhood began to shift.[73] Both fertility and infant mortality rates declined throughout the nineteenth century, and many urban White middle-class children began attending school for longer durations.[74] Instead of viewing their children as "little adults" who had economic value, White middle-class parents began to sentimentalize and protect children from the outside world.

Nevertheless, the legal protections afforded to young people have historically varied based on race, class, and gender. Although a small number of urban White middle-class children began devoting increased time to education during the nineteenth century, for instance, industrialization and the commercialization of agriculture increased the demand for other children's labor.[75] Many children—including children of color, working-class children, and immigrant children—continued to work in physically demanding, exploitative, and abusive conditions in farms, mills, factories, mines, canneries, and sweatshops.[76] Because these working conditions helped generate wealth for White men who were business and property owners, more upper-class families began hiring domestic servants—often girls from working-class and immigrant families. By the late nineteenth century, children's income typically accounted for approximately 20 percent of a family's income, and teenage sons sometimes made more money than their fathers.[77]

It was not until the mid-twentieth century that the White middle-class notion of a prolonged and protected childhood was extended to all children. This was partially a function of the Great Depression: as adult unemployment skyrocketed, many adults began to view young people as competition for jobs. With child labor reformers also advocating for schools as a way to solve the "working-class" problems of poverty and crime in urban areas, children began to leave the paid labor force and spend more time in school.[78] During this time, school boards and state legislatures also increased the compulsory education age to sixteen years, which helped mark "teenagers" as a distinct age category.[79] As they began to spend more time in age-graded institutions like schools and in extracurricular activities like sports, it became increasingly normative to view young people as "economically useless" but "emotionally priceless."[80]

Today, children are largely unable to secure citizenship rights on the basis of their "productivity" or "self-sufficiency." To the contrary, children who engage in "productive" or "self-sufficient" activities are stigmatized in the US.[81] Parents can incur significant legal and financial ramifications for giving their children "too much" independence. This is evidenced by the public re-actions to and media representations of language brokers discussed earlier in this chapter. Indeed, when children take on "adult responsibilities," people often use terms like "adultification," "parentification," "false maturity," and "role reversal" to suggest that children are not following the "normal" de-velopmental trajectory.[82] In contrast to the children of the past, then, young people today have far fewer socially valued ways to contribute to their family's well-being. Instead, childhood and adolescence are widely conceptualized as transitory phases that young people pass through on their way to becoming an adult. Children's "worth" remains contingent on their future potential; as "adults in the making," most of their daily activities are organized around their chronological age and centered around their formal education.

In a society where children are assumed to have capabilities that are dif-ferent from and inferior to those of adults, young people's perspectives and experiences are rarely taken into account, even when they are at the center of public policy debates. In fact, making claims about young people's "inno-cence" and highlighting their potential is often the only way to ensure that children receive protection, rights, and recognition in society. For example, pro-immigrant activists and politicians who advocated for Deferred Action for Childhood Arrivals (DACA) positioned children who are undocumented immigrants as deserving of rights due to their "innocence." They argued that it was unfair to deny children access to education and jobs as a result of "illegal" decisions made by their parents, and highlighted their potential to achieve the American Dream.[83] When announcing the policy, President Obama stated, "It makes no sense to expel talented young people, who, for all intents and purposes, are Americans—they've been raised as Americans; understand themselves to be part of this country—to expel those young people who want to staff our labs, or start new businesses, or defend our country simply because of the actions of their parents—or because of the inaction of politicians."[84]

Language Brokers moves beyond viewing children as passive recipients of "American" values. By bringing intersectionality theory more squarely into dialogue with the social studies of childhood's tradition of highlighting children's agency, I show how young people contest multiple inequalities through their work as language brokers. While doing so, I offer a new understanding of the ways multiply marginalized young people experience exclusion and claim membership in society.

Throughout, I highlight three reasons why working-class immigrant language brokers of color offer an ideal empirical window for understanding how the margin acts as both a site of oppression and resistance. First, translation work requires children of immigrants to interact with people who are in positions of power and play key roles in shaping the distribution of resources in society (including teachers, landlords, police officers, health care providers, and other gatekeepers to social services). Second, these translation encounters often take youth outside of the racially segregated neighborhoods where they live and attend school, such as when they accompany their parents—who often work as nannies, gardeners, house cleaners, janitors, and security guards—to predominately White and wealthier spaces. These translation interactions, especially those that take place outside working-class immigrant enclaves, often heighten youth's experiences of social exclusion. Consequently, language brokering has the potential to foster what sociologist Carla Shedd calls youth's "perceptions of injustice," or a sense of recognition that their lives are different from those of White middle-class families.[85]

Third, language brokers' lives are situated at the intersection of multiple forms of inequality. On the one hand, their status as bilingual speakers allows them to access resources monolingual immigrants might lack. On the other hand, adults often interact with youth, especially girls of color, in condescending and patronizing ways. As a result, bilingual language brokers, who symbolically and literally stand in between their immigrant parents and

English-speaking adults during translation encounters, are poised to "see" how numerous and intersecting structural barriers—including racial, age, class, gender, and linguistic inequalities—shape their family's life. These forms of inequality, moreover, are likely to be less visible to other Americans, including White people, adult immigrants, and immigrant youth who primarily spend time in racially segregated spaces. Ultimately, as this book makes clear, youth creatively make use of their marginality and their in-between position as bilingual children of immigrants to secure social citizenship and mitigate intersecting inequalities that they experience during translation encounters. Their experiences challenge the conventional way we think of marginalized children's position in society.

TALKING TO LANGUAGE BROKERS

Language Brokers takes readers inside the daily lives of Mexican and Korean American youth as they use their bilingual skills to access basic citizenship rights for their families. To do so, I draw from eighty in-depth interviews with working-class Korean and Mexican American young people who grew up translating for their parents. As I conducted interviews with the youths, it became clear that they found interpreting for healthcare providers and police officers particularly difficult. Consequently, I spoke with twenty English-speaking healthcare providers about their experiences with young language brokers and conducted six months of ethnographic research at a police department in Southern California. This data allowed me to gain a deeper perspective on the routine forms of inequality embedded in these two key institutions. My findings confirmed what language brokers shared with me about their experiences; still, I have purposefully decentered adults' perspectives in this book to ensure youth's experiences and voices remain at the forefront of my analysis. I have also avoided editing the youths' quotes, as editing risks reinforcing assumptions that there is a "standard" way to communicate, or that they are less skilled at speaking English than adults.

Over 90 percent of my interviewees' parents worked in low-skilled, low-wage service occupations. None of the respondents' parents were homeowners, and 90 percent of the respondents qualified for free or reduced-fee lunch programs at school. The vast majority of working-class children in this study thus come from "hard living" families, meaning their parents' low-wage occupations without benefits make it difficult to purchase a home and maintain a stable life.[86] Parents' work varied. Ninety-five percent of Korean American respondents had at least one parent working in an urban ethnic enclave, which often included a business owned by Korean immigrants. Indeed, studies indicate that it is typical for working-class Korean immigrants in Los Angeles to work for co-ethnic entrepreneurs.[87] Their occupations included hairdresser, manicurist, server, security guard, salesperson, and cashier. Korean Americans in my sample also lived in and attended schools in areas of Los Angeles where levels of segregation from Whites were moderate or even low.[88] In contrast, Mexican Americans were far more likely to live and attend school in Latinx-majority neighborhoods with high concentrations of poverty—which is consistent with broader patterns of racial segregation in Los Angeles.[89] Their parents were heavily concentrated in the low-wage informal economy that takes place in Los Angeles's affluent suburbs;[90] 80 percent of the Mexican American youth I interviewed reported at least one parent who worked as a nanny, gardener, or construction or maintenance worker. Such racialized divisions within their immigrant parents' occupations created different types of translation encounters for immigrant youth, which—as I show in this book—have important implications for the ways youth enact and challenge the meaning of *American* during their interactions with English-speaking adults. I include more information about sampling and methodological approach in the appendix.

I used several strategies to increase rapport with young people before and during interviews. In addition to speaking about my own experience serving as a language broker for my immigrant parents, I spoke about the importance of documenting their experiences in their own words and expressed gratitude for their willingness to participate in the research process. I began each interview by asking questions about popular culture, hobbies, shopping, and their neighborhood. When talking about these topics, I indicated my desire to attain competency in their social worlds and allowed them to direct the conversation. I also asked follow-up questions about themes they raised to help signify my interest in their perspectives. After each interview was finished, I asked respondents to contact me if they wanted to talk again. Twenty respondents were interviewed more than once. Respondents often appeared more relaxed during follow-up interviews, as indicated by their increased use of profanity and colloquial forms of speech when we spoke for the second time.

All the youth I interviewed resided in Los Angeles, where 49 percent of the population is Latinx and 15 percent is Asian American.[91] Further, in Los Angeles, more than one in three residents was born outside the United States and nearly one in three residents is classified as "limited English proficient" (LEP). (Eighty-three percent of Latinxs and 76 percent of Asian Americans speak a language other than English at home, and 48 percent of Latinxs and 43 percent of Asian Americans are classified as LEP.) Since 1973, California's legal code has required state agencies to provide bilingual services if they serve a "substantial" number of people who need them, but bilingual-services audits consistently find that most local agencies fail to comply with the federal and state laws ensuring language accessibility.[92] When coupled with its linguistic diversity, Los Angeles thus serves as a strategic methodological site to examine the effects of institutionalized forms of language inequality on immigrant youths' lives.

OVERVIEW OF THE BOOK

Language Brokers identifies, in vivid detail, the resilience children of immigrants cultivate when attempting to present themselves and their families as worthy of full citizenship rights. Based on interviews with English-speaking healthcare providers and ethnographic data I gathered at a police station, chapter 2 explains how social forces set the stage for young people to serve as their parents' language brokers. What are the circumstances that prompt public-facing institutional agents like police officers and healthcare workers—who act as gatekeepers in determining individuals' ability to access crucial social services—to rely on young people as language brokers? How do these agents perceive and respond to non-English-speaking adult immigrants of color and their bilingual children? In spite of their ostensive commitment to fulfilling everyone's right to well-being, public-facing institutional agents in these busy and underfunded institutions tended to view immigrants of color, especially the poor, as undeserving of full social citizenship rights by virtue of their inability to speak English. In a society where English fluency is an identifiable marker of one's ability to "assimilate" into an American society, in the perspective of institutional agents, those who "fail" to speak English are responsible for making their jobs unnecessarily challenging. Since many of these institutions are overcrowded and underfunded, institutional agents claim that they have little choice but to prioritize efficiency over equality by relying on children of immigrants. Consequently, even while having doubts or concerns about young people's competency and abilities, institutional agents see children of immigrants as the fastest and easiest option to increase efficiency. In chapter 3, I show how children of immigrants are alert to the harsh realities, including racialized nativism and poverty, that their parents experience on a daily basis. Capturing the breadth and depth of young people's empathy and concern for their parents, I argue that children's language brokering is externally imposed and socially enforced; children of immigrants attempt to solve structural problems their families encounter during everyday translation encounters.

In chapter 4, I continue to examine the ways a lack of citizenship rights shapes young people's experiences by showing how their desire to provide language support for their parents conflicts with their school responsibilities. Because school practices are based on White middle-class values, and educators expect youth to primarily devote their time and energy to educational pursuits outside school, working-class youth of color are placed in a difficult double bind when attempting to juggle family and school responsibilities. This double bind is especially salient during crisis situations, in which youth have to "drop everything" to help their parents navigate issues such as housing instability, legal problems, and medical emergencies. Although age expectations embedded in school practices make both Korean and Mexican American youth think that they do not have a typical "American" childhood, different racialization processes contribute to their senses of inadequacy. Working-class Mexican American youth reported that their teachers problematize their childhood and family lives and assume that their parents do not care about their children's academic success. However, these feelings of inadequacy were even more intense for working-class Korean American youth, who worry their teachers and peers deem their parents insufficiently "Asian." Through this analysis, I highlight the mismatch between school expectations based in White middle-class values and the racialized realities imposed on working-class immigrant youth, who are left feeling "different" from other students.

Chapter 5 demonstrates how language brokers, who regularly encounter racialized nativism as well as age and class inequalities during translation encounters, adopt different strategies of resistance while speaking on behalf of their parents. These strategies include (1) *passing* as an "American" adult by speaking on the phone when possible; (2) *shielding* their parents from racial-ized nativism by omitting parts of exchanges; and (3) *posing* as "professional" to sound like White middle-class people. Taken together, these strategies of resistance illustrate that children of immigrants are not passive recipients of "American" values, as assimilation theorists have long suggested. Instead, children creatively use their simultaneously elevated and subordinated po-sition as bilinguals to present their families as "normal" Americans deserv-ing of full citizenship rights. I call this process "doing American" from an outsider-within position. In addition to highlighting the importance of in-teractions in reproducing social inequality, youths' strategies call attention to how the margin, as a social location, can create moments of resistance and empowerment.

Whereas most immigration research has examined how culture shapes immigrants' assimilation outcomes, chapter 6 reveals how children of immi-grants put culture to use when attempting to claim membership in the US. I introduce readers to the concept of "inclusion work," which shows how chil-dren of immigrants selectively deploy the cultural repertoires of "deserving immigrants" to validate their presence in the US. Inclusion work uncovered in this study includes "Americanizing" their families' migration journey, con-structing their families as collective and hardworking, and presenting them-selves as productive citizens. Interestingly, inclusion work varies based on immigrants' race, with Mexican American youth deploying a wider range of "good" immigrant repertoires to contest controlling images of their families. In the context of heightened immigration hostility, their reconstructed "right kind of family" stories serve as a justification that their hard work and self-sufficiency will one day be rewarded with full citizenship rights. However, because inclusion work reinforces the myth of the American Dream and the moral boundary between "deserving" and "undeserving" immigrants, youths' attempts to redefine their position in the US paradoxically diverts attention from the very structures responsible for their daily struggles.

In chapter 7, I revisit the question of citizenship by asking why children of immigrants, who see and feel the effects of multiple inequalities in their lives, remain committed to proving their "Americanness." I argue that, to the extent that the nation holds immigrants accountable for solving what are actually systematic problems, children of immigrants will continue to "do American," face difficult double binds, and engage in inclusion work. I end this book with a discussion of the practical steps we can take to ensure immigrant families in the US receive full citizenship rights. There is much to learn about the experience of language brokers who navigate multiple inequalities. Their efforts at brokering belonging not only reveal the contradiction between our national ideals of equality and the everyday realities of exclusion faced by immigrants of color, but these endeavors also underscore the importance of fostering a society that acknowledges our interdependence.

TWO ENGLISH-SPEAKING INSTITUTIONS IN A MULTILINGUAL CITY

"Rafael Gonzales, are you here?" James, a police officer working the front desk at a precinct in Southern California, crossed Rafael's name off the wait list as the man stood to approach the desk. As the phone rang, James signaled for Rafael to wait.

James listened momentarily, then dangled the receiver in front of his coworker Martin as the disembodied voice continued to speak.

"The caller speaks Spanish," James said with a shrug. Martin sighed loudly, picked up the phone, and began speaking in Spanish.

The phone rang again. This time, James answered by asking if the call was an emergency, then put the caller on hold. He looked to Rafael, still waiting near the desk.

"Habla español?" Rafael asked.

James, who told me that he had taken two years of Spanish in high school, quickly glanced at Martin, but his coworker was still on the phone. He returned his gaze to Rafael and began in a loud, slow voice, "Muy, muy poquito." Rafael responded in rapid Spanish while James squinted, attempting to parse Rafael's reason for coming into the police station.

"Tell tu amigo to go away. He is loco!" James exclaimed to Rafael, his eyes once again darting toward the still-occupied Martin.

The door swung open, and a boy, who I later learned was thirteen, ran in. After briefly glancing around the station, he approached the desk.

Rafael's face lit up. He introduced the boy as Angel, his bilingual son. Speaking in Spanish, Angel apologized to his father for being late. Still trying to catch his breath, he repeated himself in English so that James would understand.

"I am sorry I am late," he said. "I had to talk with my teacher after school."

"Yeah, you are late!" James agreed with relief. "Now, tell me what your dad is saying."

Angel said his father was there to report a theft. Rafael suspected that his friend, who knew where he kept cash in his house, had stolen from him. When Rafael confronted his friend, he became upset and started cursing at Rafael. With Angel translating, James guided Rafael through the process of filing a police report, then explained that Rafael could report the loss on his tax return.

Over the six months I spent conducting participant observation research at this police precinct, I frequently observed children of immigrants interpreting for their parents; I'd seen the same in the medical settings where I interviewed nurses. In some ways, the presence of young people in hospitals and police stations was unsurprising. Despite serving different functions in society, these institutions primarily exist to ensure that people have access to social citizenship rights that ensure their health, safety, and well-being in situations when urgent assistance is required. Because institutional agents—gatekeepers controlling access to resources, information, and opportunities—in both settings routinely handle sensitive information, accurate and efficient communication is crucial. Translators help ensure that people's fundamental rights are met when people speak a different language than the public-facing institutional agents.

Indeed, the importance of having a translator was evident in the way that Angel—who facilitated communication between his Spanish-speaking father and an English-speaking police officer—helped streamline the efficacy of this predominately English-speaking police station. Thanks to Angel's bilingual skills, James was able to quickly complete his key responsibilities (providing information and directing the victim to resources) and Martin, upon whom other officers relied for help with the Spanish-speaking public, had his workload momentarily lightened. Angel's translation bridged the gap between his father being told his friend was "loco" and his father accessing real assistance that helped ensure Rafael's well-being and safety in the US.

That's how it looks for language brokers when everything goes right. However, many language brokers I interviewed identified police stations and hospitals as two of the most difficult places to translate.[1] In addition to being busy, crowded, and intimidating places, young people told me about jarring interactions with institutional agents who were demeaning, condescending, and hostile toward them and their parents. Research jibes with their accounts, confirming that monolingual, English-speaking adults employed in public-facing jobs in institutions like police stations and hospitals often express negative views about children's language-brokering activities.[2] Rather than assuming children are competent to discuss sensitive information and maintain their composure in high-stakes situations, authorities more often assume that children are "innocent" and "naïve" and thus need to be shielded from the realities of the "adult" world.[3] Especially in situations where communication is urgent and pertains to sensitive information, children's language-brokering work breaches normative US assumptions about children's and adults' capabilities. Nonetheless, young people like Angel frequently step into the role of language brokers within these institutions.

To investigate the circumstances under which public-facing institutional agents like police officers and healthcare workers must rely on young people as language brokers, this chapter assess those agents' perceptions of non-English speaking adult immigrants of color and their bilingual children. As I will demonstrate, in spite of their ostensible commitment to fulfilling everyone's right to well-being, the public-facing institutional agents I observed and interviewed in these busy and underfunded institutions tended to view low-income immigrants of color, especially women, as undeserving of full social citizenship rights by virtue of their inability to speak English. Rather than relying on official, state-mandated translation services, institutional agents— who have little choice but to prioritize efficacy over equality—come to see the bilingual children of immigrants as the fastest and easiest solution to communicating with adults who primarily spoke languages other than English.

Ultimately, language becomes a key mechanism through which critical and public-facing institutional agents exclude non-English-speaking immigrants from accessing fundamental rights and services.

"LANGUAGE BARRIERS" IN IMMIGRANT-FACING INSTITUTIONS

It was an unusually cold and rainy afternoon in Southern California when I arrived at the police station. Again, a pair of officers stationed at the front desk were making their way through a wait list. The lobby was packed. A Latinx woman, sitting with her three sons and an infant, handed her phone to her older children to keep them from running in circles around a waiting area that lacked toys or other diversions.[4] She repeatedly left the station to calm her infant. There was a man speaking in Chinese with a teenager, presumably his daughter, as she gestured at various places on a form he held. And a Black woman navigated her wheelchair around the rows of chairs and made her way to the front desk. After straining to reach up to the station's sign-in sheet on a high counter convenient only for adults who could stand, she told me that she'd been waiting for over an hour, and there were still five people ahead of her.

An Asian woman walked into the station with tears running down her cheeks. One of the officers pointed at the sign-in sheet. She sighed and attempted to regain her composure while adding her name to the list and selecting one of the lobby's few remaining vacant chairs.

"Jaeeun Park!"

Two hours later, around 4 p.m., her name was finally called.

Jaeeun rushed to the front desk and began speaking in a rapid mix of English and Korean.

The officer raised his hand to interrupt her.

"Wait, we need a Korean translator here!" he called out, looking over to where I stood, several feet away.

Jaeeun's face lit up.

"Korean?" she asked.

"Yes, how can I help you?" I asked in Korean.

Jaeeun responded in a hushed voice. Although immigrant women are often afraid to report incidents of domestic violence to the police, Jaeeun told me she had missed a whole day of work while attempting to obtain a restraining order against her husband.[5] In fact, this was her second time visiting the police station today. The first time, one of the officers instructed her to go to family court. There, she was instructed to return to the station to file a police report. Hence the second visit. Because Jaeeun did not have a car, she had spent the entire day walking and transferring between multiple bus lines to travel from her house to the local police station to the city courthouse and back again. Since it was nearing the end of the business day, I suspected Jaeeun would not have enough time—even if she successfully filed the requisite police report—to return to the courthouse to file for a restraining order.

"These officers keep on sending me to wrong places," Jaeeun said in Korean as she wiped tears from her eyes.

Before I was able to interpret, James interrupted me. He cupped the telephone receiver with one of his hands.

"Hey, how do you say 'Wait' in Korean?" he asked me.

"Say ki-dah-ryo-ju-se-yo," I responded.

"What? Ki-what? That's so long. Why can't it be simple like *wait*? Never mind."

"I am going to put you on hold," James said into the phone. He then pressed the hold button and asked me to take the call after I finished speaking with Jaeeun.

Jaeeun, still speaking in Korean, told me that nobody had made an effort to listen to her. "This one police officer just took out a piece of paper with the court address and yelled, " 'Go here! Okay?' That's it," she said.

The well-being of poor people of color is entangled in the actions and whims of variety of institutions. Most government agencies operate according to "normal" business hours, which makes it difficult for individuals with inflexible and irregular work to access these services. Successfully accessing services is also contingent on an individual's ability to procure documents or records produced by another arm of the state—a process that, as research has shown, requires a considerable amount of time, resources, and energy.[6] For example, because the court system views police records as crucial pieces of evidence in legal proceedings, Jaeeun first needed to file a police report to ensure she had sufficient "proof" to go to the family court to obtain a restraining order against her husband. Consistent with the findings from other studies,[7] institutional procedures added to the difficulty Jaeeun faced in trying to secure basic resources to ensure her safety.

That this web of institutions is primarily English-speaking makes things infinitely more difficult for immigrant women like Jaeeun. After missing work and spending hours on public transportation, she found police officers were quick to assume that she had shown up at the wrong place; it's entirely possible that, on her first visit to the station, the officers misunderstood Jaeeun's needs, and their manner with her discouraged her from asking follow-up questions to clarify. I noted, over the six months I spent at the precinct, how officers— the majority of whom were tall, broad-shouldered, and imposing—attempted to communicate with non-English speakers by using large and dramatic body gestures, simplifying their language, and speaking loudly. Coming from an armed and uniformed authority figure, this exasperated performance would surely seem dismissive and intimidating. It's no wonder Jaeeun told me that everyone was yelling at her. And it's no wonder that, in the end, Jaeeun was unable to access the resources that could have helped her ensure her well-being in a timely manner.

Interestingly, non-English speakers were not the only ones left feeling unheard in these situations. The police officers, nurses, and doctors I spoke with unanimously said that language barriers were among the biggest "problems" they encountered at work. This trend was exemplified by Mathew, an English-speaking police officer who said that "language barriers" made it "really difficult to deal with almost everyone who comes into the station." Similarly, Alicia, who had previously worked as a nurse in North Carolina and Georgia before moving to Los Angeles, told me "language barriers" made "patients" more "difficult to work with." "I think it's more of California thing," she mused.

Sabrina, a delivery and labor nurse with fifteen years of experience, felt the same. She began her interview by exclaiming about how much she loved being in a position where she regularly had opportunities to "advocate for patients, take care of people's health, and help the poor." However, she said that she often felt "frustrated," "inadequate," and "upset" because she was unable to "communicate effectively" and "do the nursing education" within a context like Los Angeles, where "over 70 percent" of her patients didn't "speak English."

An intensive-care-unit (ICU) nurse named Karen extended the "communication barrier" to a "cultural mismatch" as she described workplace challenges. She gave the example of ICU visitors trying to "keep feeding" patients, seemingly unable to "understand" that intubated patients could not eat solid foods. "I think it's in the culture. I think they believe that if you eat, you get better," Karen said. "And, they always massage the patients. Massaging is big thing in Korean culture."

Korean immigrants are not the only group of people who believe that eating nutritious food will help patients recover quickly. Nor are Koreans the only ones who use massages as a means to improve blood circulation, reduce muscle tension, or relax during stressful situations. Regardless of their "culture" or ethnicity, many people also bring homemade food to hospitals for loved ones. Many patients find the hospital's bland offerings unappetizing. Furthermore, I regularly noted the paucity of affordable and culturally appropriate food when I interviewed nurses in hospital cafeterias in predominately Latinx and Korean neighborhoods.

Rather than recognizing institutional flaws, including the lack of adequate translation support, Karen assumed "Korean culture" was to blame for miscommunications. Perhaps for this reason, Karen—who worked in the city with the highest Korean American population in the US—did not try to improve her ability to care for patients by learning basic Korean. Nor did she worry that she might otherwise overlook important warning signs that could indicate a deterioration in critically ill patients' conditions. Instead, she said that she could get "far" with a few Korean words and "body language," demonstrating her approach to me by pointing at an imaginary feeding tube, shaking her head, then pointing to her stomach. "'Are you hungry? I will feed you,'" Karen said in a slower and louder voice.

Despite her attempts at proving she could adequately communicate by dropping one or two key words from patients' languages into her questions, it was unclear whether Karen could reliably determine which language a patient might speak. Although she had been describing the difficulties of interacting with monolingual Korean speakers, Karen began speaking Spanish and Korean interchangeably when demonstrating how she asked patients whether they needed to use the restroom: "Do you want to go to bathroom? *Baño*? *Hwajangsil*?"

Across my interviews and observations, I noted that police officers and nurses rarely sounded concerned about the level of services or care they were able to provide to people who spoke a language other than English. Instead, they often told me how much more difficult and time-consuming it could be to interact with such clients. For example, Grace, an ER nurse told me that the doctors and nurses are "very, very busy. It's fast paced here. It's constantly moving. But, we have about 80 percent that can't speak English. There is a lot of misunderstanding and that makes everyone angry."

These "communication issues" were compounded by reductions in governmental budgets, a process called retrenchment that is part of a broader trend of deregulating and privatizing services that fulfill fundamental human rights. For example, Jason, a veteran police officer who started his career in the 1970s, said that he now had to "multitask a lot more than before" because the number of callers and people visiting the station had significantly increased while the staffing levels decreased. This was especially the case for police departments in low-income communities as they are largely funded by property, business, and sales taxes. And yet, despite recognizing the problems associated with underfunded institutions, Jason regularly complained about the Spanish speakers who made it difficult for him to convey information. Reminiscing about "back in the old days," when most people he dealt with spoke English, he said that Spanish speakers who called about "every little thing" made his job "challenging." Similarly, many nurses discussed the additional administrative tasks they had been tasked with as the number of hospital support staff had dwindled over the years. Caitlin described the "recent healthcare trend" in which hospitals like hers worked to "minimize costs and maximize profit." Because "cutting costs means cutting labor," she said she and "other support staff" were "always running around." Most days were "busy enough" that she barely had time to "deal with" patients who were "English speakers," let alone take the time to understand patients who primarily spoke other languages.

Essential service providers knew they worked in a city in which the majority of residents spoke a language other than English, but virtually none of them criticized their employers for failing to uphold people's rights. It was noteworthy, for example, that police officers expressed frustration with having to depend on "unreliable" volunteer translators, rather than acknowledging California's legal mandate concerning translation services and their station's breach of that law. Similarly, it was striking that these English speakers seldom contemplated whether they should strive to become more proficient in a second language. Instead, they labeled non-English speakers as "difficult to deal with" and held them responsible for intensifying the already demanding nature of their jobs.

The nurses who fleetingly mentioned interpreters generally said it was "impossible" to regularly utilize language services when caring for patients.

Rachel, an emergency department nurse, commented, "It is impossible to provide a thousand-plus language resources for different immigrants."[8] Others described telephone interpreters as "inefficient" and "cumbersome"—ill-suited to the fast pace of their work. One of the nurses, Mary, at least recognized that her hospital was not living up to its obligations to ensure equal access to non-English speakers under California law; she said that non-English speakers could "file complaints with the federal or state agencies" because she and her colleagues rarely used translation services. Nonetheless, she said there wasn't "much" anyone could do to change the status quo.

"It's ICU, and doctors are too busy to call the [hotline] and wait for the translator to show up on the phone," she said with resignation. In effect, essential-service providers regarded formal translation services as yet another layer of bureaucratic red tape, seemingly designed to minimize the risk of potential lawsuits rather than to facilitate the flow of their daily duties. Julia, for example, explicitly acknowledged the legal, not interpersonal, benefits of relying on telephone interpreters, which she knew hospitals were "technically" required to use. She said that recording the medical interpreters' names and badge numbers via phone had the added bonus of protecting healthcare providers from potential lawsuits. Otherwise, patients could claim that "nurses did not explain the procedure."

There was good reason to suspect that nurses weren't adequately explaining the medical procedures. They were relying on limited vocabulary and gestures, and they knew that patients might be able to understand only one or two key words. Nonetheless, Julia said her hospital "hardly" used telephone interpreters because it was a "waste of time." Plus, she intimated that there was only so much she could do to change the behavior of doctors, who—by dint of their position within the occupational hierarchy—were afforded more power and status than nurses. Julia said that doctors, "always in a hurry," rarely wanted to "wait for the interpreters to interpret everything" unless they were legally required to, such as when they were "trying to get consent." "If they are just generally asking how patients are doing, they don't have to use the phone," she said. "Once in a while, I ask doctors to use the phone when it becomes too difficult to carry on a conversation, but you can get in trouble [with the doctors] for talking too much."

Certainly, as suggested by the healthcare workers I interviewed, time is of the essence, especially in ICU units, emergency rooms, and maternity wards.

Patients' health would be jeopardized if workers delayed treatment or missed subtle signs that indicated a deterioration in their condition. And yet, taken-for-granted policies and procedures in underfunded and crowded hospitals make it difficult—if not impossible—for non-English speaking patients to effectively communicate their needs. Instead of blaming the institutions or suggesting ways to improve, many institutional agents I interviewed implicitly or sometimes explicitly condemned a growing immigrant population who couldn't speak English. In the end, language became a pivotal tool employed by institutional agents to marginalize non-English-speaking immigrants, barring them from essential rights and services.

BILINGUAL STAFF

As we saw with James and Martin, one way that healthcare providers and police officers attempt to resolve language barriers is by relying on bilingual staff. Many of these bilingual providers demonstrate more empathy and understanding toward those who primarily speak another language, either because they themselves are immigrants or have family members who primarily speak a language other than English. For example, Heejin, a bilingual nurse who grew up and attended a prestigious nursing school in Korea, told me that she viewed interpreting as her "responsibility." In part because it had been "very difficult" for her to "learn English" in advance of obtaining a nursing license after immigrating to the US, she said she "always [took her] time with Korean patients." Otherwise, she said it could be "terrifying" to "end up in a place where nobody speaks your language" for patients who are "physically sick," going through "multiple surgeries," and "vulnerable." Although patients need to be able to "ask questions" and "find out what is going on with [their] body," she had noticed that many monolingual Korean patients opted against communicating with nurses unless the nurses addressed them in Korean first. Patients are "so happy to see me, and they start asking a lot of questions," she grinned.

Heejin's own experiences of being an English-language learner weren't the only factor contributing to her willingness to slow down and explain things to patients. She was also cognizant of the way that other nurses—the majority of whom were White women—could be condescending and hostile toward immigrants. For Heejin, managing her "relationship" with her "coworkers" was one of the most difficult work tasks. She shared several stories that indicated other nurses' disdain toward non-English speakers. The other nurses, she suspected, "think I am just playing with them or something," and it seemed to her that charge nurses purposely "isolated" and "excluded" her by slotting her into the "worst night shifts." Despite the pride she took in providing care to Korean patients, this treatment left her feeling "lonely" and "rejected."

Rosa was another bilingual nurse who "did not mind translating" for her patients. Unlike Heejin—who came to the US as an adult—Rosa moved from Mexico when she was eight years old. Unlike many other 1.5 generation immigrants, she became fluent in Spanish as a result of the years she spent as a young language broker. Years later, Rosa said that Spanish-speaking patients always reminded her of her mother. Rosa thus took it very "personally" when the nurses and doctors spoke to a patient "in English really fast, knowing that this patient is struggling to communicate." "Maybe they've had a bad day, but I need to think about my parents and what they've been through in this country," she said.

At this point in the interview, Rosa's cell phone began ringing. Rosa glanced down and told me she needed to take the call. It was her neighbor, who had just moved to the US a few months earlier. Since her neighbor primarily spoke Spanish, Rosa was helping her enroll her child in school. After taking the call, Rosa picked back up, telling me that, as much as she disliked seeing her coworkers gloss over non-English-speaking patients' questions and concerns, she could also "understand" their "point of view." "It's hard for everyone," Rosa said. The hospital had scant triage space, and it took "teamwork" to ensure patients were seen "as soon as possible." And it wasn't as if she could readily communicate with every patient herself. When she had "a Korean patient," she needed "Korean nurses to help [her] too." Especially on "a very busy day," Rosa said it was often more efficient for her to "go in and translate" than wait for a telephone interpreter. Although it was "extra work" that fell "outside of [her] job description," it was the only way to prevent patients from "waiting all day" to be seen.

For nurses like Heejin and Rosa, bilingualism is an asset. It enables them to ensure that all patients, regardless of the language they speak, receive the best care possible. Although hospitals do not formally compensate bilingual nurses for this additional work, their commitment to translating stems from an awareness that English-speaking institutions are difficult—if not impossible—for monolingual immigrants to navigate without a translator. To them, the extra effort to secure non-English speaking patients' rightful institutional resources appear to be a form of what sociologist Adia Wing-field calls "equity work."[9] Similar to the way that Black healthcare providers often attempt to give back to their communities at a time when healthcare organizations are prioritizing efficiency and profits, many bilingual nurses I interviewed viewed their bilingual skills as a means of ensuring hospitals maximized the number of patients they could see and help.

Not all bilingual workers, however, expressed an unwavering commitment to performing equity work on behalf of their employers. Understaffing in underfunded institutions means that all nurses, regardless of the language they speak, have to take on additional responsibilities; bilingual staff without institutionalized language support can get frustrated with just how much extra work they are expected to do. Valentina, another bilingual nurse who spoke English and Spanish fluently, was blunt about the ways "coworkers and doctors always asked" her to perform uncompensated work that wasn't included in her job description. "We talked about it" at staff meetings, she said, "and some [nurses] are very unhappy about it. Because when they are busy and someone just calls them and asks them to translate, it can be upsetting."

Still, racialized and gendered power dynamics in hospitals leave bilingual nurses—the majority of whom are women of color—with little choice. Oftentimes, these requests come from doctors, who are more likely to be White men. Crystal, an ICU nurse who spoke Korean and English fluently, said it was nearly impossible to "say no" to doctors who asked her to perform unpaid translation work. This was especially the case with one of her hospital's ER doctors, who regularly expected her to "leave her patients" on the fourth floor so that she could translate for his patients on the hospital's first floor. Crystal implicitly acknowledged that the racialized and gendered occupational hierarchy between nurses and doctors cast her into the role of being a doctor's "personal translator." Instead of telling him she "was too busy to translate for him," she often "had to find someone to cover [her] patients and go down to ER to translate for his Korean patients."

Similarly, being bilingual generally adds to the work of the frontline but lower-status police officers who work at the precinct's reception desk. Martin, whose translating for his coworkers was described earlier in this chapter, was one of the few bilingual officers in this public-facing role. Relatively new to the position, he was often the first officer to greet people who came up to the front desk. Upon meeting me, Martin told me how proud he felt every time he put on his uniform. "We all do that," Martin said as he turned to another officer standing next to him—"look at ourselves in the mirror and show up to a party with our uniform on. Right?"

Seemingly eager to prove his capabilities to more senior officers, Martin always arrived at the station fifteen minutes before his shift began. Whereas many officers let the phone ring when they were busy, Martin always answered and placed callers on hold if he was helping someone else. During downtime, other officers retreated to a lounge area near the back of the lobby, where they chatted and relaxed. But Martin always remained at the front desk, seemingly ready to take on more responsibilities than other officers, especially more senior officers—the majority of whom were White men.

Because Martin rarely complained, it stood out when, one day, he loudly sighed while recording handwritten reports into the station's electronic system. He nodded in the direction of the pile of police reports. "You see this pile?" Martin whispered to me. He shifted his gaze from the stack of reports to a senior White officer, chatting and laughing with the (White, male) supervisor a few feet away. "And he has nothing to do."

Considering that Martin was already shouldering more responsibilities than other officers, he told me he sometimes felt "frustrated" when he "stepped into translate" or "take on Spanish speakers." He understood that Spanish speakers "want to speak to someone who speaks their language," but the "unequal division labor" within the station felt "unfair." Due to his subordinate position in the organization, he knew he couldn't say no, especially when his supervisors asked him to "take the call" or take on "Hispanic civilians."

Supervisors and coworkers often automatically assume that Latinx and Asian American police officers and healthcare providers are bilingual by virtue of their ethnicity —another source of frustration. For example, Kevin, a Latinx police officer who was born and raised in Los Angeles, told me that he grew up speaking Spanish with his grandmother. Since the police academy did not require bilingual officers to pass a formal competency exam, he had "sold" his bilingual skills during his job interview. During his first few weeks on the job, however, he told me that he quickly realized he wasn't as fluent in Spanish as he thought. He felt flummoxed when his White coworkers assumed he would be able to translate specialized language—such as "Miranda rights" and "probable cause"—from English into Spanish while in the middle of performing other aspects of his job.

Unlike English monolinguals who assume they can get by on body language, Latinx and Asian American workers are often acutely aware of the risks of speaking to patients in a language with which they are not familiar. Isabel, a Mexican American nurse, told me she encountered "a lot of racism" in the hospital where she worked. Because she looked "Mexican," the doctors and patients "automatically assumed" she spoke Spanish. But, as a third-generation Mexican American who had grown up in Los Angeles, her Spanish was "not good" and she worried that someone might sue if they were to experience "a complication from the surgery" after she attempted to explain the procedure and its risks.

In recent years, as budgets have gotten tighter and labor shortages more acute, hospitals have increasingly relied on nursing aides and health technicians to fill support positions. As a result of broader systems of inequality, employees in these lower-status and low-wage positions are more likely to be immigrants and thus, more likely to bilingual themselves.[10] Oftentimes, hospitals pay nursing aides low hourly wages for performing physically and emotionally demanding tasks that are nonetheless vital to maintaining patients' comfort, safety, and well-being. As a result of institutions' failure to provide sufficient language support for their patients, the nurses I interviewed also occasionally expected bilingual nursing aides to perform the additional labor of translating for patients. If they were desperate for a translator, nurses said they turned to custodians and food service staff, too.

While I did not interview any nursing aides or hospital support staff, their lower position within workplace hierarchies likely amplifies the frustrations reported by many of the bilingual nurses I interviewed. Bilingual staff are constrained into performing unpaid work that falls outside the scope of their job description. Nonetheless, performing this invisible labor is crucial in ensuring hospitals are able to maintain efficiency at a time when institutional resources are scare.

SIZING UP CLIENTS

As noted above, nurses are well aware that, under California state law, patients have the right to file for medical liability or medical malpractice if healthcare providers' negligence causes injury to the patient. However, few healthcare providers, especially those who worked in hospitals located in low-income neighborhoods, sounded overly concerned about potential lawsuits from patients who primarily spoke a language other than English. Instead, they generally considered immigrants of color as unlikely to file complaints or lawsuits against their institutions.

In fact, despite feeling frustrated at the difficulties of communicating with non-English-speaking patients, many nurses (and the handful of doctors I interviewed) tended to describe first-generation immigrants as "nice," "docile," "subservient," "passive," and "cooperative." They also said these patients were "grateful," "more appreciative," and less "demanding" than English-speaking patients. Caitlin, a nurse who described "Asian patients" as "docile," remarked that their inability to "speak the language" increased the likelihood that they would "just accept what is going on" and "follow your orders," while Olivia said that it was "much more unlikely" that patients would "complain or ask to speak to the charge nurse" if they spoke only "broken English." Conflating English facility with being American, Olivia added that these patients tended to be "more cooperative" than "Americans," who "will complain about everything without blinking an eye." Sabrina agreed, describing immigrants as more "subservient" and "a lot more passive" and saying that non-English speakers were more likely to "just follow" along and to ask fewer questions than "American" patients. Speculating that it might be a "generation thing," she added that "first-generation immigrants" and "little ladies from Guatemala" were often "grateful and thankful for whatever [they] can get."

Although most nurses left gender unmarked, it was often clear that they were referring to women when they described immigrants as docile and passive. Indeed, in the rare instances when a nurse called non-English speakers "aggressive," it was in reference to immigrant men. For example, Nicole, an ICU nurse, said it was "frustrating" and "hard" when she ran into "communication issues" with patients. Instead of "cooperating" and following her instructions, she said that patients often became "mad," "aggressive," "agitated" and "combative." Although she did not explicitly identify the patients' gender for the most part, she said, "If they want to go to bathroom, I have to tell them, 'You can't go because you fractured your bone.' Then they get mad because you are not letting them get up. And this one time, this patient didn't understand me, so he ripped the IV."

Such statements made clear how difficult it is for non-English speaking patients to access basic social provisions—such as proper medical treatments and care—within busy institutions that tacitly allow sexism and racialized nativism toward patients to remain largely unchecked. Instead of pointing patients in the direction of complaint forms translated into different languages, English-speaking authorities like Sabrina had the impression that non-English-speaking immigrants—especially women—would remain "thankful" for whatever service they received.

And yet, this did not mean that everyone is passed over or overlooked in the name of efficiency. English monolinguals who are White seem to have an easier time being heard. This pattern was exemplified one afternoon when a White man walked into the police station with a young girl in tow. Although all the officers at the front desk were busy speaking with other people, the man walked straight up to Officer Martin and interrupted.

"Sir, I will be right with you, but please sign your name first," Martin said.

The man glanced at the station full of people and wrote his name—Chad—on the wait list, muttering, "We are going to be here forever."

In this station, located in a mostly low-income, non-White neighborhood, I observed, at most, a handful of White people come in on any given day. Rather than taking a seat, Chad continued to stand at the front desk, occasionally interrupting the police officers. For instance, after skimming the wait list, he asked, "Do you usually get this many people?" His behavior appeared to be distracting to the officers, who kept looking in his direction. When Officer Martin finally called Chad's name, the source of his impatience became clear: his stepdaughter, who was Mexican American, had been physically abused by a teacher at her school.

It was relatively rare for people who came into the station to report incidents that involved child abuse. However, Officer Martin responded in a way that aligned with the station's tendency toward following jurisdiction and protocol. He told Chad the matter required school police attention, then began searching on his computer for the contact information for the district's police department.

Whereas many other people I observed tended to accept the officer's instructions, Chad pushed back. "I already tried the school police," Chad said.

Martin explained more fully that school-related issues fell outside the precinct's jurisdiction, but Chad refused to take no for an answer.

"Can I speak with your supervisor?" he asked.

Martin waved to his supervisor, who asked Chad and his stepdaughter to come into his office. After about fifteen minutes, the station filled with the sound of laughter as the supervisor—also a White man—opened his office door. Chad and the supervising officer laughed all the way back to Martin's desk, where they interrupted his work with another person. Then the supervisor instructed Martin to call the school district's police department and ask them to file a report for Chad. He waited with Chad until Martin hung up the phone several minutes later, at which point he instructed Chad to pick up the police report from the school district's police station.

Although I did not witness Chad's conversation with the supervisors, his move to speak to a higher-up enabled him to access the resources he needed. In the end, the police officers smoothed out the step of filing a police report for Chad, even as they knew that this case did not fall under their jurisdiction. Although it is likely that this outcome occurred due to his unwillingness to take no as an answer, he was also able to present his case as more urgent and serious in a space full of English-speaking White men.

Healthcare providers I spoke with also understood that there are patients whose status enables them to more easily access the care to which they are entitled. Indeed, despite identifying language barriers as one of the "biggest problems" they encounter at work, nurses often described rich, educated patients—who deployed English to communicate their needs and status—as the hospital's most difficult patients. For example, Rosa contrasted "less educated people" who might "yell or curse" with the difficulties of interacting with patients who are "more educated." Although they were polite to nurses' faces, these patients were far more likely to "write a letter" or "talk to the charge nurse" if they felt unsatisfied with the treatment they received.

"If patients are highly educated, they will tell you the plan of care," Rosa said. "They won't listen to you but tell you what should happen with their labor. Because they have more education, they think that they are superior [to their] nurse."

Other nurses described "rich people" similarly. Kim, who worked in an

ICU, said that rich people not only "question everything that you do," but they "also act like their relatives are the only patients in the hospital." Instead of recognizing that nurses have "other patients" to help, they are quick to "complain" unless you "go check up on them every five minutes." "They don't care about other people," she said. "It's all about me, me, me."

While I did not observe "rich" and "educated" people interacting with nurses, research has found that upper-middle-class people are far more likely to advocate for themselves in ways that coerce institutions to address their needs.[11] Indeed, a key part of having their needs met is having and using the right language to complain to supervisors. Knowing that "rich and educated" patients are more likely to complain and file lawsuits, nurses often described preemptive attempts to placate them. Nicole, for instance, took a deep breath before describing the way that nurses were often "scared to take care of rich people" because they "might get sued."

Although most nurses avoided making explicit reference to race, some nurses interchangeably used the phrases "rich people" and "White patient." For example, recall Sabrina, the delivery room nurse who described the "little Guatemalan lady" as "submissive." She said that "the more difficult" patients tended to be ones with "more money." They often treated nurses like a "waitress" who is there "to serve them" and "expect doctors to check up on them more often." "That's a joke, but it's true," Sabrina said. "So, if they are more educated, they have more questions. They look up [information] on the internet before they come into the hospital. So, our White patients are more difficult."

Crystal was also among the handful of nurses who explicitly mentioned Whiteness when describing her most difficult patients. She dubbed "picky, entitled, and very wealthy" patients—who tended to be donors' family members or doctors' "friends"—as "VIPs." She said these VIP patients were "almost always White patients." Given their status, the "hospital administration" tended to make "special accommodations" to accommodate their "unusual demands." By way of example, Crystal cited a time when her hospital allowed a "VIP" patient to store flowers and gifts in a separate hospital room. And because ICU policies often prevent patients from having more than two visitors in their room at a time, this patient's guests used this second room as a private waiting area. The actual work of pleasing VIP patients, moreover, often fell on the shoulders of nurses—most of whom were women. Although the hospital usually assigned one nurse to two ICU patients unless someone was "really sick," Crystal also said this same patient—who was "not that sick"—had "one nurse" to "care" for them and stayed in the "ICU longer than they needed to." "When they finally moved out of ICU, they requested the same ICU nurse, so she followed them to a different unit," Crystal remembered.

To be clear, Crystal's hospital did not go out of its way to ensure all educated White people received "special treatment." Still, because a small fraction of White people holds the majority of wealth in the US, it is not coincidence that these "VIPs" were almost always White. And although Crystal said it was "unfair" that "management allowed this to happen," she and other nurses expressed far less concern when non-English-speaking immigrants—who were mostly people of color—received an inadequate amount of institutional resources, such as the translation services to which they were legally entitled. Instead, nurses who worked in busy and underfunded hospitals sounded frustrated when non-English speakers "wasted" hospital resources by attempting to communicate their needs. As evidenced by their tendency to characterize non-English-speaking patients as "docile" and "submissive," nurses implicitly coded immigrants of color as perpetual foreigners—they weren't entitled to this same level of care because they weren't Americans.

This assumption that basic social citizenship rights should be reserved for "real" Americans became clear near the end of Sabrina's interview. I warned Sabrina that my next question might be difficult to answer. "What can be changed to make your job easier?" I asked.

Considering that Sabrina spoke at great length about how educated rich White people were her most difficult patients, I expected her to discuss specific protocols the hospital could implement to distribute resources more equitably. I was wrong. She said that immigrants were the ones who could make her job easier.

"This is not a difficult question," Sabrina responded without hesitation. "Learning English is the simplest and easiest solution. If I move to France, I have to learn how to speak French." Rather than wanting to enforce immigrants' rights under the law, Sabrina blamed the non-English-speaking immigrants for failing to speak English—something she seemed to think was a simple, straightforward process though she was monolingual herself.

Taken together, it was clear that nurses primarily worried about meeting the basic social citizenship rights of those patients they believed most likely to file complaints or lawsuits—those who were rich, educated, and tended to be

White. Consequently, they preemptively afforded wealthy White people more than their basic share of rights. This left even less time and energy to be divided among the rest of the patients, especially non-English speakers of color the nurses deemed "docile." Blaming immigrants' inability to speak English for the series of inequalities they revealed shows that these institutional agents inevitably prioritized profit and efficiency over equality. They simply didn't have enough time and energy to provide social citizenship for all.

RELYING ON BILINGUAL CHILDREN OF IMMIGRANTS

When I met healthcare providers for an interview, it was common for them to start the conversation by talking about their frequent interactions with children of immigrants acting as their family members' translators. For example, Lisa, an ER doctor, knew that my research was about child language brokers, and so she began, "We get that a lot, especially with Hispanic population. They bring little kids all the time and ask them to translate."

As I've shown, in busy institutional contexts where English-speaking agents view professional interpreting services as inefficient, they instead rely on bilingual staff for ad hoc translation services. The second-best choice is frequently a child.

"Just today, I had a forty-year-old patient who spoke Spanish," Lisa said. "I told her, the patient, to sit on the edge of the bed, but she could not understand. Her daughter was ten years old, and she speaks Spanish, so she was doing all the translation."

It was unclear why the child was with her mother that day, but in an ER, it was always possible that the mother had a crisis and, without the time to line up childcare, was forced to bring her along. But, like other institutional agents, Lisa assumed this girl was present in order to translate.

Joyce, a nurse who also worked in the ER, confirmed that she saw children interpreting for their parents "all the time." In fact, it was so normal that doctors often "would not make the effort" to talk to non-English-speaking patients. Instead, they defaulted to speaking with a patient's son or daughter. "Doctors come [in the room] for the non-English-speaking patients and ask us, 'Is the son here, daughter here?' Because they know that sons and daughters might speak English, so he wants to speak to them," Joyce said.

In fact, easing effective communication was the primary reason English-speaking agents so readily turned to children to broker conversation. Instead of using her "broken Spanish" to convey very "limited information" to her patients, Crystal said, bilingual children enabled her to "explain a lot more." Where she might otherwise only be able to instruct a non-English speaker to "take this medicine," the presence of a bilingual child allowed her to explain "why they are getting this medication, what this is for, and what side effects there might be," as well as "what is going on with the patient" and "the long-term plans" for their health.

Daisy, another nurse, also said it was "nice," "convenient," and "productive" when a non-English speaker brought a bilingual child with them to the hospital. If she could "rely on bilingual family [members] or children," she could gather information about a patient's condition and medical symptoms faster. When children were around, Daisy could also ask "multiple questions to evaluate patients' progress" and "explain" procedures in more depth. "It saves me time," Daisy said.

Despite relying on bilingual children "all the time," English-speaking agents often reported feeling ambivalent or uncomfortable about doing so. It felt "off" to ask young people to translate in settings where adults were accessing critical and urgent services, and some worried that the medical information was too difficult for young people to comprehend. A nurse named Nicole said they were "not supposed to use" "young children" as translators because they are "too young to process complicated information." Nonetheless, Nicole admitted that she and other staff relied on children "all the time without even thinking about it." It was "faster." She didn't have to go around looking for hospital's "housekeeper" or her bilingual coworkers, who "do not always love to help out."

Other institutional agents expressed similar beliefs. They said that young people needed to be shielded from some of the information communicated to their family members. Molly, a nurse, told me that she didn't want to have to tell children that "your mom is dying." Jack, a police officer, also worried that expecting young people to communicate sensitive details about criminal investigations could be "too much to bear" and "not suitable for their age." "In theory, you are not supposed to use kids," he said.

Several monolingual, English-speaking nurses I interviewed also worried that young people might purposely omit information when interpreting for their parents. Recalling a time when a child did not want to tell her father that he had cancer, Claire said to me, "She was withholding information. So, sometimes, I don't like to use children too much because they say something that I didn't say. They say, 'You are not dying,' but that's not what I said. In an ideal world, I will not use a child, because they are not honest with you," she said.

Of course, English-speaking agents were cognizant of the fact that they didn't work in an ideal world. Claire, an ICU nurse, told me that waiting for a telephone interpreter would slow her down in an "extremely busy" institution. Relying on "children who were right there" was often the "fastest" and "easiest" way to "resolve the communication issue." According to English-speaking agents, when they used language brokers, those seeking institutional services ended up receiving faster and better care.

UNEQUAL ENCOUNTERS

In the US, those who "fail" to learn English are constructed as a burden to society and a threat to national unity. This prevalent view is reflected in opinion polls. The vast majority of Republicans—96 percent in 2016 and 89 percent in 2020—believe that speaking English is the most important feature of "being truly American."[12] Most Democrats—87 percent in 2016 and 65 percent in 2020—agree. Indeed, Americans deemed all other characteristics—such as sharing US customs and traditions or being a Christian—as less important markers of American identity than speaking English. Even being born in the US is less tightly coupled with notions of truly belonging in America than the ability to speak English. In some ways, these results are unsurprising. After all, there is a long history of an English-only movements in the US. When combined with populist rhetoric deployed by politicians and mainstream depictions of immigrants in the media, learning English is widely assumed to be an important precursor to becoming an American.

In a social and political context where language is perceived as an identifiable marker of one's ability to "assimilate" into the American mainstream, essential-service providers—who work in busy, crowded, and underfunded institutions—often avoided explicitly stereotyping immigrants based on their race and gender. They also opted not to criticize their workplace for neglecting to uphold immigrants' rights. Instead, they often said they have little choice but to prioritize efficiency over equality and blamed immigrants for making their jobs unnecessarily challenging. While doing so, they used Asian and Spanish languages as indicators that low-income immigrants of color, especially women, are undeserving of full social citizenship rights due to their "failure" to learn English. Even essential-service providers who briefly acknowledged state-mandated language assistance for non-English-speakers assumed that it would be burdensome or impractical to use formal interpreting services on a regular basis. Ultimately, despite working in a city where most residents speak at least one language other than English, essential-service providers assumed that those who speak languages other than English would remain "docile" and "grateful" for whatever amount of assistance they received.

Instead of relying on formal interpreting services, healthcare providers and police officers often attempted to bridge language gaps in busy, crowded, and underfunded institutions by enlisting the assistance of bilingual staff. However, bilingual staff—especially those who occupy lower-ranking positions within these organizations—often felt coerced into performing unpaid "equity labor"[13] that is devalued within English-speaking institutions. Furthermore, there was a limited number of bilingual staff, and staff who were conversationally proficient in Spanish or Korean sometimes lacked the specific terminology to translate complex medical or legal jargon.

In the absence of readily available adult translators, institutional agents often viewed children of immigrants as the next best option. Many doubted children's capabilities but asking children to translate spared English-monolingual workers the effort of repeatedly seeking out bilingual staff's language skills. This approach also led to quicker and higher-quality patient care. It broadened the range of instructions or explanations that these agents could offer since they no longer had to rely solely on gestures and their limited Spanish and Korean vocabularies. Essentially, bilingual children of immigrants play a pivotal role in ensuring the ongoing operation of English-speaking institutions.

Undoubtedly, the hospitals and police stations in this study offer only a partial glimpse of the broader landscape of English-speaking institutions. These establishments, situated in low-income and racially segregated neighborhoods of Southern California, cannot be taken as representative of all hospitals and police stations in the US. However, Southern California—especially Los Angeles—presents a strategic site to understand how language intersects with other forms of inequality to prevent immigrants of color from receiving full citizenship rights. No single racial or ethnic group constitutes a majority in the state of California. A majority of residents of Los Angeles primarily speak a language other than English, and Spanish and Korean are among the most widely spoken languages. If a region with such extensive linguistic and racial diversity is unable to offer crucial services to immigrants, healthcare facilities and law enforcement agencies in other areas of the US may be even more inclined to withhold resources from monolingual immigrants of color who "fail" to speak English.

Nonetheless, we should not automatically assume that essential workers themselves are to blame. As illustrated in this chapter, essential service workers operating on the frontlines contend with various forms of discrimination stemming from their relatively low rung in both organizational and societal hierarchies. The issue primarily stems from federal and state policies that direct resources away from low-income neighborhoods and toward affluent, predominantly White suburbs. In resource-rich areas, there are often fewer people seeking services and more staff to ensure that institutions and governmental agencies maintain their efficiency. In contrast, in neighborhoods and areas where governments have redirected resources away for the past century, there is an increasing demand for services but a dwindling number of staff to provide them.

Although essential-service providers operate within institutions that prioritize efficiency over equality, attributing the need for change to immigrants deflects attention away from profound social inequalities in the US such as underfunded and overcrowded public institutions. The seemingly simple solution of expecting immigrants to learn English masks a myriad of economic, political, and cultural forces that systematically exclude immigrants of color from receiving fundamental social citizenship rights. There is also a dearth of language support, affordable housing, safe and reliable childcare, and jobs that offer living wages, flexible work schedules, and adequate health insurance. Moreover, the disproportionate attention given to wealthy, White, English-speaking individuals even within these crowded and underfunding institutions exacerbates the issue, leaving even fewer resources to be distributed among the remaining patients. Within this context, assigning blame to working-class immigrants of color—especially women—for "failing" to learn English is essentially placing responsibility on those who bear the most pronounced consequences of larger structural inequalities. Even if all immigrants did speak English, these broader social problems would persist. And speaking English fluently would not resolve other structural problems that working-class immigrants of color regularly encounter, such as racialized nativism and sexism.

The multiple and intersecting structural inequalities that low-income immigrants of color face in the US is a topic I examine greater detail in chapter 3, which delves deeper into the everyday realities that immigrants of color encounter in a so-called nation of immigrants. When the state fails to ensure everyone's fundamental citizenship rights are met, language brokering becomes a "normal" family responsibility for bilingual children of immigrants.

THREE BECOMING LANGUAGE BROKERS

Hemi, a sixteen-year-old, was the eldest child of working-class Korean immigrant parents. She spoke English and Korean fluently and described herself as a jovial soul with a keen sense of humor. After we found a place to sit in the back corner of a crowded Korean coffee shop near her school, Hemi—who was sitting a triple berry smoothie—playfully warned me that she was going to "speak Konglish" to me "here and there." She began describing how "normal" and "natural" it had been for her to become her family's language broker when she was seven years old—shortly after her family immigrated to the US.

"Life was tough, very tough when we first came to the United States," Hemi said. "We had to learn very quickly that things aren't the same as it was in Korea. We knew that we were all we've got."

Upon their arrival in Los Angeles, Hemi recalled that her family had squeezed into a small one-bedroom apartment in Koreatown. Her mother, a "superwoman" who had never worked outside their home in Korea, quickly found a job as a server in a Korean restaurant. She also shouldered numerous responsibilities around the house. She cooked, cleaned, went grocery shopping, and managed the household finances. In contrast, Hemi's father encountered a rough patch in his quest for steady employment in the US.[1] Despite having worked steadily as a teacher in Korea, Hemi said that her father's ability to "be the breadwinner" was momentarily disrupted by the move. A "mainstream" job remained beyond his grasp due to his limited English proficiency.

"I remember him venturing out every single day in search of work," Hemi recalled. A deep sigh escaped her lips as she recounted the impact of her father's under- or unemployment on their family. Hemi occasionally caught glimpses of her mom crying "because she was so scared." "It just broke my heart," Hemi said. "We didn't know what to do. We were buying the cheapest things we were able to find. We rarely went to the shopping mall because my mom would just sew clothes for us."

After months of relentless job hunting with no breakthroughs, Hemi's father made a pivotal decision to "start from the bottom." Relief infused her voice as Hemi said, "Thank God he didn't give up. He found a job as a dishwasher in a Korean restaurant."

Since her parents worked constantly and hardly knew any English, Hemi said that it took them a while to navigate the intricacies of enrolling their children in nearby public schools. Initially, Hemi and her siblings spent a significant amount of time alone at home. "We would just stay home trying to learn English by reading books and watching TV," Hemi said. She and her brother would also "test each other." Sometimes they played a game they called "speed bingo," which entailed learning at least twenty English words per day—a skill that was helpful once their parents' started to receive "so much" mail. "My mom thought it would be a good idea for us to use all these materials as a study tool. So, we would use the dictionary, and by the time my parents came home at night, we would have all the letters translated," Hemi said.

Hemi recalled sitting next to her mother and helping her go through the mail. As she translated, she would get her mother's "feedback" to make sure "everything made sense to her." Like other young people I interviewed, Hemi said that her English skills "dramatically improved," especially as she began interacting with English-speaking peers and teachers at school. Now, almost a decade later, her English-speaking skills were "very good"—an accomplishment she was quite "proud of."

By comparison, Hemi knew her parents had fewer opportunities to practice speaking English. They mainly interacted with other Korean immigrants at work and still struggled to grasp the intricacies of the language. "They were so busy, so they didn't have time to learn English," she said.

"Did you wish that your parents learn English?" I asked.

"No."

"No? That would not make your life a bit easier?"

She paused for a moment, as if she were attempting to discern why I was asking a question with an answer that seemed obvious to her. "It would be nice if they can go to school and learn English," she said. "There is that pressure for immigrants to learn English. I mean, people think it's so easy to learn a new language. But unfortunately, not everyone gets that opportunity and time, you know."

I nodded affirmingly as she continued speaking.

"My parents, like all immigrants, struggle every day. They have jobs. They are trying to provide for the family, so trying to learn English will stand in the way of that. But I became good at it. It's just easier for me to go through the mail and translate."

When asked to name the places where she served as a translator for her parents, Hemi's face lit up. "Everywhere!" she exclaimed. Ticking off locations on her fingers, she said she translated at the mall, the doctor's office, Walmart, small claims court, the school, the emergency room, the apartment manager's office, and the pharmacy. "Wait. That's eight. Right? There are more," she said. Hemi continued describing different English-speaking adults she regularly spoke with, which included agents from credit card companies, car insurance agencies, the cable company, the electricity company, the bank, the DMV, and the social security office.

Hemi's responsibilities didn't stop there. Since her parents toiled long hours in the service industry to scrape together a modest living, Hemi began assuming additional domestic duties at home. She often lent a helping hand to her brother and her US-born sister, assisting with their homework and preparing simple meals like Kraft macaroni and cheese.

Yet, as she recounted her encounters with monolingual English speakers over the years, Hemi's smile gradually faded. She had met "kind people," but many others were "condescending," "impatient," "dismissive," and "abrupt" in their interactions with both Hemi and her parents. Hemi recalled a "disturbing" encounter with a nurse when her mother went to the hospital attempting to seek relief for relentless migraines.

"What did she say?" I inquired.

Hemi's voice rose, and she spoke slowly, mimicking the nurse's tone as she spelled out her instructions letter by letter to "get on the scale." "Why yell at my mom like that?" Hemi asked. "It's hard not to get upset when it's my mom. She acted as if she were an adult scolding a child." Hemi paused and then continued speaking in a calmer and more measured tone. She wished she could have said to the nurse, "Please, don't speak to her that way. I'm here. Talk to me."

Hemi's parents were not the only working-class immigrants of color who faced racialized nativism—that is, hostility and antagonism based on their perceived foreignness.[2] Nor was her family unique in experiencing financial precarity. It was striking how all the language brokers I talked to repeatedly recalled how their parents were "mistreated," "disrespected," and "looked down upon" for speaking a language other than English. Nor was it a coincidence that Hemi's parents wound up with low-wage jobs and struggled to make ends meet. Scholars have consistently demonstrated that people of color often end up working in low-status jobs after immigrating to the US.[3] In addition to working long hours, they often face exploitative working conditions and lack access to benefits like employer-subsidized health insurance plans.[4] This trend applies even to immigrants of color who attained college degrees and held lucrative careers in their country of origin.[5] Despite their prior experience, they are often excluded from racialized workplaces that require English proficiency.[6] And because institutionalized racism and linguistic discrimination have historically prevented immigrant men of color from earning a family wage, immigrant women of color—including those without formal work experience outside the home prior to migration—often find feminized, labor-intensive jobs to help supplement their partner's under- or unemployment in the US.[7]

In a nation where language becomes a racialized mechanism to exclude immigrants of color from receiving basic citizenship rights (as discussed in chapter 2), Hemi—like other young people in this study—attempted to make up for her family's lack of a sufficient safety net herself. Witnessing the multiple inequalities her parents faced in the US instilled a strong sense of determination in Hemi, who came to believe it was "natural" for her to help ensure her family's well-being and, at times, survival. Furthermore, as Hemi's skills as a translator improved, she became increasingly invested in helping her parents access a variety of resources they otherwise would have been denied. Over time, her family responsibilities gradually expanded to include other dimensions of care work that her parents did not have time to perform, such as cooking and taking care of her younger siblings.

This chapter considers how the children of immigrants like Hemi come to think of language brokering as "normal" in a society where children are seen as "incompetent" and "naïve." Consistent with the perspectives of the healthcare providers and police officers I introduced in chapter 2, children of immigrants viewed being a language broker as an effective way to ensure their parents could communicate with institutional agents in the busy and overcrowded institutions they navigated. And yet, when they stepped in as language brokers, they witnessed the range of social problems their families were experiencing and became accustomed to developing individual solutions to larger structural inequalities. Ultimately, language-brokering work was both externally imposed and socially enforced by the lack of social citizenship rights afforded to working-class immigrant families of color.

STEPPING INTO THE BROKERING ROLE: CHILDREN OF IMMIGRANTS AS PARENTS' "MOUTH AND EARS"

Language brokers were always perplexed when I asked, "Why do you translate for your parents?" Nearly all the children I interviewed answered this question by saying it was "normal," "natural," and "ordinary."[8]

Edson, a fourteen-year-old Mexican American, responded with raised eyebrows and a puzzled look. "Why do I translate for my parents?" he asked. "I never thought about that, but to me, it's common sense: they need my help."

Another child, seventeen-year-old Mina, paused for a moment as if to determine why I had asked such an unreasonable question. "I am good at this. I am like their mouth and ears. It's my responsibility," she answered.

Most language brokers could not even recall when they started translating. Minho, a fifteen-year-old Korean American youth, said, "Honestly, it's just an everyday thing that I don't recall the very first time. They needed me and I was there." Young people often engage in more mundane forms of language-brokering work than speaking to healthcare providers and police, such as ordering pizza, interpreting television shows, or speaking to retailers.[9] And yet, partly because the process of becoming their parents' "mouths and ears" was gradual, young people rarely spoke about more routine forms of language brokering when asked about their earliest interpretation memories. For many youth, moments in adult-centric spaces like hospitals, police stations, and pharmacies served as what sociologist Arlie Hochschild calls "magnified moments."[10] Stakes were high, and so these memories stood out. Further, while children of immigrants described their language-brokering work as "normal," they also knew that adult authorities did not perceive their work as "normal," especially if they had started speaking for their parents in adult-centric spaces at a young age. For example, Danbi, a fourteen-year-old Korean American, recalled visiting an emergency room with her mom when her five-year-old sister had a high fever. "I was a little kid at the time, so of course people did not take me seriously. People there really wanted to talk to my mom," she said. But, as she remembered, her mother had been unable to find someone to translate. After one of the receptionists "failed" to find a bilingual person, Danbi, who was eight at the time, stepped in.[11]

Assuming their parents would use formal translation services if they were available, few young people recalled requesting them. Amy, a fifteen-year-old Korean American, was one of the only a handful who recalled a time she had asked if someone who spoke Korean was available. "Most people want to speak with an adult, and I was very young at the time," she said of a memorable pharmacy trip with her parents. "So, I asked if anyone speaks Korean, but they said no. I had to do it."

Alda, a seventeen-year-old Mexican American, said she was "really young" ("maybe eight or nine years old") and "still learning English" when she first translated for her parents at a police station. They went to report a robbery, and Alda recalled, "I was hoping that someone there speaks Spanish. Someone brought this bilingual officer, but his Spanish was so bad. I was better at [interpreting]."

As reflected in Amy's and Alda's statements, some young people did not show up to these adult-centric institutions intending to serve as an interpreter for their parents. Not only did they know that these spaces were not child-friendly, but they recognized that being a child diminished their chances of being heard. And yet, young people often witnessed adults struggling to communicate, which in turn compelled them to interpret for their parents. At least in the beginning, serving as their parents' "mouth and ears" seemed a "natural" way to speed up the process in English-speaking institutions.

Schools provide other examples of high-stakes language brokering. For example, Suejin, a fifteen-year-old Korean American, remembered one of her earliest memories of translating for her mother when her younger sister got into a fight at school. "My mom had to show up even though she was working at the time and can't speak English." Suejin was ten at the time.

Suejin was a straight-A student who was pursuing a slate of extracurricular activities ranging from cheerleading to band. When asked if her parents attended any of her school events, she seemed surprised. "Oh my gosh, rarely. When I was younger, I literally begged them to come. I do a lot of activities in school, but they never came."

"Why couldn't they come?" I asked.

"Well, according to them, I do too much. There are holiday concerts, these games, that games, but they just didn't have time."

After a pause, she continued, "American parents always go to children's events, so I wanted them to come." Although it was a "big deal" for Suejin, she quickly realized her mother didn't "fit in" when she showed up at one of holiday concerts. Her mother couldn't communicate with anyone—including her teachers—and looked "very uncomfortable." Suejin felt "so bad" that day that she "got over" wanting her mom to attend subsequent events. "I can't do that to my mom," she said.

Even when the vast majority of students in their school had Spanish-speaking parents, young people still reported that English-speaking school officials offered limited interpretation support. Maria, a sixteen-year-old Mexican American, said: "My elementary school had a lot of immigrants, mostly from Mexico and Guatemala, but most teachers could not speak Spanish. Looking back, it's kind of messed up that they did not have any Spanish interpreters. So, when my mom had to talk to my teachers, I had to translate."

When asked how her mother might have felt during such meetings, Maria demurred, "I am sure she felt embarrassed. People make all sorts of assumption about people who can't speak English. Like, they are ignorant or simply lazy because they are not willing to learn English. My mom is aware of that, but how can she help her children if nobody speaks Spanish?"

Children of immigrants in this study learned early on that their teachers understood caregiving as an adult, primarily maternal responsibility. As young people like Suejin and Maria reported, their schools were organized around the assumption that all parents, especially mothers, were available and able to participate, even though many immigrant parents worked in low-wage jobs that required long hours. With such work schedules, it was difficult for these parents to meet the institutional demands—at least in the way the schools expected mothers to do so. Amplifying the power differences between English-speaking school authorities and working-class immigrant parents of color, the very same institutions that expected parents to participate in their children's education generally failed to provide language services. As a result, even when they missed work to show up, immigrant mothers—in the eyes of children—looked "uncomfortable," "embarrassed," or could not easily "fit in."

In their research with immigrant parents in the United Kingdom, education scholars Gill Crozier and Jane Davies found that educators often referred to immigrant parents as "hard to reach" and criticized their lack of involvement in their children's lives.[12] In other words, educators, like healthcare workers and police officers, framed immigrants as a *problem*. And yet, as Crozier and Davies note, it is English-speaking institutions that are often "hard to reach" for immigrants. Institutions overlook the everyday lives of working-class immigrants and fail to provide sufficient language support. In this context, it becomes "normal" for bilingual youth to "help" their parents by filling an institutional void.

"I AM NOT GOING TO GIVE UP": CIRCUMSTANCES, GENDER, AND SIBLING DYNAMICS

I met Gabriella, a sixteen-year-old Mexican American, in front of the building where my office was located. Her mother, who had long black hair flecked with gray, walked Gabriella a half mile from their apartment to the university campus, then sat on a nearby bench outside to wait for her daughter. Gabriella flicked her ponytail over her shoulder and waved at her mother, who smiled at me. I smiled back. When we got to my office and began our interview, Gabriella described herself as her mother's "number one translator." She said that her mother was "strong" and "strict" and had "always wanted me to learn Spanish so I can communicate with her." Plus, Gabriella recalled, her mom told her, "People will always expect Mexicans to speak Spanish," because "you are not White."

"She would get me to read and write verses from the Bible and summarize [them], write it in my own words in Spanish," she said. "It was annoying back then, because [the] Bible itself is hard to understand, and I was a child. I remember thinking it was so useless because I didn't need it for anything else. But, when I was seven or eight, I started helping my mom with translation."

Carefully, Gabriella noted that her mother never "forced" her to translate. "I was one of those curious kids. I didn't like being unaware. I was committed to helping my family," she said. She was also more "mature" and "reliable" than her siblings, both of whom were younger. "My brother was clueless about what was going on in the family," Gabriella laughed. So, when translating duties arose, they went to her.

Still, for her, like other youth I interviewed, translating was not, initially, an easy task to pick up. Around age seven, Gabriella accompanied her mother to the doctor's office. The receptionist spoke to her mother in English, telling her they had to "register her as a new patient." Gabriella stepped in and told her mother, in her own words, that they had to "write her name in the computer." She smiled as she said that she quickly realized that people "purposely use difficult words so we don't understand. Some jargon is extremely hard to understand. Some technical medical terminologies were definitely out of my range of knowledge. It was also difficult to find proper words in Spanish." Gabriella further described feeling "anxious," "nervous," "inadequate," and "guilty" as she tried "to convey her ideas and her pain to this person." Nearly a decade later, Gabriella remembered how she fretted, "Maybe I am not doing it right."

Even though Gabriella felt "flustered," she told herself, "I am not going to give up." Indeed, she said, such early moments of difficulty "forced" her to "learn Spanish and English quickly." Because Gabriella knew that she was "desperately needed," "appreciated," and "valued," she would "research the terms and try to find the equivalent in Spanish" in a dictionary so that she would be prepared in the future. Gabriella even opted to take an AP Spanish course in high school to improve her written Spanish skills.

"I became very proficient in a year or two based on that experience," she said. "I am way more comfortable translating now. . . . I still come across words that I don't fully understand. But, if I don't understand it in English, I will ask for an explanation."

Language brokers reported feeling "great," "relieved," "delighted," "gratified," "satisfied," and "proud" as their language proficiency increased and they successfully obtained resources for their families. They felt "important," "appreciated," "respected," and "valued" within their families, and it motivated them to learn more and improve. In moments when young people like Gabriella gained the opportunity, in their view, to contribute their skills to help their parents, it likely helped them acquire language proficiency faster than others their age. Language brokering was a hands-on learning opportunity that required them to apply their knowledge to real-life scenarios with the goal of helping people they deeply cared about.

While both boys and girls undertook language-brokering responsibilities, I found that girls particularly assumed tasks that demanded a keen attention to detail. While Gabriella said she became her mother's interpreter because she was a "good" child who was more "mature, "curious," and "reliable" than her younger siblings, her perceived personality, interest, and commitment to helping her mom was gendered. Indeed, studies consistently demonstrate that immigrant daughters like Gabriella are more likely to get recruited to fill the "family work" for their parents, in part because adults often assume that girls are more mature, responsible, and detail-oriented than boys.[13]

Although language brokering often required girls to shoulder a disproportionate amount of the family's chores and caretaking responsibilities, girls who became language brokers often reported gaining respect and status within their families. For instance, Minju, a seventeen-year-old Korean American, became her family's translator at age seven, when they moved to Los Angeles from Korea. This responsibility made sense at the time. Minju's younger brother, in addition to being only five years old when their family immigrated, was more "introverted" than her. Perhaps because her brother could not speak English, "he didn't talk to anyone" when he started school. She said that when he entered middle school, however, he became quite "rebellious." According to Minju, "he would skip school and never did well," which made her parents feel "sad."

Similar to Gabriella, Minju's status as smart, competent, and responsible child compounded as her brother's perceived incompetency increased. Her brother's so-called bad behavior seemed to encourage her parents to value and appreciate her "good" behavior even more. In fact, Minju frequently compared herself to her brother throughout her interview. Whereas her brother was "like a D average student," she was "always the student of the month." Her status as the one who "always did the translation" emerged in contrast to that of her brother, who "failed" the family. Perhaps because adults often assume biological forces are preventing boys and men from assisting with household tasks,[14] Minju said that her parents "never asked [her] brother for help."

"Now, he can't do anything by himself, because I was the one who always did the translation for my mom and my brother!" Minju exclaimed.

Boys who were language brokers experienced the duty differently. They often described language brokering as a "family responsibility" that allowed them to assert themselves as men. Josh, a nineteen-year-old Mexican language broker who grew up with a single mother and two siblings, said that he "matured" faster than his younger brother and sister because he was the "man of the house." Unlike his younger brother and sister, who were "a bit spoiled," always "having fun," and "didn't care about what was going on in our family," Josh felt like there was "more pressure" for him to "feel strong" and "protect" his family. "My mom always told me, 'Josh, you are the man of the house,'" he said.

Much like Gabriella and Minju, Josh perceived language brokering as helping him "mature" faster. Yet, Josh linked his family responsibility and adult identity to a gendered form of respect. Although it could feel like a huge responsibility, Josh indeed gained status within his family by acting older than his age while translating.

Such divisions of labor among siblings were not always permanent. One interviewee, a seventeen-year-old Mexican American named Justin, told me that although he had always done a "little translation, like translating at restaurants" when he was younger, his older brothers had always "translated more serious stuff, like talking to the apartment manager." Yet, by the time Justin was fifteen, his oldest brother had married, and his second-oldest brother was in college. When their father started working as a general contractor and needed more regular interpretation skills, "Well, my brothers were not there anymore," Justin remembered. "So, I went to see my dad's clients when they needed estimates, call them to make an appointment, and sometimes translated complaints."

Over time, many young people's responsibilities gradually expanded. As they became familiar with their parents' schedules and responsibilities, young people, especially girls, often began reminding their parents about doctor's visits or other important due dates, such as rent or credit card payments. "Even though I started as a translator," recalled Hemi, "more and more I took on the role as a decision maker and caretaker. I think I pretty much run the household now. Like, I go through all the mail and set aside important renewal notices and bills to pay. It involves making a lot of mental notes to myself."[15] Victoria, a sixteen-year-old Mexican American, also mentioned, opening the mail and "taking care of bills and renewal notices."

In general, serving as their parents' language brokers seems to make young people's relationship with their parents stronger. Josephine, an eighteen-year-old Mexican American, described translating as a way to "connect" with and "get to know more about" her "busy parents." Similarly, Gina, a Korean American, said that translating "forced" her to have "more conversations" and "talk about a lot of stuff" with her parents about school-related topics, which included "letters from school," "PTA meetings," and upcoming "vacation schedule[s]."

"I think that was a key way for us to have more conversations and connect," Gina said. "Because once you start talking about these documents, it leads to other conversations, like 'What's going on with my school?' and 'How are my teachers?' It also forced me to know more about their health and work situations. I think that kept us close."

Despite having different family circumstances, gender identities, and sibling dynamics, all these young people shared a role that helped make them active social agents. None of them gave up, even when they became discouraged or frustrated at their inability to speak multiple languages fluently. Instead, in part because the stakes were high, they strategized and developed skills that their siblings and other children their age lacked.[16] Rather than "naturally" having feelings of affection or feeling obligated to help their parents, structural circumstances—as well as their parents' perceptions and praise of their abilities—helped foster their bidirectional family relationships. For children of immigrants, language brokering is a process through which they gradually begin to contribute their labor and skills to their families.

TRANSLATING SOCIOECONOMIC CLASS

Both by being exposed to adult, institutional conversations and by developing stronger relationships with their working-class immigrant parents through their language-brokering activities, the young people I met in this study learned about parents' financial struggles, which in turn further motivated their desire to put their bilingual skill and knowledge to use. This became clear when I interviewed Sandy, a high school junior whose single mother had worked in a Korean grocery store since they had moved to Los Angeles ten years ago. She said that translating made her "closer" to her mom because "there were no secrets between us." "Everything was out in the open," Sandy explained. "If she was struggling with money, I knew it."

When asked to elaborate, Sandy recalled a time she "discovered" her mother's rapidly compounding credit card debt. "My mom asked me why she had to pay this charge, like she was not sure why there was extra fee, and that's why I called the credit card company for her," she said. "They explained to me that when she pays late, there is this extra fee. And so, I can see in the charge that it's, like, late fees after late fees, and my mom wouldn't pay like, the whole bill and would only pay the minimum because she didn't have the money to pay. So, I realized like, oh, my family is really struggling financially." Sandy, who explained her mother's financial circumstances to the credit card representative, was ultimately successful in reducing the late fees. "I felt a big relief," Sandy said. Certainly, her mother did, too.

Jaime, a sixteen-year-old Korean American who immigrated to the United States when she was nine, also learned about her family's financial struggles while translating. Although her older brother had mostly served as their monolingual parents' language broker, a life change had precipitated her movement into this role. After Jaime's mother filed for divorce and left with Jaime's older brother, Jaime started helping her father more. One of the first times she translated for him she was tasked with calling the unemployment agency—he'd been laid off. The unemployment agent initially insisted on speaking with her father directly but eventually allowed Jaime to ask her father questions about his financial situation.

"I think my dad was feeling really uncomfortable, but I had to find out why he got laid off, how much money he has in his bank account, and if he's looking for a job right now," she said. "What else? There were so many questions, and it was really complicated, and they wanted to know everything about my dad, literally."

Despite being a complex and difficult translation task, Jaime successfully interpreted all the questions. She also recalled feeling "thrilled" several weeks later when her father started receiving unemployment payments in the mail. Although she was "worried about what will happen next," learning about her father's precarious condition further motivated her desire to help. Instead of asking him "any questions," she felt compelled to perform what she described as her "job" of "speaking for [her] father." After all, the translation encounter had revealed how much her father's status as a "breadwinner" had "suffered" after migrating to the US. Jaime assumed her father—who was a "prideful person" and had immigrated to "provide better life for his family"—found it "humiliating" to now be in a position of "relying" on her and having her know about his financial struggles.

"I don't even want him to have to ask [me to translate]," Jaime said. "I should just automatically provide the help he needs. It's my family responsibility, and it's the right thing to do. We have to take care of each other."

John, who was born in the US, had also witnessed his Korean American parents' precarious financial situation firsthand. When I interviewed John, a senior in high school, he politely told me that he could speak with me for only an hour. He didn't want to risk being late for his part-time job as a cashier at a local video store. Although he often felt tired and stayed up past midnight trying to finish his homework, John shared that he had recently started toying with the idea of taking on a second part-time job. His single mother, who worked as a beautician, would have preferred that he focus on school, but he knew they needed the money after he translated a "three-day notice to pay the rent or quit" that had been tacked onto his family's apartment door.

"I asked my mom if we [would] have to move out, but my mom said not to worry about it," John said. "But then, when I went to the apartment manager's office with my mom, I had to translate for her. Why she missed the due date and all that. My mom was literally begging for the extension." Despite feeling like he "wanted to cry," John kept his feelings for himself. Assuming that his mother already felt bad about their finances, John "calmly" interpreted for her. Thanks to his efforts, their apartment manager granted them an extension. "I was like, 'Thank God, we are not getting kicked out of the apartment,'" John said.

Many young people thought their parents tried to hide their money troubles initially, but translation forced the family secrets into the open. Amy, age fifteen, had grown up in Korea until she was nine. She remembered, "When we were in Korea, I didn't really know that my parents were having a hard time financially." Although she had been "happy" to hear that her family was moving to the US, she quickly realized that the move meant that her parents couldn't "easily hide these secrets" anymore. "Here, I was the first person to know it, because if they got a parking ticket and didn't pay, I am the one who tell them. If their checks bounce back or if they get that final notice, I have to tell them about it."

Like Amy, many young people admitted that they often opened mail because it was easier for them to sort, read, and "take care" of the letters on their parents' behalf. However, as Amy's response suggests, "taking care" of these bills also requires children of immigrants from working-class families to "see" adult problems in print. More often than not, translating is a reminder of their family's financial struggles.

Carlos, a seventeen-year-old Mexican American, recalled hiding his feelings of shock whenever he translated documents for his parents, including his mother's bank and credit card statements. Although Carlos reported that "it was pretty scary" to learn that his mother was paying only the minimum balance and high late fees for overdrawing her bank account, he never asked his mom "why she was so behind." Because Carlos knew that she was having difficulty "keep[ing] up with all these payments" despite working long hours, he decided to "help [her] out" by putting his translating skills to use. He called the bank and spoke with a representative, who agreed to waive the overdraft fees his mom had accrued.

At first, the financial struggles young people describe can seem to merely reflect individual hardships. But one can miss the forest for the trees by characterizing the parents' financial problems as personal struggles. Working-class immigrant parents' compounding credit card debt, bank fees, unemployment applications, and eviction notices are clear indications of systemic issues. Federal or state policies that guarantee access to a living wage, subsidized or rent-controlled housing, or job security would help stabilize these working-class families' lives. Because language brokers were the "first person" to know and see these larger social problems, they used their bilingual skills to help their parents fill out unemployment applications, reduce bank fees, and negotiate with landlords. In doing so, these young people attempted to address the structural problems that affected their families.

ENCOUNTERING RACIALIZED NATIVISM

Although young people may fear that they are unlikely to be heard because of their age, the fact that other adults treat their parents like children is far more troubling. Jiho, a seventeen-year-old Korean American, referred to a time when he interpreted for his mother after his younger brother got into a fight at his school. "As soon as [the teacher] realized that my mom didn't speak English, I felt this condescending attitude," he said. "He stopped looking at my mom and made her feel like she is not there. He only addressed me, and I kind of disliked that."

"Did he treat you nicely at least?" I asked.

"No. He sounded frustrated. He sounded like he just wants to tell us that my brother is bad and just be done with us." Jiho noted, "I was a little kid back then." Jiho told me that he got used to adults like this teacher who do not treat young people with respect. "But, my mom is not a kid. He treated her like that—little kid, you know. Her opinions don't matter kind of thing. If someone is having a conversation, I feel like people should address the whole crowd. Just because my mom can't speak English, that shouldn't be a reason for you to ignore that person completely."

Although Jiho felt "uncomfortable" knowing that his mother was "excluded from the conversation," he didn't know what to say. "I didn't know how to tell the person, 'Hey, you know, like look at my mom, too. My mom is here.'"

Jiho didn't have power, he recognized, to "change other people." But he still reflected on what he could have done to include his mother in the conversation. "I think as an interpreter, I want to find a way to improve that, you know. I want to be a better interpreter to my mom in the sense that even though I am the one who talk most of time, I still include her, the person I am interpreting for."

Similarly, Leticia, an eighteen-year-old Mexican American, said that her mother had been treated like "a kid" during an interaction with a doctor eight years earlier. As Leticia had tried to describe her mother's back pain, she had been greeted with a "patronizing" tone that "made it seem like she was not in the room." Leticia lowered her voice to imitate the male doctor. "He would tell me, 'Your back pain is just regular back pain and you kind of have to deal with it.' And my mom would say, 'No, I feel X, Y, and Z,' and I would explain to the doctor what my mom said. And he will be like, 'Whatever.' He won't listen to what my mom has to say. So, it's incredibly dismissive."

"Adults tend to do this to a kid," she said. Instead of "digging into" the problems and listening to their concerns, she said that adults often "think that a child is incapable of understanding the nuances" of adult conversations and ignore their "little comments." And yet, her mom was not a child. Although her mother had repeatedly attempted to tell doctors about her "really bad pain," Leticia said it took about eight years before her doctor to "finally" took her "seriously." By this time, however, her mother's health problems had compounded. In addition to discovering "two broken discs," the doctor realized that her mother's spinal fluid "had been leaking for eight years." "So, not only they had been dismissing her, but they were negligent!" Leticia exclaimed.

Research has demonstrated that gender, race, and class shape individuals' access to healthcare services in the United States. Because physicians rely on biomedical diagnostic tools as well as their own opinions to evaluate patients' pain, they often recommend different courses of treatment depending on who reports the symptoms, thus leading to unequal treatments.[17] For example, due to the long-standing medical belief that women are "hysterical" and "anxious," as well as the notion that women can tolerate or manage pain better than men can, physicians are less likely to validate and subsequently to undertreat women's pain.[18] These biases are even more likely to affect women of color, who are often perceived as uneducated, inarticulate, and angry in comparison to White women.[19]

At the same time, language intersects with other forms of inequality to make young people feel as if their parents are treated like "little kids." As demonstrated in chapter 1, healthcare professionals often express gendered and racialized expectations for immigrant women of color, especially those who can't speak English. Nurses often anticipate that these patients will be docile, subservient, and grateful for any care they receive. However, as young people's experiences made it clear, English-speaking institutional agents began expressing frustration or dismissing patients' concerns as soon as they observed these patients speaking a language other than English. Language thus become a mechanism through which critical institutions like hospitals exclude immigrant women of color from being treated with respect and in ways that ensure their well-being.

Previous research also indicates that women of color, especially immigrant women of color, often report feeling belittled or rejected, or they blame themselves for the substandard medical care that they receive.[20] Considering the findings of this research, as well as what I describe in chapter 1 based on my interviews with healthcare providers, it is very likely that Leticia's mother's gender, race, and language shaped the interaction she had with her doctor, and that Leticia was correct to feel that the doctor infantilized her mother, dismissed her pain, and ultimately prolonged her misery. These negative interactions likely affected both Leticia and her mother's dignity and subsequent ability to trust the health care system. Indeed, research consistently shows that people of color report lower levels of trust in their personal physicians than White people do,[21] and that their sense of mistrust is the result of their past experiences of being discriminated against during healthcare encounters.[22] In the end, many people of color stop seeking help or are left suffering until their symptoms become too advanced to ignore. Leticia's mother, for example, received help only after a visit to the emergency room. Leticia was "infuriated" by the treatment of her mother.

Young people also recalled times when police officers infantilized their parents. For example, Abelinda, a fifteen-year-old Mexican American, spoke of a day when police knocked on her door to inquire about a criminal incident that her neighbor had reported seeing. The police officer asked Abelinda's mother if she had seen three men using drugs in their apartment building's parking lot several days earlier.

When Abelinda told the police officer that her mother did not see them, the police responded, "Tell your mom that if she lies, she will get in trouble." Abelina said that this made her feel "thrown off." "He is the one who needed our help, but he was pretty much threatening us—as if my mom did something wrong," she said. "I don't know if it's because my mom is Mexican, or if it's because she is a small woman. Or maybe it's because she doesn't speak English. He totally looked down on my mom, like she is a kid lying to an adult or something."

Other bilingual young people I talked to also recalled encounters where their parents had been treated like they were "stupid" or "dumb" for not being able to speak English. Jooyoung, a fifteen-year-old Korean American, had this experience. Dressed in a bright yellow tank top and black jeans, she offered me a bag of Doritos as I joined her in her school cafeteria after classes. She said she served as her parents' language broker "pretty much everywhere and anywhere." "I got used to translating now. It doesn't bother me." What bothered Jooyoung were the "arrogant" English-speaking people she had to deal with.

When I asked her if she had encountered anyone who had made her experiences difficult, her disposition shifted. She began speaking in an angrier tone. "Are you kidding?" she asked. "Plenty of times, and every time it makes me sick. I always felt like they were talked down upon, my parents, because they don't know English. Whether it was the hospital or mall, there were always employees who would be obviously rude whenever we needed to ask a question. It was ridiculous because I speak fluent English and I can hear them."

She then paused for a few seconds as if she was trying to find the right words to describe these experiences. "You know, it seemed like our ethnic identity followed us everywhere," she said.

"Can you give me an example?" I asked.

"It's usually White Americans. So, this lawyer. He was super racist. He was keep repeating, 'Do you speak English?' Really loud to my mom as if she is deaf. I heard him mumbling something like, 'People in this neighborhood need to learn how to speak English.'"

The incident left Jooyoung feeling "angry" and reminded her that "Americans" think that "people in this neighborhood, like our family, are stupid" and that "they do not belong here." Jooyoung added, "I never really had a chance to say something, but it is definitely something that I won't ever forget."

Indeed, racist and nativist encounters were hard to forget. Jungmi, another Korean American, also described an encounter where her mother was treated as "stupid." It was at Target. Jungmi said, "A White woman yelled at my mom, telling her to go back to China," she said. "My mom didn't know that this woman was in line ahead of her even though [the woman] went to go grab something else. She was just an ignorant woman because my mom is not even from China. I was so upset and wanted to yell back, but I didn't want to make a scene."

The cashier was also rude, Jungmi said. When her mother reached the front of the line, she attempted to ask the cashier about the price of one of the items, the "rude" cashier "frowned" at her mother and yelled, "'What?'"

"I think my mom's mannerism or her broken English make people think that she is stupid," Jungmi said. She said she felt "bad" and "angry," but it reminded her that she has "to be there" for her mother all the time. "If I am not there, people will treat my mom like she is trash," she said.

Mexican Americans also consistently described encountering racialized nativism during translation encounters. Their parents were regularly perceived as un-American or "stupid" for "failing" to speak English. For example, when I asked Antonio, a fifteen-year-old Mexican American, to talk about a difficult brokering incident, he immediately recalled a time when he was working with his dad, a handyman, in "some mansion" when he was eleven. He described the encounter with the mansion's owner in vivid detail, four years after the fact.

"He asked my dad a question, and he couldn't understand. So, I got in to help and translate. But I overheard the guy talking mess to another guy."

"What did he say?" I asked.

"He said, 'I don't know why these Hispanics are in this country when they don't even understand the language.'"

"He said that in front of you?"

"Yes, he was whispering, but I heard him saying that Hispanics are just a waste of time and space."

"Did you say something to that guy?" I asked.

"No. I was only eleven at the time. I just felt sad that they would look down on people because of a language that he doesn't know. I wanted to hurt those guys and stand up for my dad, because my dad is a good worker. He's a professional at what he does, but just because of the language barrier and just because he is Mexican, they are willing to talk down on him."

The narratives of the youth in this context vividly illustrate that speaking a language other than English acts as a signifier of being "un-American," putting their parents in a position to be infantilized, harassed, and dismissed. As Jungmi's and Antonio's experiences demonstrate, parents speaking an Asian language or Spanish is sometimes met by remarks that they don't belong in the US, or they should go back to where they came from. Even in a city where the majority speak a language other than English, Asian languages and Spanish were subject to social control and became a trigger for both overt and covert racism. These interactions effectively barred them from attaining social citizenship.

Reports from Korean and Mexican Americans about translation encounters revealed a racialized difference in their experiences with nativism. In comparison to Korean Americans, Mexican Americans were far more likely to report being stereotyped as "lazy" or "uneducated" or as "criminals."

Such was the case for Carlos, who grew up in a Latinx-majority neighborhood with a high concentration of poverty. Like most of the Mexican Americans I interviewed, Carlos often served as a language broker in predominantly White suburbs, where his parents engaged in informal service work. When I asked about his translation experiences, Carlos said that he often had to mediate interactions between "American" employers who often "yelled" at his father, a gardener, for being "lazy."

Carlos also remembered an incident when a police officer pulled over his father, who was driving a pickup truck through a wealthy suburb, for "being Mexican." "This officer pulled us over for no reason. I mean for no reason!" Carlos exclaimed. "He was like, 'What are you doing in this neighborhood?' I felt that we were discriminated especially because he asked us to get out and searched the car, even though I clearly stated to him we had nothing to hide. I just felt terrible, like, 'Why are you singling us out for no reason, man?'"

"So, did the officer let you and your dad go?" I asked.

"Yeah, but we got out of the car, and my dad could not say anything because he didn't speak English and he was afraid that he would get deported. He would not let me ask too many questions, but I wanted to ask, 'What did we do wrong?' I wanted to be like, 'Why are you fucking searching my dad's body for so long?' I felt bitter because I wanted to let him know that I am aware of this discrimination." In the end, Carolos just told the officer, "We are just here to work." He was relieved when the officer left and remained "thankful" that he had been there to translate for his dad.

Gloria was a nineteen-year-old Mexican American community college student. When asked if she had ever met someone who made her translating experience difficult, she said, "Oh gosh, yes, constantly. Where do I start?" She recalled a time she accompanied her mother to a local Starbucks to fill out a job application. "My mom is always ignored in public settings because she can't speak English and did not graduate from college and stuff. When I was about twelve years old, I saw this sign from Starbucks looking for an employee. I wanted to apply for it, but I thought maybe I had to be eighteen, so I asked my mom to apply, so we went there to get an application. The lady then asked if my mom was a graduate. . . . I asked that lady, 'Graduate of what?' And, she said, 'A graduate of college.'"

When I expressed surprise, Gloria said, "I know! That was my response. But, honestly, at this time, I was slightly embarrassed for my mom because of my mom's education level. She only went up to the fourth grade before she had to drop out to help maintain her family. So, I timidly answered the question and said that my mom never graduated from middle school." Gloria vivid recalled the lady's reaction: "This lady was so taken aback and had this look like she is disgusted or something." Gloria voice trembled as she continued, "She sounded angry when she said, "Ignorant people can't work here." As if "this wasn't enough to insult us," when Gloria and her mother were walking away, "she muttered something about a low-life, dirty Mexican." Gloria's emotion welled up as she shared, "I was so mad. Come on, I knew someone who never graduated from high school but worked in Starbucks. Why do you need the college graduate to make coffee?"

Gloria told her mother that the lady probably wanted someone younger, like a college student, because she knew that her mother understood the words *college* and *education*, and she did not want her mother to be ashamed that she did not have a college degree. She told me that she was "furious" because they went to the Starbucks to simply pick up an application; they were not ready to "be interviewed by a random racist lady."

Indeed, Gloria's life was a constant battleground against prejudice and discrimination, and this incident was just one tile in a mosaic of similar encounters. Too often, she found herself staring down individuals whom she could only categorize as "racists." Their reactions were shockingly consistent: a profound disbelief upon discovering that she, a Mexican immigrant, was pursuing a college education—as if such an achievement were an anomaly for someone of her background. These racialized attitudes toward Mexican immigrants cast an enduring shadow over her role as her mother's translator, a role she regularly played while her mother worked as a house cleaner. Gloria recalled one such incident with remarkable clarity, her voice trembling with the weight of the memory. "It happened in a nice, upscale suburban neighborhood," she began, painting a vivid picture. "There was this White lady, all decked out, who accused my mother of stealing expensive jewelry." Her eyes brimmed with tears as she continued, "It was a heartbreaking experience." When I asked Gloria to delve into her thoughts about why people mistreated her and her mother, she didn't hesitate for a moment. Frustration and sadness etched across her face, she declared, "People think Mexicans steal stuff . . . and never go to college!"

Regardless of their immigration status, Mexican Americans also reported being categorized as "illegal" immigrants. Alejandro, a nineteen-year-old Mexican American, was born and raised in Los Angeles. Yet, when he was translating for his mother at a parent-teacher conference, his teacher recommended he and his mom attend a "DREAM Act workshop" for potential DACA recipients and their parents. He described how "pissed off" he was: "Just because I am Mexican, she assumed that I don't have paper[s]."

THE SOCIETAL FORCES BEHIND LANGUAGE-BROKERING RESPONSIBILITIES

Duty is a powerful cultural force. It serves as a compelling motivation that encourages individuals to make decisions, contribute their expertise, and sacrifice to fulfill the needs of others. This sense of commitment, however, does not emerge in a vacuum. It is shaped by daily interactions, institutional norms, and the broader cultural context in which people are embedded.[23] For this reason, some family members feel more of a sense of duty than others. In the United States, for example, institutions are organized around the assumption that parents, particularly mothers, have the primary duty of caring for their children. A key institution where this expectation is imposed on mothers is the educational system, which operates under the assumption that children grow up in a nuclear White middle-class family headed by a breadwinning father and a devoted mother—what sociologist Dorothy Smith calls a "standard North American family."[24] Schools, for example, implicitly assume that all parents—especially mothers—are available and able to participate in their children's school activities, including after-school programs, open houses, parent-teacher organizations, and field trips.[25] Schools also expect mothers to intervene when students fall behind in homework,[26] are diagnosed with learning differences,[27] or are suspended.[28] As a result, mothers often devote an enormous amount of energy, time, and resources to caring for their children, which can conflict with their ability to ascend the ranks in professional careers and leave them feeling ambivalent when family and work commitments pull them into different directions.[29] If mothers fall short of societal expectations, they often face scrutiny and criticism—a tendency that ignores the fact that some mothers have more resources and time to devote to their children's upbringing than others.[30]

Although they have received less attention within existing research, there are also societal expectations of the "ideal" childhood. Many people in the US believe that children—who, by default of their age, are presumably innocent and naïve—should be shielded from the complexities of the adult world. As a result, when young people assume "adult responsibilities," they often encounter surprise, sympathy, concern, and occasionally even criticism from adults. In these cases, parents are often criticized for exposing their children to adult content that will result in their children growing up "too fast."

Given these prevailing societal expectations, one might assume—as mainstream reporters often have predicted—that children of immigrants would harbor resentment toward their parents (see chapter 1 for more information). After all, the children of immigrants I interviewed were acutely aware of adults' tendency to regard them as incapable of being skilled translators. It was also difficult for them to decipher complex sentence structures and jargon. And yet, the children of immigrants I interviewed seldom said that their language-brokering duties resulted in a role reversal between themselves and their parents. Nor did they blame their parents for not mastering the English language. Instead, the children of immigrants I interviewed tended to describe their responsibilities as a natural extension of their "family responsibilities." Some even characterized their language-brokering work as a labor of love, which underscored the profound emotional bond that fueled their sense of duty toward their parents.

However, it's important to recognize that children of immigrants do not come to view their language-brokering responsibilities as "normal" overnight. Instead, social circumstances help to shape the sense of duty they feel toward their family. As these young people accompanied their parents to English-speaking institutions, they quickly discovered the way language can function as a racial signifier. It was a tool employed by English speakers to single out, mistreat, discriminate against, and draw a boundary between "American" and those labeled as "foreigners." Since language was a mechanism through which English-speaking institutions excluded their parents from securing their basic citizenship rights, the children of immigrants I interviewed felt compelled to speak for their parents.

As young people begin to serve as their family's language broker, they start to witness the harsh realities of their parents' lives. This motivates children of immigrants—especially girls—to learn more sophisticated vocabularies. In addition to seeing their parents experience financial hardships, they see their parents being infantilized or becoming the target of racialized nativism.[31] As their proficiency in translation grows, language brokers garner increased status and recognition from their parents. This recognition comes hand in hand with the opportunity to spend additional quality time with their family. Over time, these language brokers also begin to anticipate their family's needs and take on essential household responsibilities, potentially a reason why girls in immigrant households often end up shouldering a greater share of chores and dedicating more time to household tasks than boys do. Eventually, it starts to feel "normal" or "natural" for bilingual children—who feel they have no choice but to become competent and adept at performing "adult" responsibilities—to serve as their parent's "mouth and ears."

Although Korean and Mexican American youth both witnessed their parents encountering racialized nativism, their parents were not racialized in the same way. Mexican Americans are more likely than Korean Americans to encounter situations where they or their parents are seen as "lazy," "criminal," or "uneducated." Considering that immigrants who speak Swedish, Dutch, or Gaelic in the US are not treated in a similar manner,[32] young people's experiences demonstrate how languages can function as a proxy for race, leading to differential forms of exclusion for people of color.

Children's language-brokering work is a response to the limited citizenship rights provided to immigrants of color. In a capitalist society that has historically relied on Asian and Latinx immigrants as a source of cheap labor, the working-class children of immigrants I interviewed described parents who battled irregular work schedules, low wages, and physically demanding jobs. Their parents rarely had access to employer subsidized healthcare plans or retirement savings accounts. Their families also lacked access to childcare, safe and affordable housing, or translation support. Although it felt "normal" to the language brokers I interviewed, their experiences exposed the harsh realities immigrants of color regularly confront in a nation that prides itself on being comprised of immigrants. Contrary to this nation's core values, it has become the responsibility of children of immigrants to ensure that their parents' basic needs are addressed. And, as I show in the next chapter, the burden on youth to address structural problems becomes even more pronounced when their parents experience a crisis. When legal entanglements, housing instability, or medical emergencies arise, language brokers often have to "drop everything" to navigate these systemic issues. In these situations, their family responsibilities sharply conflict with White middle-class expectations embedded in schools, which ultimately leave language brokers in a difficult double bind as they attempt to juggle both school and family responsibilities.

FOUR THE DOUBLE BIND IN LANGUAGE BROKERS' LIVES

It was drizzling on the day David, a high school senior, met me in a café. Before entering, however, he paused to briefly examine his reflection in the glass. Retrieving a black cloth from his pocket, he cleaned his glasses and tucked his colorful polka-dot umbrella under his arm. His gaze swept across the bustling coffee shop, taking in the sight of students hunched over textbooks, professionals engrossed in their laptops, and chattering groups of friends. Spotting me, David gave a warm, albeit slightly fatigued, smile and stepped inside. We shared a quick greeting in Korean before heading to the counter to place our orders. His choice, without hesitation, was an Americano—a strong, "no-nonsense coffee" that he said matched his "straightforward personality." It was his favorite brew, and he said that he could undoubtedly use its caffeine kick today.

"I only got about five hours of sleep last night," David told me in a voice that was tinged with exhaustion.

As we settled into our seats, he quietly sighed and began explaining everything that was on his plate. He was in the midst of preparing for his college applications—a process that he said was "both exciting and overwhelming." For the next twenty minutes, we spoke about his college aspirations. He shared his concerns about his sophomore-year grades, particularly in biology, which had dipped from a B to a C- halfway through the year. He leaned forward and said that the roof in his family's apartment had started leaking and had demanded his attention during a crucial exam period.

Although he had been only fifteen years old at the time, David confronted the management company and accused them of infringing on his family's tenancy rights. Nevertheless, he said that discussing the situation with their apartment manager had been one of the most "challenging" and "draining" translating experiences he had ever encountered. David vividly recalled how, on multiple occasions, his parents asked him to notify the management company that the roof was leaking water whenever it rained. Each time, the manager would offer his parents vague reassurances like "Okay, okay." And yet, the leak would reappear during the next downpour. The manager's dismissive attitude deeply irked David. He felt as though his parents' requests "were not being taken seriously." In David's eyes, the manager's refusal to acknowledge his parents' concerns stemmed from the fact that he was communicating with a teenager instead of a bona fide adult.

Although he recognized that his age affected how others perceived him, David remained undeterred. Despite the manager's assumption that his family's concerns could be brushed aside, David turned to the internet and "googled like crazy." He learned that tenants in California have the right to refuse to pay rent if their landlords don't fix a problem in a timely manner. "I wrote the letter stating that we are not going to pay the rent if they don't fix their problem soon," he recounted.

When asked whether his parents gave input about the content of the letter, David said that his parents had asked him to be polite. They expressed concern about the possibility of "getting kicked out of the apartment" if he was too persistent. This balancing act between honoring his parents' wishes and rectifying what he saw as an unjust situation placed David in a delicate predicament. After promising his parents that he would "try to sound professional" and "not be rude," he undertook the task of crafting the letter by himself.

Once the manager finally fixed the roofing issue, David felt relieved and accomplished. However, the process of persuading the apartment manager to make the necessary repairs had proven to be an arduous and time-consuming ordeal. David had dedicated numerous hours to what he described as a "family responsibility," which had required him to extensively research tenant rights and craft multiple iterations of the letter. This commitment also came at a cost—he found himself lacking the time to attend to his own schoolwork. Ultimately, the experience had left David feeling frustrated by his conflicting desires. He yearned to assist his family but also harbored a strong desire to excel in school. Acknowledging how difficult a balancing act this could be, David said, "I am torn between wanting to help all the time and wanting to focus on my own work. It's hard."

As discussed in chapter 3, children of immigrants often embrace their language-brokering duties wholeheartedly. Like David, the other young people I interviewed regularly described language brokering as a "natural" way to help their parents or as a "family responsibility." However, as exemplified by David's experiences, this did not mean that language brokering was the only task that children of immigrants were expected to perform. As a high school student, David was also expected to dedicate approximately thirty-five hours a week to his high school classes. He was also expected to devote additional time after school to completing daily homework assignments and studying for exams. These taken-for-granted school policies pose a challenge for young people like David. Despite his best efforts to balance family and school commitments, David grappled with mixed emotions concerning his dual roles as a child of immigrants and a student, particularly when he encountered conflicts between what he perceived as his family obligations and his school responsibilities.[1]

In this chapter, I demonstrate the challenging tightrope that working-class immigrant youth must walk when their familial duties conflict with their school responsibilities. Because schools expect youth to primarily devote their time and energy to educational pursuits, these language brokers often find themselves grappling with a sense of inadequacy as they endeavor to balance both. This double bind becomes especially pronounced in times of crisis, which require young language brokers to "drop everything" to help their parents navigate pressing issues such as housing instability, legal troubles, and medical emergencies. While both Korean and Mexican American youth wrestle with these feelings of inadequacy, distinct racialization processes within the school system contribute to their divergent perceptions about why their childhoods seem "atypical." For working-class Mexican American youth, their frustration springs from teachers' racialized assumptions that their parents are apathetic about their academic achievements. In comparison, although working-class Korean Americans also grapple with the sense of injustice embedded in middle-class expectations about academic success, Korean American youth worry that their teachers and peers might judge their parents as insufficiently "Asian." These contrasting racialized perceptions amplify their feelings of otherness and inadequacy as they navigate the intricate balance between their family responsibilities and the expectations of the school environment. Through this analysis, I underscore the mismatch between age-based and White, middle-class expectations embedded in school practices and the realities of working-class immigrant families' lives, which leave young people feeling a profound sense of being caught in a double bind.

BALANCING FAMILY AND SCHOOL WORK

Yolanda, a sixteen-year-old who described herself as a proud Mexican, migrated to the US when she was six years old. We spoke about her family while sitting on a park bench near her home. The wind swept Yolanda's curly dark brown hair in front of her dimpled smile as she politely reminded me at the beginning of the interview, "I have one hour and a half to chat, so let's begin."

Without further ado, we began by speaking about her parent's lives. Recalling their first few years in the US, Yolanda said, "At first, my parents struggled getting jobs. My dad has always been a hard worker; in Mexico, he worked in the fields as a farmer. He would leave really early in the morning and come home late."

"When we got here to the US, it was no different," Yolanda continued. "He would wake up early, catch the first bus, and go to Home Depot. He would stand there for the entire day, hoping someone would pick him up for any type of labor. He was willing to work on anything that he was told to do. Some days he was lucky and had construction jobs, but other days, it was slow, and he would come home disappointed."

Yolanda then described how her mother's life changed after migrating to the US. She said, "In Mexico, my mom was a stay-home wife. She would cook, clean, and take care of my needs. But coming to the US, we wouldn't be able to survive with only one paycheck, so my mom had to find a job too."

Yolanda's mother eventually worked as a house cleaner with the help of her aunt, who was already cleaning houses for a living. She said, "There were some [clients] that took advantage of her and wouldn't pay her at all. There were also some who were really nice, and she continues to work for them as we speak."

Describing language brokering as a labor of love, Yolanda said, "My parents still work hard to put food on the table, and it would suck if I say I can't help them. I can't ask them to rely on strangers for help when I know that my parents can't speak English. Whenever I translate for my parents, I don't expect to get anything back because if I am able to help them out, then I will do it without hesitation. It's really a labor of love and I will always be there for them."

It was clear that Yolanda shouldered a significant amount of family responsibilities. She was always willing to be there for her family and didn't expect anything back. Although she listed more than ten places where language-brokering work took place, there was not a hint of resentment in her voice as she described it. Instead, she said she was happy to be a "third parent" when following her mother to her younger siblings' parent-teacher conferences and teacher-requested meetings.[2] She also recalled feeling proud about the time she, as an eight-year-old, had negotiated her mother's cleaning fee up from $80 to $100.[3] "The lady was impressed because I was really young and I was able to translate and negotiate," Yolanda said with a smile. "So, at the end, she kindly said, 'You got it, young lady. *Cien* [one hundred] it is.'"

Yolanda, like other youth described in chapter 3, was proud of her parents' work ethic. She was also painfully aware of how much they struggled with financial instability, sporadic employment, and low-wage jobs. And when Yolanda stepped in to translate, she, like other language brokers, also saw how easy it was for White Americans to mistreat her mother, who wasn't fluent in English.[4] Because Yolanda saw her parents struggle in the face of daunting and dehumanizing work conditions, she felt a strong sense of reciprocity about ensuring her hardworking and sacrificing immigrant family's survival.

Despite framing her work as family responsibility, Yolanda knew her responsibilities were not seen as normal by the larger society. By calling herself a third parent or highlighting a time when she surpassed age expectations by successfully negotiating with her mother's employers, she acknowledged that idealized notion of American childhood did not include her life experiences.

An hour and fifteen minutes into the interview, I reminded Yolanda that we were running short on time. Before we wrapped up our conversation, I asked about her career plans. She said her parents had always told her that "they came [to the US] and struggled because of their children's education." Yolanda's father, for example, often reminded her that "the best present for me and your mom is for you to be successful in school." Her father's advice closely paralleled what Yolanda's mother told her. Yolanda recalled a conversation they had when Yolanda was about eight years old. Her mother had said, "If you don't have education, you have to live like me, cleaning other people's houses."

The thought of cleaning other people's houses for the rest of her life "traumatized" Yolanda, but her mother did not have to warn Yolanda about the harsh realities "low-educated Mexican immigrants living in America" experience. "I see it every day," Yolanda said.

These experiences left Yolanda feeling determined to strike what sociologist Robert Smith has dubbed an "immigrant bargain."[5] She wanted to repay her parents for their struggles in a new country by achieving upward mobility. "I am going to be an elementary school teacher, because that would make my parents proud," she said.[6]

Since our interview was cut short by her busy schedule, I offered Yolanda my phone number in case she wanted to schedule an additional interview. I received a phone call from her a few days later. When I answered my phone, Yolanda was crying.

"Are you okay?" I asked.

After a pause, Yolanda said, "Not really. I just yelled at my parents. I think I am going crazy."

"What happened?" I asked.

Yolanda let out a huge sigh.

"Nothing," she said. "Just everyday things, really. But today, it was just too much. I lost it. I told them I am a student. I have to study for my test. I can't do everything. I am just one person."

Once she had regained her composure, Yolanda explained why her day had been "too much." The day had started like any other day, she said. She came home from school around 4:00 p.m. After washing the dishes, she began going through the mail. She set aside a vehicle registration notice and made a mental note to remind her father to send payment to the DMV in the next three months. Then she called her mother. Her mom asked Yolanda to call a client. The client had paid Yolanda's mom $120 for the five hours it had taken to clean the client's sprawling, five-bedroom house in the Hollywood Hills, which was $80 less than Yolanda's mother should have been paid. Yolanda called the client, who began complaining about how long it had taken Yolanda's mother to finish her job. The client thought it should have only taken three hours for her mother to clean the entire house instead of five.

Yolanda listened patiently. By now, she had spent years listening to her mother repeat the mantra "the customer is always right." She had also developed a strong sense of how long it would take to clean any given house. There was no way her mom could have completed such a large job in three hours. Yolanda nonetheless suppressed her frustration, even though she thought the client was being "way too rude" and "often took advantage" of her mother.

Carefully but forcefully, Yolanda pushed back against the client's "outrageous" and "unreasonable" expectations. She explained that her mother was paid hourly and deserved to be compensated for all of her work. Before hanging up, the client declared, "You know what? I cannot communicate with your mother because she can't speak English. Tell your mother she is fired."

Yolanda was furious. However, she put her own feelings aside as she began heating up tamales for her younger brothers. She attempted to turn her attention to her homework while sitting at the kitchen table with them, but before long, she was distracted once again. She heard water dripping in the bathroom. She left the kitchen to investigate, only to discover that the toilet's pipe had broken. Water was seeping out of the bathroom and soaking into the adjacent hallway's carpet.

Yolanda frantically called the landlord, who did not answer his phone. When the landlord finally called back an hour later, around 8:00 p.m., Yolanda explained the problem and asked him to fix the toilet as soon as possible. He agreed but was upset that the carpet was ruined.

At this point, Yolanda said she felt drained, tired, and just "wanted to go to sleep." Instead of resting, however, Yolanda knew she had to prepare for an upcoming algebra test. Yolanda's grade in math class had recently slipped from an A to a B because she had too little time to study for the tests. "That is not acceptable to me," she said, "so I lost sleep over this. I was trying to get an A on my next test."

Yolanda was deep in concentration when her mother knocked on her bedroom door. She asked whether Yolanda had contacted the client. Before she had a chance to answer, Yolanda's dad also poked his head in.

"What happened to the carpet? What's wrong with the toilet? Did you call the landlord? What's this DMV notice?" he asked.

Although Yolanda usually did not feel bothered by her parents' requests, she told me she "blew up" and "lost it." She told her parents, "If you want me to do well in school, you have to stop asking me to do all this work!"

Yolanda was deeply committed to contributing her labor and excelling in school to circumvent the various forms of discrimination she and her parents, who were working-class immigrants of color, had experienced in the US. She knew that her parents, who worked hard to support their family in the US, could not navigate the English-speaking world without her help.

At the same time, Yolanda did not feel an unequivocal sense of solidarity toward her parents.[7] Nor was the "patchwork" of bringing together resources for her family[8] or striking an "immigrant bargain" seamlessly achieved. Rather than always being willing to prioritize her family work over her schoolwork, Yolanda felt like she was "going crazy." She "blew up" at her parents, which left her feeling "terrible and guilty."

Relaying the story to me a day later, Yolanda said, "What choice do my parents have? My parents struggle with work and money, and they can't talk in English."

Few would deny that everyone, including immigrants, feels a complex combination of emotions, including affection, gratitude, obligation, and resentment, toward their family at different points in their life. Yet Yolanda's mixed feelings about her family and school responsibilities were shaped by the way age intersected with other forms of inequality. Although Yolanda, who was only sixteen years old, wanted to promote her family's well-being, her ability to do so came into conflict with her position as a teenager in society, as young people in the US are expected to devote a considerable amount of time to completing homework and studying for tests. They are also assumed to have a quiet and safe place to study that is free of distractions. These are produced and reproduced through taken-for-granted school practices. By assigning homework and expecting students to study for tests, schools implicitly assume that teenagers are neither working nor shouldering significant family responsibilities outside school.

Although institutions like schools operate under ethnocentric and classed expectations about children's ability to study and complete homework, such practices overlook the reality of the working-class immigrant families' lives. Yolanda was primarily responsible for her family work because her parents worked long hours in the informal economy. Yolanda had to take care of her younger siblings because there weren't any affordable daycare or after-school programs for them to attend. Housing in the US is also a privatized commodity, meaning that families experiencing poverty, including Yolanda's, often lack access to habitable housing. Many working-class young people and students of color experience similar living and family conditions as a result of larger social problems like poverty, racism, and sexism. And as demonstrated in chapter 3, the young people in this study were uniquely positioned to witness these circumstances as a result of their language-brokering work. Ultimately, attempting to juggle everything left young people like Yolanda feeling conflicted when their family responsibilities competed with their school responsibilities.

SHOULDERING A LABOR OF LOVE DURING CRISIS SITUATIONS

As suggested by Yolanda's story and as detailed in chapter 3, young people learn to perceive their language-brokering work as a natural family responsibility. Many, like Yolanda, even report that they are happy to shoulder this responsibility. Nonetheless, Yolanda blew up at her parents when her compounding responsibilities became too much to manage. Like Yolanda, other young people report feeling especially conflicted about their family and school responsibilities in times of crisis. These situations, which range from a parent's illness to legal problems, required the young people to drop everything, including their schoolwork. Although these situations certainly do not occur on a daily basis, every young person I interviewed described a family crisis that left them feeling exhausted, drained, stressed, overwhelmed, and frustrated.[9]

Among the most common crisis situations young language brokers encounter are emergency visits to the hospital. Considering that many language brokers' parents perform labor-intensive jobs, many of these hospital visits involve work-related illnesses. Furthermore, because most of the parents do not have paid sick or medical leave, they often go to work sick or injured, which increases their risk of developing more serious health conditions.

Adriana, an eighteen-year-old Mexican American, recounted a time she visited an emergency room with her dad. She was about to study for an important chemistry test when her father, who "coughed all the time" and "breathe[d] dusts" at the construction sites where he worked, told her something was wrong with his chest. "I was scared that something serious happened to my dad because he said that he has burning chest pain, like he couldn't really breathe," Adriana said. Fearing the worst, she "forgot to change [her] clothes" and "rushed to the emergency room" with her father.

Adriana had long suspected something was seriously wrong with her father, a working-class immigrant of color. The fact that she anticipated the crisis helps illustrate how multiple inequalities embedded in workplaces and the healthcare system contributed to her family's crisis. For instance, many working-class immigrants of color are employed in jobs that do not provide health insurance.[10] Consistent with this nationwide trend, Adriana's father did not have health insurance or paid time off from work. Consequently, he had learned to live with the cough that regularly rattled his lungs. Lacking time, money, and other institutional resources, he, like many other Americans without health insurance, delayed treatment until his problems became too severe to ignore, which led him to seek emergency medical care. Partly because it is unlawful for the public ERs to deny a patient care,[11] patients like Adriana's father are disproportionally inclined to visit the ER more than any other healthcare facilities.[12] Additionally, even if they live in a neighborhood where the majority of residents are Latinx immigrants, emergency rooms are often de facto English-speaking institutions (as discussed in chapter 2), which meant that Adriana had to come along to ensure that her father could communicate with hospital staff.

Adriana's visit to the emergency room was, in her words, a "nightmare." She and her father spent hours in the overcrowded waiting room to be seen by a physician. "I kept going up to the front desk saying that my dad is in pain," she recalled. "But they didn't take me seriously. One person said, 'Everyone here is in pain.' I wanted to cry."

The experiences she recalled are consistent with the findings of existing research that public emergency rooms located in poor, racially segregated neighborhoods are understaffed and underfunded and have average wait times of between six and twelve hours.[13] However, one might wonder why emergency-room staff, who are supposed to triage patients on arrival, did not deem her father's chest pain a high-priority concern. From Adriana's story, it was unclear whether they had taken his vitals on arrival.

Although it is possible that the hospital staff had decided that he was stable enough to endure a long wait, medical sociologists have long argued that the process of labeling patients and categorizing their illness is connected to medical professionals' bias about dependency on welfare and poverty.[14] Studies have also demonstrated that medical staff often take patients of color less seriously than White patients who report pain or medical concerns, which can influence whether staff delay the treatment of people of color during an ER visit.[15] Considering that Mexican Americans are racialized as "illegal immigrants," the hospital staff's assessment of Adriana's father's ability to pay for the cost of the ER visit might have also shaped Adriana's experience. On top of these barriers, it might have been all the more difficult for Adriana, a teenager, to be taken seriously by hospital staff. As a teenage Mexican American girl accompanying a Mexican immigrant father who could not speak English, Adriana's race, class, gender, and age likely contributed to her perception that the visit was "degrading."[16]

Twelve hours later, after finding out that her father's chest pains were not related to cardiac arrest, Adriana left the hospital with a complicated mix of emotions. Despite her relief, she recalled feeling upset that her father had neglected his health for such a long time. Adriana nevertheless understood why; he had been fearing the expense of seeing a doctor. "It always comes down to money for my dad," Adriana said.

Adriana was also worried about how she would fare in school the next day. It was 4:00 a.m. She felt panicked and suspected that she was going to fail her upcoming chemistry test. "Do you think you would have said no to your father if you had known his health wasn't in immediate danger?" I asked.

"I would never say no to my dad," Adriana said. "He is working so hard to give his family a better life. I want to make sure that he gets the care that he deserves. I want to speak for my dad."

Adriana paused for a few seconds before continuing. "But I wish something like this doesn't happen right before the test, because school is important to me. I am about to graduate [from high school], and I want to go to college."

Adriana's father, who urgently needed her help, also wanted his daughter to go to college and obtain intergenerational mobility. She said, "My dad really wants me to succeed in school. He reminds me that education is the number-one solution to the financial problem. He wants me to go to college, so that I don't have to worry about money all the time like he does."

Like many young people I spoke with, Adriana refused to entertain the notion of saying no to her father, whose health was jeopardized by his physically demanding job. In fact, witnessing her family's financial struggles had only further solidified how important it was for her to do well in school. Like her dad said, education was the "number-one solution" to the financial problems they regularly encountered. Although Adriana knew that enrolling in college was a pathway to social mobility, she perceived her family responsibilities as incompatible with what was expected of her at school. Doing well in school required sufficient time and energy to study and concentrate.

Working-class Korean Americans also experienced a difficult double bind, meaning they, too, were pulled between their desire to help their parents and excel in school during crisis situations. Minjoo, an eighteen-year-old Korean American, for instance, spent a significant amount of time accompanying her father to a local hospital, where he received chemotherapy for lung cancer. While there, she felt trapped between "uncaring and busy" institutional agents and her "frustrated and distressed" monolingual father. Navigating the bureaucratic hurdles of the hospital and her father's health insurance company took a lot of time and energy, leaving her feeling underappreciated and overwhelmed.

Unlike Adriana, however, Minjoo expressed less empathy about her father's lung problems. She described her father as a chain smoker who "smokes two packs [of cigarettes] every day." Still, Minjoo quickly re-represented her father, a breadwinner and a security guard at a parking lot in a nearby Korean ethnic enclave, as a hardworking immigrant. She said, "My dad is stressed out at work. His employer just cut his hours. He is constantly worrying about his family. You know, it costs a lot of money to maintain family here."

Despite feeling resentful about her father's smoking habit, Minjoo also articulated a sense of ambivalence about her dual position as a daughter of immigrant and a student. She said, "I understand that my dad is frustrated because he can't communicate with the doctors, so I really want to be there for him." Although Minjoo wanted to be there for her father, she said it was impossible to balance the competing expectations of being her parents' "big helper" and a good student.

In addition to navigating healthcare encounters, legal problems were another common crisis that young language brokers encountered. Anna, a sixteen-year-old Mexican American, had been born in the US, but her two older brothers and parents were undocumented. While she was growing up,

Anna's parents repeatedly reminded her that she was needed and appreciated, but Anna simultaneously felt guilty for having citizenship rights that her family members were denied. After discussing how her brothers' lives differed from hers, she declared, "I was brought up to strive for the best, because I am an American-born US citizen. I have just as much opportunities as any other person in this country to achieve anything that I dream to do."

Nonetheless, she said that translating could leave her feeling overwhelmed when she had tests to study for. Referring to one incident where she had to deal with "the fake lawyer" who took her parents' money and disappeared, she exclaimed, "It was crazy, because my parents don't make that much money and gave this guy a lot of money."

Anna's parents were "super nervous" about reporting this fake attorney to law enforcement, especially because they feared deportation. Although Anna's parents ended up filing a police report with Anna's assistance, she reported that nothing happened after it was filed. "My parents were devastated, and I felt so bad," she said. "Like police weren't even that helpful, but we spent a lot of time there, and guess what? I missed school and my parents couldn't even write the note for my teacher. It was really frustrating."

Anna was unsuccessful at finding the "fake lawyer" who stole her parent's money. It was very possible that Anna's frustration stemmed from the fact that the police "weren't even that helpful." However, her experiences were also shaped by the ethnocentric and classed notions of normative childhood, expectations that are imposed on young people in school. Anna, a dependent, needed her parents' permission in order to be excused from school. Anna was distressed because her school lacked sufficient resources to communicate with her parents, who read and wrote primarily in Spanish. In short, there was a clear disconnect between what school expects of young people and the multiple forms of inequality working-class immigrant families of color experience on a daily basis, which leave young people feeling torn between their desire to help their family and succeed in school during crisis situations.

CHAIN TRANSLATIONS

For many working-class families, one crisis leads to another. Children often engage in what one language broker described as "chain translations." For example, Adriana, who had experienced the nightmare in the emergency room, said that accompanying her father to the hospital for his chest pain was "only the beginning." When her father asked Adriana to translate the medical bill a few weeks later, she was shocked by the charges. Although Adriana's father had received a low-income-family discount, the initial crisis situation inevitably created a domino effect that Adriana then had to navigate. Over the next several months, she made multiple phone calls and sent numerous faxes and letters until her father's medical bill was settled.

"I could not believe how much it costs for that one visit!" she said. "My dad was really frustrated, too, so I called for my dad and explained to one of the staff [at the hospital] that my dad really couldn't pay for the cost 'cause he's poor."

Edmon, an eighteen-year-old Mexican American who grew up with a single mom, experienced a similar domino effect. A dedicated language broker, Edmon told me that he was determined to counter the uneducated-Mexican stereotype and make his single mother happy and proud. Although "many people judge those of Hispanic origin and think that their children will not amount to anything," his mother expected him to do well in school. In fact, Edmon beamed whenever he talked about his mother, who had "a dream that [Edmon would] become an important person."

Nevertheless, Edmon told me that he had missed several days of school after his mother was injured during her cleaning job. "My translation responsibilities tripled," he said. First, Edmon accompanied his mother to the hospital. Next, he contacted his mother's client. Although his mother had been injured at this client's house, the client refused to pay the hospital bill. Edmon then contacted a lawyer to determine whether his mother qualified for workers' compensation. The lawyer, however, asked for a lump sum of money up front, which Edmon's mother did not have. Throughout all this, Edmon began falling behind in school, which left him feeling conflicted about spending such an inordinate time helping his mother.

As illustrated by Edmon's case, successfully navigating a crisis often involves negotiating with various English-speaking adults, such as doctors, lawyers, and the parent's employer. Other language brokers reported similar chain-translation encounters. For example, Joseph, a sixteen-year-old Korean American, recalled skipping his last class period to talk on the phone with his mother, who had been in a car accident.

"My mom told me that she was really scared when that guy hit her car and started speaking English to her. She wanted to explain to him that it was not her fault, but she couldn't," he said. Joseph said it was his responsibility to "step in as her advocate." Although he was committed to helping his mom, he admitted that this particular incident was stressful and that it wound up being "a pain in the ass."

"I had to call the police, and after that, I had to call the insurance company, and then the body shop. It was nonstop. I was getting frustrated because I had to be in my class instead of calling these places. My teacher would never understand why I had to do this for my mom."

Like many other language brokers I interviewed, Joseph, Edmon, and Adriana all said that their parents did not have any other option but to rely on their children during crisis situations. In reality, it is hard to believe that parents never have any other choice. Many could ask relatives, friends, or neighbors for help. In addition, studies have shown that ethnic organizations, including churches, play a pivotal role in providing social support for immigrant families.[17] However, many young people said that not only did their parents' busy schedules prevent them from fostering social capital with their communities, but their parents refused to discuss family problems with friends and relatives. These crisis situations, which tended to reveal their social class position, were viewed as private matters. For example, Youngmi, a fourteen-year-old language broker, said, "My parents don't really like to talk about their personal issues with other people." "My parents trust me more than anybody," she added.

Undoubtedly, Youngmi, like other language brokers, was called on to translate in crisis situations because she was the "trustworthy" translator who had accumulated years of experience navigating US institutions. Yet as demonstrated in chapter 3, young people like Youngmi accumulate language-brokering experiences and become their parents' most reliable translator because crisis situations require immediate action. There often isn't any other "trustworthy" or "good" translator who could step in without sufficient notice. Because most institutions in low-income neighborhoods are underfunded and have insufficient translation support, bilingual youth feel compelled to take care of their parents, especially during crisis situations.

Despite their best efforts, however, bilingual youth of color from working-class families are unable to fully compensate for the lack of institutional support. Nor is it possible for them to successfully balance their family and school responsibilities. Instead, language brokers often have to "drop everything," including their schoolwork, to help their parents in crisis situations. And because one crisis can create a domino effect of increasing their family responsibilities, some young language brokers may miss multiple days of school or have difficulty completing assignments for extended periods of time. For children of immigrants who are determined to obtain upward mobility, these chain translations leave them in a difficult double bind. Although everyone in this study experienced the double bind, race intersected with age and class, a topic I discuss next.

RACE AND THE DOUBLE BIND

The young people I interviewed told me that the difficulties they encountered balancing school and family responsibilities made them feel different from the typical American teenager. In this section, I show how race intersects with age and class to instill a lingering sense of inadequacy among the language brokers I interviewed. Because the educational system imposes differently racialized stereotypes,[18] the Mexican American and Korean American youth I interviewed reported different desires and disappointments when they were unable to successfully juggle school and family responsibilities.

Camila, whose Mexican immigrant parents worked as house cleaners, told me that she shouldered "a lot of family responsibilities." In addition to serving as her parents' "eyes, ears, and mouth," she often helped her three younger brothers with their homework. "It's hard," she said, "because my mom couldn't help us with homework ever since we were little. So it was up to me to help my brothers with their homework and projects."

Like the majority of the language brokers I interviewed, Camila knew that many of her family responsibilities were perceived as "adult" responsibilities. "Even though I am young, I think my parents treat me more like an adult because they know I am mature. That's why I am not only sister to my brothers, but I also take some of the role of a mom. That's not to say my mom is not involved in our lives. She definitely is and cares a lot about our education, but I also help my brothers out considerably."

On weekends, Camila accompanied her mother, who cleaned houses for living. At the time of the interview, she also worked at a clothing store twice a week.

"Did your parents ask you to work part time?" I asked.

"No, no, no, they actually didn't want me to work," she said. "I just started working because I needed money for myself and can help my parents. Also, last month, we didn't have enough money to pay the rent. We were behind, so we were about to get kicked out."

"Did your landlord say that to you?"

"Yeah, I translate for my dad when he needs to talk to the house owner, who picks up the rent. And my dad could not pay the rent because he didn't have enough money, so he asked me to explain to the house owner if he can wait a few days."

"How did it make you feel when you had to translate that?"

"Honestly, I just hated telling the house owner that my dad doesn't have enough money for the rent. It was embarrassing." She paused momentarily before saying, "I am guessing it might have been embarrassing for my dad, too. He had to swallow his pride and ask me for help, but on top of it, he had to ask for an extension."

When asked about how she felt about juggling school and family work, Camila had a lot to say. Although she did not want to "let the family situation affect [her]," she worried about her family. "Sometimes when I am at school, I can't focus, because I am always wondering if my dad has money for the rent," she said. "I wish I didn't know about the rent issues because it makes me worry a lot."

Tears started rolling down Camilla's cheeks as she told me how she felt about the responsibilities she shouldered. "Even though my parents told me not to worry about them, I felt like I had to take on so many responsibilities. Honestly, it felt overwhelming. There were times I just wanted to cry. I thought to myself, 'I am just a kid.'"

"Thinking about it, I never felt like I was a typical high school student," she said as she wiped her tears away. "I knew we are not the perfect American family. We are a family that struggle and have our ups and downs."

When I asked Camila to elaborate what she meant by "the perfect American family," she began speaking about how different her life was in comparison to "a rich American couple" and their two kids whom she knew. She had encountered this family while helping her mother clean a two-story house in West Los Angeles. In addition to having a swimming pool, both children had their own bedrooms. They also had a separate room for completing their homework, which was far different from Camilla's arrangement at home, where she shared a bedroom with both of her younger siblings and spent her evenings completing her homework at the kitchen table.

"Her two kids had a really nice room to study, and when I passed by their schools, they had fancy buildings with clean tables and cafeteria. It was a whole different environment than the schools you see over here in this community," she said.

Despite living in a Los Angeles community where the vast majority were working-class Latinx residents, Camila still viewed her family, which "struggle[d]" and had its "ups and downs," as different from the "norm." Instead, she identified "a rich American couple" and their two kids as the "perfect American family."[19] Scholars have consistently demonstrated that the image of the "normal American family" is ubiquitous in popular culture.[20] These ethnocentric and classed images tend to depict a White, heterosexual, middle-class nuclear family as the American ideal.[21] This imagery, moreover, serves to denigrate the life experiences of marginalized families, including poor and working-class immigrant families of color.[22] For Camila, traveling to wealthy neighborhoods of Los Angeles for her mother's job made this imagery salient and reinforced her belief that her life was different from the "typical" American teenager.

Camilla's experiences in school, however, also contributed to her perception that she herself was not a typical student. In contrast to the school she went to in a predominately Latinx area of Los Angeles, she knew the schools that "rich American kids" attended had "fancy" buildings and "clean" cafeterias.

Moreover, Camila knew that her teachers had a low expectation of her capabilities. Starting when she was young, many teachers had judged her and her parents harshly. Recalling the "racist" teachers she had encountered over the years, she said, "I remember that as soon as my teachers realized I was from Mexico, they would expect less of me."

"Can you give me an example?" I asked.

"When I was a kid in first grade, my teacher said, 'You are Mexican, so you cannot read higher-level books.' And it stuck with me all this time. If I didn't do something well enough, I would always go back to what she said, and I would think, 'She was right. I cannot do this.'"

Existing research demonstrates that educators often perceive Mexican

American students as less intelligent than White and Asian American students.[23] Research also shows that educators make their racialized expectations clear when interacting with students in school,[24] which Camila herself had experienced in first grade. These negative interactions stuck with her. As time went on, she also began to perceive her teachers as uncaring. And rather than asking for help, she suspected her teachers wouldn't—or didn't want to—"understand."

"I realized that my teachers don't understand what we have to go through," Camila said. "Or they don't want to understand. They just don't care. They weren't okay with my family. They always kind of made me and my family feel like we are below them."

When asked to elaborate, Camila recalled a time her brother had an asthma attack. When his inhaler did not have its desired effect, her mother rushed him to the emergency room. Camila missed half a school day to translate for them. Shortly thereafter, Camila's teacher called home and asked her parents to come in for a meeting, a meeting that Camila described as "hostile."

"I could tell they were judging my family because my parents aren't educated as they are," she continued. "I always felt like they were demanding, like my parents don't know any better. This one teacher didn't even think that I was translating correctly, so she kept saying, 'Are you sure you told them what I said?'"

Although Camila, acting as her parents' translator, attempted to explain her absence from school, her teacher wasn't sympathetic to her family's situation. The teachers "didn't understand why my parents didn't know English," she said. "They did not understand why I had to miss school. I mean, my brother had an asthma attack!"

Considering that family practices are highly racialized in the US, Camila's experiences pointed to the ways in which educators not only perceive Latinx students as lacking academic ability but also hold Latinx parents and students accountable for their "abnormal" family lives. Research has demonstrated that educators tend to blame low-income parents, especially Black and Latinx parents, when students miss or fall behind in school.[25] Camila experienced school as a hostile institution,[26] where "demanding" teachers who did not seem to care or understand their students' family lives attempted to correct her and her parents' behavior. These experiences contributed to Camila's lingering sense of inadequacy and led her to believe that her family was not perceived as normal.

Camila was not unique in this regard. When explaining what made their family less typical than that of the average American student, other Mexican American youth also described being treated like they were stupid and said their teachers problematized their families. This was especially the case of Mexican American boys, who reported that teachers were quick to penalize them.[27]

Sergio, a Mexican American boy, described himself as "outgoing but also introverted." Sergio liked socializing but also liked "staying in" and having some time to himself.

"Do you get paid to translate for your parents?" I asked.

"No way!" Sergio said, laughing. "I would be a rich man if they had paid me."

After regaining his composure, he said it was his responsibility to help his parents, who would "feel lost" without his translation abilities. "I know how to speak English and Spanish, so I should help. My parents would feel lost without me," he said. "Even adults need help at times. Everyone needs some help."

Sergio said that age didn't always determine who needed help. Although his language-brokering work had made it clear that "everyone needs some help," this didn't mean that he thought his childhood was "normal." Instead, he told me he knew "more than [he] was supposed to know" about his parents' lives.

"I am the oldest, so I grew up fast," he said. "I honestly think that I did know more than I was supposed to know. I remember having to call electric or gas companies because my mom had not paid the bill on time, and they were going to cut the electricity and gas. I would have to explain the situation, which made me feel uncomfortable."

Like most youth, Sergio had mixed feelings about translating. Despite reporting feeling good, needed, and appreciated, he also recalled moments when he felt uncomfortable. This discomfort stemmed from dominant perceptions of childhood, which construct adults as being the ones who are supposed to know more than children. As a result, age played a crucial role in shaping his feeling about the type of language-brokering work. Indeed, as discussed earlier in this chapter, these age-based expectations about young people's typical responsibilities were reinforced through Sergio's daily experiences at school. Sergio said that juggling language-brokering work was even more difficult when these responsibilities competed with his schoolwork.

"I struggle with the same stuff that all teenagers go through, like just trying to graduate and get out [of high school]," he said. "Growing up and being a teenager, you sometimes get annoyed and bothered by [translation work]. And sometimes I would be mean about it. Like, I cannot live according to my parents' schedule, because even the teenagers have their own schedule. I have my school exams and homework."

Although Sergio said that it was natural for teenagers to "get annoyed" and "bothered by" language-brokering work, it was clear that school sets the standard against which young people's childhood or teenage years is measured. In addition to assuming that all students have plenty of time to study for exams and to do homework, Sergio's teachers played a pivotal role in shaping how he evaluated his own childhood. Sergio's memory was etched with a poignant recollection of a time when a teacher singled him out and labeled him a "slacker."

One day, Sergio fell asleep in a history class. He had been "too tired" to pay attention because he had stayed up late the night before to complete his homework after helping his father, who worked as a painter, translate for several prospective clients. Sergio awoke to the feeling of water splashing onto his face. To his horror, his teacher had used a plant sprayer to wake him up, which made the entire class burst out laughing.

Although he attempted to tell his teacher that he had been up late dealing with "some responsibilities at home," his teacher brushed aside his concerns. Sergio rolled his eyes as he recounted his teacher's advice. "You have to let your parents know that you are a student," he mimicked, his voice dripping with sarcasm. "If you want to graduate, there has to be a limit," he added, expressing the frustration he had felt at the time.

Like Camila and the vast majority of Latinx youth in this study, Sergio was attending a school where the majority students were low-income Latinx children of immigrants. Within this context, Sergio was not unique in spending time after school providing language and financial support for his family. In fact, some teachers in low-income districts recognize that their students are more likely to come across hardships that make it more difficult for them to concentrate and complete homework in a timely fashion.[28] Despite this recognition, however, educators often racialize students' circumstances and blame students of color for lacking willpower or the necessary grit to keep up with the pace of school.[29] This seemed to be the case with Sergio's teacher. In addition to mocking him in front of class, she had made him feel like he was a slacker. She had also implicitly condemned his parents for failing to provide Sergio a "proper" childhood as she reiterated the expectation that school should come first. Telling Sergio that he needed to limit the amount of assistance he provided to his parents ignored the reality of his situation.

"I don't think teachers get me," Sergio said. "They just don't try to get to know us, you know what I am saying?"

I nodded as Sergio continued speaking.

"They always make me feel like there is something wrong with me and my family."

All the young people I talked to knew that schools expect students to prioritize schoolwork. They were also keenly aware of age-related expectations embedded within school and other institutions, which assume that parents are the ones looking after their children. Given their awareness about age expectations and in light of their regular interactions with teachers who racialized and problematized their school performance and family lives, Mexican American youth anticipated that their teachers would not fully understand their realities. Lacking trust in educators, many Mexican Americans were critical of and reported feeling anger toward educators who left them feeling as if there was something wrong with their childhood and family life.

Korean American language brokers did not think that they had a typical American childhood either. When compared to Mexican Americans, however, Korean Americans, who were more likely to go to school with middle-class White and Asian American students, were far more likely to talk about how educators racialized them as model minorities. As a result, rather than feeling anger toward their teachers, young working-class Korean Americans felt more unfit when they were unable to live up to their teachers' seemingly positive expectations about their academic capabilities.[30]

Jinju, a high school sophomore, is representative of this pattern. Jinju, who migrated to the US when she was ten years old, lived in a Los Angeles suburb with a "decent school district." Her school was one where the majority of students were White and Asian Americans, and 32 percent of students were experiencing poverty.

I met Jinju in front of a bustling ice cream store where she worked part-time after school. Although her shift did not start for another two hours, she ran into the shop to make me a strawberry and banana smoothie, something she proudly proclaimed she was "very good at making." She briefly winced as she handed me the smoothie, however, explaining that she had recently started feeling sharp pain in her wrist and fingers. She suspected this pain was from repeatedly scooping hard ice cream for hours on end.

As we sipped our drinks, she began telling me about her family. Her mother was "lucky" enough to be employed as a manicurist shortly after immigration to the US. Her father, however, was currently unemployed. He had spent the last several years hopping from one low-wage job to the next. He had worked in a range of occupations over the years, ranging from factories to dry cleaning. Without a second income to supplement her mom's wages, it was difficult for her family to pay their monthly rent.

Jinju began witnessing her parents' hardships firsthand once she mastered English and started translating more regularly for her parents. "Because I translate for my parents all the time, I got to know about parents' situation a lot more. I know we are in a very tough situation right now. My mom sometimes pays late fees [for her credit card] because my dad doesn't have a job," she said.

Like other language brokers, Jinju avoided asking her mother too many questions about their financial circumstances. "My mom is going through a lot right now. I don't want to ask my mom because she is stressed out. I go to her work a lot and try to help out. I answer the phone calls and get people through the cashier. When American people come, I will be the one who is going up to them and say, 'How can I help you?' I want to help her as much as I can."

Despite wanting to help her mother as much possible, Jinju, like many other language brokers, was acutely aware that her life was different from the lives of her friends. She knew their parents didn't "depend on them as much."

"They are just like teenagers," she said. "They would talk about boys while I talk about my part-time jobs. Their focus is all about having fun. While they went out to play, I had to work. They worried about their SAT scores and other school subjects and grades. That's not the only thing I worried about."

"What do you worry about?" I asked.

"My parents' financial situation is unstable, so I worry about the future of my family. I do envy my friends sometimes for not worrying about financial matters. They don't have to help their parents. They can just focus on school.

Every month, I see all these credit card statements and bills, and it's not fun to always worry about them."

Teenage life in the US is defined as a time when young people are supposed to focus on school and have fun with their friends.[31] As demonstrated in this chapter, schools help reinforce this distinction between adult and teenage responsibilities by assigning homework and expecting students to devote their free time to studying and preparing for college admissions exams. Even when schools offer youth opportunities to pursue internships or part-time jobs, there are strict restrictions on the number of hours and the amount of money young people can earn. Young people thus often volunteer or work for course credit instead of earning a regular salary.

As Jinju's experiences suggest, however, these practices can leave working-class youth feeling different from everyone else. This is especially the case for young people like Jinju, who attend schools alongside more affluent youth. Unlike her friends, whose parents had more time and resources to devote to their children's schooling, Jinju had a part-time job. Whereas she tried to help out her parents as much as she could and was worried "about the future of my family," her friends were teenagers who talked about boys, focused on having fun, and "went out to play." Their biggest concerns were about their SAT scores and grades.[32]

Yet for Korean American youth like Jinju, the racialization of Asian American students' academic achievement intersected with class and age to shape her understanding of the "typical" childhood. And teachers played a crucial role. For instance, Jinju told me that her teachers had "no idea about [her] family life" and often assumed that her exceptional academic performance was a reflection of her Korean parents' "unconditional support." Being seen as a student with "devoted Korean parents" who assisted with her academic pursuits at every step contributed to her feeling frustrated and different in comparison to both her Asian and White classmates.

"My Korean friends have tutors, but I have to do everything by myself when it comes to my homework," she exclaimed. "My teachers thought I was good at math because I am Asian. 'Oh because you're Asian, you should be good.' I am actually good at math, so I fit the stereotype, but I felt cheated. I hated it because I worked so hard when it came to math. It was also my passion because there are more jobs out there if you are good at math. Like, it's very practical. My parents' financial situation is unstable, so it makes me more ambitious in terms of my own career." "Money becomes a big deal," she added. "It's not everything, but I can't go to college and not make money, so I have to be more proactive."

Although I did not interview Jinju's teachers, research shows that educators often hold higher overall expectations about the academic capabilities of Asian American youth.[33] Educators, for instance, often racialize Asian American youth as "smart" students. Their exemplary academic performance in all subjects, but especially math, is regularly attributed to their upbringing, as their parents are assumed to devote a significant amount of money, time, and energy to their children's education. For young Asian Americans like Jinju, however, devoting time to a subject like math was a way to increase her chance of obtaining a job that would allow her to earn more money. Moreover, when Jinju said that math is a "practical" subject, she implied that some professions are largely inaccessible to Asian Americans due to racial discrimination. By comparison, there are "more jobs out there" for Asian Americans in other professions, such as ones that require workers to be good at math. Nevertheless, Jinju "hated" that her teachers assumed that she had an "Asian" childhood. Jinju felt as if teachers were unaware of the way that social class intersects with race to shape Asian American youths' academic experiences. They were unaware of the additional work she had to put into earning exemplary grades in school, especially in math.

Importantly, Jinju's regular contacts with educators who imposed the Asian stereotype had shaped the way Jinju perceived and interacted with her parents. Referring to the time when she was distracted from completing her homework because her parents needed help translating a credit card statement, Jinju said, "They bother me especially when I am doing my homework. I am so concentrated, but I get really distracted when they come in and ask me. I am like, 'Dude, can't you see my homework? Leave me alone.' Sometimes I think, 'Can't my parents be more like other Korean parents who always care about their children's education?' That's when I am showing [my parents] that I am so annoyed, I will be like 'Why?' and give them an attitude. Ahhh, oh my gosh, so that's really frustrating."

Clearly, Jinju, like Mexican American language brokers, knew that schools and their practices excluded the experiences of working-class immigrant youth of color because they revolved around White middle-class values. And yet, whereas Mexican Americans were critical of educators' negative evaluations of their family life, Korean Americans like Jinju were more likely to compare their life to that of more privileged Korean/Asian American youth. Consequently, instead of feeling angry, working-class Korean Americans felt more inadequate than working-class Mexican Americans did for not being able to live up to their teachers' expectations. The seemingly positive stereotypes of Asian American youth thus served as subtle yet powerful mechanisms of control.

Similarly, Jerry, a sixteen-year-old Korean American, also compared his family to other, more privileged co-ethnic peers. Partly because Jerry had regular cross-class contact with middle-class Korean American youth, he believed it was less common for Korean Americans to experience financial precarity. He also thought he was unique in spending so much time assisting his parents, which became clear when he repeatedly described his parents as not being "typical" Koreans throughout his interview.

After Jerry uttered the phrase "typical Korean" for the third time, I asked him to explain what he meant. He furrowed his eyebrows, as if he automatically assumed I would understand what he meant. Speaking to me in a slow voice, as if I were having trouble comprehending him, he said that all the other "Koreans" drove expensive "Mercedes." His dad, however, owned a "beat-up old Hyundai."

Hyundai, a South Korean car manufacturer, is one of the most popular brands in Korea. In Jerry's eyes, however, driving this old, "beat-up" car paradoxically made his working-class parents *less* Korean. Owning a Mercedes, a German car that sells for tens of thousands more dollars than a Hyundai in the United States, was what he expected from the "typical" Korean in Los Angeles.

Another thing that made Jerry feel less "typical" was that expectation he encountered at school that revolved around parents being actively involved with their children's education. Similar to other young people in this study, Jerry told me that his working-class immigrant parents rarely attended his school activities. Unlike "typical Korean parents," his parents were not "tiger moms" or "helicopter parents." Instead of criticizing the school practices, which did not take into account his working-class immigrant family's circumstances, however, Jerry was angry at his parents.

"They didn't even come to my middle school graduation," he said.

"How did it make you feel?" I asked.

"I was mad, but I just decided not to attend the ceremony. More and more, I think I am getting used to it. I just don't even bother telling them about my school stuff."

Being able to engage in "helicopter parenting"—the practice of paying enormous attention to children's lives and being ready to jump in to solve problems—is closely related to social class.[34] For this reason, it was unsurprising that Jerry, like many of the other working-class Korean Americans I interviewed, expressed an acute sense of inadequacy when comparing his life with the lives of other privileged peers whose parents appeared wealthier and more available than his own.

Although Jerry projected his feelings of frustration onto his parents, in reality, schools fail to account for the lives of working-class families. For instance, parents with unpredictable or irregular work schedules may find it challenging to participate in a ceremony like graduation, which supposedly marks a monumental milestone in students' lives. However, events like graduation are often scheduled during "standard" business hours. Considering that professionals are more likely to have flexible work schedules or paid time off from work, Jerry's experiences highlight how working-class children of immigrants get "used to" what Raymond Williams identified as a "structure of feeling" or "actively felt and lived" inequalities.[35] Jerry was initially "mad" when his parents were unable to attend his middle school graduation and had subsequently stopped bothering to tell them about his "school stuff."

And yet race intersects with class and age to shape the sense of inadequacy schools impose on working-class Korean American youth like Jerry. For instance, Jerry, who was "barely passing" his classes, frequently interacted with educators who assumed that all Asian Americans do well in school. "I don't get how teachers automatically assume that because you are Asian, you have do well in school," he said. "There are a lot of Asians in my school who don't get an A in math, but there is always that pressure."

In part because of the racialized expectations that were imposed on him at school, Jerry rarely sought help from his teachers when he had difficulty balancing "responsibilities between home and school." Just the other day, it had been "difficult" to find time to complete his homework because he had spent three hours on the phone trying to help his parents sort out Medi-Cal benefits. "That's when I compare my life with Korean kids who are better off than me," he said. He briefly paused. "It's hard for me to tell anyone this is what I am going through." "People might think, 'What is wrong with your parents?'"

The fact that Korean Americans evoked stereotypical meanings of Asian families as being model middle-class minorities was noteworthy. Mexican American youth I interviewed, whose socioeconomic circumstances were similar to that of the Korean American youth I interviewed, rarely compared their lives to middle-class co-ethnics. Instead, because educators racialize Mexican Americans as lazy and stupid and problematize their childhoods for presumably having parents who do not care about their children's academic success, Mexican Americans express a sense of anger. In comparison, although Korean Americans also feel the sense of unfairness encoded in middle-class educational expectations about academic success, they experience their family circumstances in differently racialized terms. Because educators often racialize Asian Americans as "smart" students whose parents devote significant amounts of money and energy to their children's education,[36] Korean Americans in this study expressed a sense of disappointment. Recognizing the distance between their families and the pervasive image depicting Asian families as the model minority, Korean American youth described a heightened sense of inadequacy, thus showing the powerful role of seemingly positive stereotypes in shaping young people's desires and disappointments.

RETHINKING AGE-BASED WHITE MIDDLE-CLASS STANDARDS IN SCHOOLS

Of the thirteen young people introduced in this chapter, eight are girls and five are boys. Seven are Korean American and six are Mexican American. Some attended schools in more urban areas of Los Angeles, whereas others attended schools in the suburbs. Some of their parents and siblings were undocumented.

Despite their differences, institutionalized inequalities shaped the ways they made sense of their family and school responsibilities. In a nation where institutions routinely fail to provide a sufficient safety net and language support for working-class immigrant families, all the youth I interviewed stated that it was their family responsibility to translate for their parents. Young people's desire to contribute their labor for the sake of family well-being, however, exists in tension with what is expected of young people in school. Children of immigrants are keenly aware that institutions, including schools, expect their families to adhere to top-down intergenerational relations, where parents are always the ones imparting resources to their children. They also know that young people, by default of their age, are supposed to have "carefree" childhoods that revolve around school. Nonetheless, because institutions fail to provide sufficient resources, including language services, working-class immigrant parents of color have a hard time prioritizing such expectations, especially in times of crisis. Largely excluded from English-speaking and racialized workplaces, parents instead have labor-intensive, low-paying jobs without benefits where they have to work long hours. Because young people in this study vividly witnessed the multiple forms of inequality that their parents experienced through their language-brokering work, their desire to do well in school to repay their parents' struggle in a new country was amplified.

And yet it was especially difficult, if not impossible, for them to complete homework, study for tests, and attend school during crisis situations. In these situations, language brokers have to "drop everything" to help their parents navigate English-speaking institutions, including hospitals or police stations in low-income neighborhoods, which, as I discussed in chapter 2, do not have sufficient translation support. Lacking resources to fully navigate flawed institutions and juggling time-sensitive issues that often involve chain translations, many language brokers are caught within a structurally imposed double bind. Torn between their twin desires to help their family and to achieve upward mobility, the young people I interviewed felt like they didn't have the typical childhood.

However, working-class Mexican American and Korean American youth experience the double bind in differently racialized ways. Although most youth I interviewed felt like their lives were different from those of the "American family," working-class Mexican American youth described their experiences of interacting with teachers who racialized them as stupid or slackers. Consistent with the results of existing research,[37] their teachers harshly judged their parents for being negligent, which left Mexican American youth feeling frustrated and upset with educators who overlooked or ignored the realities of their lives. In contrast, scholars have shown that educators often racialize Asian parents as middle-class model minorities who offer their children significant parental support. The pervasiveness of this imagery in the educational system was something that the working-class Korean American youth I interviewed were fully aware of, which left them with an acute sense of inadequacy for having families that could not adhere to this seemingly positive stereotype. Ultimately, age and race intersected with class to shape young people's understanding of family and school responsibilities.

Unlike the outwardly negative racial meanings that Latinx and Black people endure, the seemingly seductive model minority stereotype portrays Asian Americans as living proof of the American Dream or the idea that anyone can pull themselves up by their bootstraps and make it in the US.[38] And yet, as scholars have long argued, this stereotype works as disciplinary measure and fails to grant Asian Americans full citizenship rights. In addition to pitting Asian Americans against Black and Latinx people, who have allegedly failed at pulling themselves up by their bootstraps, being elevated to the exemplary position of model minorities helps divert attention away from structural inequalities Asian Americans experience in school.[39] Rather than feeling angry at the school system or racist authorities, which, as Victor Rios has argued, can lead to politicization,[40] the findings shows that model minority stereotype can make Asian Americans feel as if their families are personally responsible for being different from the American norm. As sociologist Lisa Park argues, "For Asian Americans, deviation from the model minority ideology implies not only a moral shortcoming due to their own individual failure, but also separates them from the American norm, thereby reinforcing their foreigner status."[41]

As long as the nation continues to hold everyone accountable to normalized White middle-class notions of citizenship, young people's desire to help their families will continue to conflict with their academic pursuits and place them in a double bind. And as I show in the next chapter, multiple inequalities that youth shoulder on a daily basis also prompt young people to develop various interactional strategies to solve structural problems.

FIVE DOING AMERICAN FROM AN OUTSIDER-WITHIN POSITION

"I am American. I was born here. I love being bilingual."

Maria, a sixteen-year-old Mexican American, told me that she enjoyed translating for her Spanish-speaking parents. They often praised her for being both "smart" and "very articulate." She loved being bilingual. And as someone who was born in the US, she identified herself as American. This, however, did not mean that people outside her family saw her in the same way.

Maria oscillated between sounding empowered and frustrated when describing her language-brokering work. Her mixed emotions were partially shaped by an awareness of how people "disrespected" her mother. Asked to provide a specific example, she told me she "got super angry" at a police officer who perceived her mother as an illegal alien when she attempted to report a hit-and-run collision in which she was involved. Though the encounter at the police station had happened three years earlier, Maria's memory clung to it with a vividness that made it feel as if it had unfolded just yesterday. The officer had automatically assumed that her mother was the one who had done something illegal.

"My mom forgot to bring her new insurance card," Maria said. "So, when I translated this to that police, he was like, 'Tell your mother that in this country, it's illegal to drive without the insurance.' He then went on and on about the consequence of driving without insurance and a driver's license. I never said my mom drives without the insurance card! But I kept my tongue. I just told him that she meant to [bring it] but forgot."

In addition to opting against challenging the officer, Maria omitted parts of the conversation when translating the police officer's instructions. Rather than telling her mom that the officer had assumed they were illegally driving without insurance and a driver's license, she said, "Let's go get your insurance card. He said we need to bring the insurance card to file the report."

When they came back with the new card, Maria interpreted the questions on the police report for her mother.

"We had to draw the cars on the form, too. I drew the other car so much bigger," Maria grinned from ear to ear as she recounted the moment.

"Can you tell me why you did not tell your mom about what the police officer had said?" I asked.

"What is the point?" Maria shrugged as she said, "I didn't want my mom to get mad."

When I asked why she did not challenge the police officer, Maria said something that many other Mexican language brokers told me. "My mom can't speak English," she said, "so people automatically treat her like she is stupid. And here is her little daughter trying to speak for her mom. He won't take me and my mom seriously because we are Mexicans and I am a kid!"

Despite being known as the smart and articulate child, Maria's accumulated experience of translating for parents taught her early on that her voice would not be taken seriously. Through numerous translation encounters such as these, where age, race, and gender inequalities shape English-speaking adults' perceptions of language brokers' competency, Maria came to know herself as a "Mexican," a "little daughter" and "a kid."

These early experiences had a lasting impact on her. Over the years, she had developed new strategies to avoid having her credibility as a translator called into question. One strategy was to speak on the phone whenever possible. "I don't want them to see me," Maria said.

People often judge others based on social characteristics like race, gender, and class. Because social status and esteem are differently conferred in everyday interactions, people often develop strategies to pass as normal or to help ensure that others perceive them as competent.[1] In fact, sociologists have long argued that this is one way that the social order is reproduced. People "do" gender, class, and racial differences during everyday interactions because these omnipresent categories are used as measuring sticks against which individuals are evaluated.[2]

Less attention, however, has been paid to understanding how people who are at the margin—in this case, the social location of being a young working-class immigrant of color—draw on their accumulated knowledge to resist inequality in everyday life. Yet people who are living at the intersection of multiple systems of oppression often develop ways to observe inequality that is less visible to dominant groups in the society.[3] In other words, what Patricia Hill Collins calls the "outsider-within" position enables social actors to resist inequalities of power and make "creative use of their marginality," thus potentially changing social order.[4]

Indeed, Maria's story reveals how the margin can be a site of both repression and resistance.[5] Despite being an American by virtue of her birthplace, Maria learned early on that her social position as a daughter of Mexican immigrants limited her ability to obtain full citizenship rights based on her accumulated experiences as a language broker. Rather than "doing" difference in ways that fully reproduced the social order,[6] she used her simultaneously subordinated and elevated position as a bilingual speaker to resist inequality during translation encounters. For example, knowing that her mother would become upset about the racialized nativism they had encountered at the police station, Maria opted against translating everything the police officer said. Furthermore, after discovering that being perceived as a "kid" or "Mexican little daughter" negatively affected her ability to be taken seriously while translating for mother, Maria strategically used the phone instead. At the end of the day, these strategies helped ensure that Maria was successful in securing crucial resources for her family.

In this chapter, I explore the strategies that language brokers like Maria use when attempting to provide social citizenship for their family members. How and with what consequences do bilingual immigrant youth of color like Maria use their outsider-within status to navigate and resist multiple inequalities when translating for their family members? How do these strategies provide them with the resources that would otherwise be limited or inaccessible to their family members? To answer these questions, I identify three strategies language brokers draw on when attempting to prove their competency as "professional" American adults: *passing*, or using the phone and their English fluency to hide their age and race; *shielding*, or censoring and filtering microaggressions to ensure their parents maintain their composure when they encounter racialized nativism; and *posing*, or enacting the behaviors, vocabularies, and mannerisms valued by middle-class adults. By describing these strategies, I argue that children of immigrants respond to age inequality and racialized nativism by "doing American." In other words, they draw on their outside-within position to enact normative understandings of Americanness in hopes of gaining full citizenship rights for their families.

PASSING AS "AMERICAN" ADULTS

As demonstrated in chapters 3 and 4, language brokers encounter multiple inequalities when attempting to help their family members access housing, educational, legal, financial, commercial, health, and employment resources. Through their accumulated language-brokering experiences, language brokers learn that their social position as children, as well as racialized meanings depicting their monolingual parents as "undeserving foreigners," negatively impacts their family's ability to access resources. As a result, many intentionally use what Erving Goffman described as an avoidance strategy, or a defensive measure that prevents them from encountering discrimination.[7] Rather than speaking to English speakers face to face, many bilingual youth attempt to pass as "American" adults on the phone.

The way language brokers attempt to pass was demonstrated by Mina, a Korean American girl. I met Mina on a scorching summer day in a local park. As Mina made her way to the bench where I was seated, I noticed that her straight hair, peppered with red highlights, was damp with sweat. She was breathing heavily as she paused to push her thick glasses up the bridge of her nose. After taking a moment to catch her breath, she explained that she had run more than two miles from her school because she was so anxious to chat with me. As she introduced herself, she said she was an "expert translator," a phrase that other language brokers also used.

Mina was shorter than most other seventeen-year-olds, but her lively spirit, enthusiastic demeanor, and booming voice made her appear larger than life. We jumped right into discussing "all these annoying people" she had met while translating for her parents, a job she had started doing shortly after moving to Los Angeles from Korea at age eight. Although Mina initiated the conversation topic, I sensed some hesitation as she began sharing her experiences.

"Who are these annoying adults?" I asked.

"Adults who think they are better than kids." She paused momentarily and said, "It's really annoying when some people think you are just a kid. I understand that's how adults think [about young people], but I am just trying to help my mom, you know?"

"Can you give me an example?"

Mina sighed and told me about a time she had endured a two-hour wait at the DMV with her mom. "I think I was about ten years old," she said. "I went to DMV with my mom because her registration card didn't come in mail for like three months. The lady there didn't listen to me carefully. She was speaking to me in that kiddie voice, saying something like it takes more than a month for the registration card to arrive."

Mina rolled her eyes. She continued describing her encounter with the DMV agent in vivid detail. "What part of 'more than three months' didn't she understand?" Mina asked. "I repeated that it has been more than three months, and she didn't even bother to look it up on her computer to see if it was mailed out or not. She went on a two-minute rant about how I need to be patient and just wait."

Despite having been told in a "kiddie voice" to be patient and wait, Mina called the DMV a few days later. She learned that the registration card had indeed been mailed out over two months ago. It turned out the card was lost in the mail. The new card the DMV agent mailed to Mina's mom arrived within a week.

After this incident, Mina realized an important lesson: it was easier to translate over the phone, as it allowed her to sound more like an adult. She said, "I know all of my mom's intimate information by heart. [When I talk on the phone], I feel more powerful because they take you more seriously 'cause they think they are speaking with an adult."

Many children, regardless of their racial background, occasionally try to act or sound like an adult to gain respect from others.[8] Yet shouldering what many Americans consider adult responsibilities in adult-centric settings like the DMV had made Mina highly aware of the widespread societal perception that children are naïve, innocent, impatient, and incompetent. For this reason, it was likely not a coincidence that the DMV agent asked Mina to "be patient and just wait." The agent's usual clients were not ten-year-old girls, leading to a mismatch between Mina's capabilities and the way adults held her accountable to widespread understandings of chronological age in everyday actions. While accruing expertise as her family's translator, Mina developed a strategy to offset the risk of having the limited status of childhood ascribed to her. Using the phone helped Mina give the impression that she was an expert, thereby ensuring she was successful in securing resources for her family.

There is, however, a specific type of adult that young people attempt to emulate when they attempt to pass on the phone. Language brokers want to pass as an *American* adult. Such was the case for Jennifer, an eighteen-year-old Korean American, who was cognizant of the way that Asian Americans are racialized as perpetual foreigners.

"I hate it when people ask you, 'Where are you from?'" Jennifer said. "And I go, 'I am from Los Angeles,' and they ask you, 'Where are you really from?' I am sure all Asian people who were born here had the same experience, even though they speak English fluently."

She shook her head and continued speaking. "You know, some White people come up to you and go, 'Ni hao ma,' and I am like, 'I don't speak Chinese.' And they are like, 'Konnichiwa.' I speak English. Hello?!" She waved her hand. "I don't even try to tell these people I am Korean."

"Why not?" I asked.

"Because people think that all Koreans are FOBs."

Jennifer was highly aware that people often perceive Asian Americans as FOBs, an acronym for the pejorative phrase "fresh off the boat." This stereotype, which depicts Asian Americans as perpetual foreigners who just immigrated to the US, shaped the way Jennifer and her family were perceived. Because "normal" Americans are expected to speak English fluently and without accents, Jennifer, like the vast majority of Korean American youth I spoke with, knew that her Korean immigrant parents were especially vulnerable to racialized nativism as a result of their limited English proficiency.

In fact, although her parents spoke "basic" and "simple English to get by," Jennifer said they preferred not to speak English for fear of sounding like an "idiot." "My parents are very conscious of their accents," she said, "because the moment they try to speak [English], some people give them this dirty look, like they are idiots."

Given her accumulated experiences of navigating racialized translation interactions where one's competency was judged by the ability to speak English fluently and without a "foreign" accent, Jennifer had learned to equate Americanness with Whiteness. This became clear as she recalled a time when she asked a customer-service representative for a refund over the phone. "When people just hear me, they are nicer," she said. "The representative was so apologetic. That never happens to me when I translate in person. If you speak without accents, and if they don't see you, then they think I am White."

Although Jennifer attempted to speak without an accent, there is no such thing as "standard" English. No matter how unmarked a person's language may seem, everyone has an accent. As Rosina Lippi-Green asserts, "Every native speaker of English has some regional variety, with the particular phonology of that area, or a phonology which represents one or more areas for some people."[9] In the minds of bilingual children, however, standard English is a colorless and accent-free language spoken by White American *adults*. As a result of their cumulative experiences of navigating adult-centric institutions where language is racialized, young language brokers gradually realize that English-speaking adults are more accommodating and "nicer" when they are not interacting with a "foreigner" or a "child." To reduce the effects of the age and language discrimination, language brokers, who conflate "talking White," "sounding like an American," and speaking without an "accent," opt to use the phone to pass as White American adults.

Given their awareness of how their age and race play into translation encounters, many children of immigrants reported that translating over the phone reduced their anxiety. This was especially the case for girls, who, as existing research has shown, are less likely to be perceived as intelligent or competent public speakers than boys are.[10] Some children echoed what Jinju, a fifteen-year-old Korean American, said: "I don't know why, but I can talk better over on the phone. I don't get intimidated because the other person doesn't see me." It is possible that children of immigrants, especially girls, actually communicate better over the phone knowing that others will be less likely to write off their capabilities. Indeed, studies have shown that when people become aware of negative racial and gender stereotypes concerning their group, they often become anxious and fail to perform at their maximum.[11] However, it is important to note that when young language brokers cover their age and race behind the phone, adults are less likely to dismiss their concerns, thus increasing their chance of accessing resources for their family.

Mexican American youth had similar experiences of attempting to pass as American adults on the phone. They, too, had learned early on that race, gender, and age shape how English-speaking adults treat them. Yet in comparison to Korean Americans, who are often racialized as middle-class minorities, Mexican American youth are more likely to encounter racism during in-person financial transactions, such as when they attempt to help their parents purchase or rent expensive items. Accordingly, when attempting to inquire about advertised goods, Mexican language brokers reported that they were especially successful in using the phone to offset the extent to which they were judged as coming from a financially unstable family.

Flora, a sixteen-year-old Mexican American, exemplified this pattern. Despite being born and raised in Los Angeles, she said in a sarcastic voice, "Of course people think I am just Mexican no matter how many times you tell them I was born here."

Like many language brokers, Flora had mixed feelings about her language-brokering work, which were partially shaped by an awareness of how her credibility as a translator was regularly called into question by adults. Through her accumulated experiences of translating for her parents, she had learned that she looked like "a Mexican little girl." However, over the years, Flora's position as an outsider-within helped her realize that the phone was a valuable tool to ensure her success when accessing services her family needed. For example, she recalled going into a car dealership in an affluent, predominately White area of Los Angeles called Culver City with her mother. They walked in and stood by the door, expecting a salesperson to greet them. "But we were just sitting there, and nobody came to help us!" Flora exclaimed.

Several minutes later, Flora sat down on a "shining leather couch" in what seemed like a waiting room. She then tried to make eye contact as one sales representative after another passed by them. She even attempted to wave her hand in the direction of one of them.

"Were they busy assisting other customers?" I asked.

"No, absolutely not." Flora was firm in her reply.

"So they were not busy but did not ask if you need help?" I asked.

"I swear, this man saw us but purposely looked away," Flora said through clenched teeth.

It was not a coincidence that Flora, a Mexican American girl, reported feeling invisible at the car dealership. Research consistently finds that automobile retailers respond differently to potential buyers depending on their gender and race.[12] Car salespeople, the majority of whom are White men, might have assumed that Flora and her mom would not have enough money to purchase a car or that they were waiting for Flora's father to arrive.

Although this was not the first time Flora had felt ignored during a translation encounter, her experiences at the car dealership left her feeling especially resentful and angry. It had taken her mother, who used the bus to travel across Los Angeles from one cleaning job to another, a long time to save up enough money to purchase a car. What was supposed to be a celebratory milestone, one that signaled their family's success as hardworking American immigrants who were presumably pulling themselves up by their bootstraps, quickly soured.

Flora's mother wanted to go to another dealer. But Flora devised an alternate plan. As they were walking out of the dealership, Flora suggested, "'Let's call them and see what they say. I sound White, right?'" She grew more relaxed as she recalled what happened next.

"So then they were like so nice on the phone. All of sudden, they had so many cars available for us to buy!" Flora made an appointment to meet with a representative. Several days later, they went back to the dealer. This time, she and her mother drove off the lot in their newly purchased green Corolla.

Although all Mexican American youth found using the phone to be especially helpful when speaking for their parents during financial transactions, Mexican American boys encountered a different form of gendered racism. Whereas youth like Flora felt invisible, Mexican American boys felt hypervisible. The gendered difference in Mexican American youths' experiences was exemplified by Vincent, a dark-skinned seventeen-year-old who was over six feet tall and had tattoos covering his muscular arms.

Growing up, Vincent had learned at an early age that he was a target of racial profiling. His neighborhood was viewed as dangerous and police regularly stopped and harassed residents, including Vincent. What was ironic to Vincent, however, was that he faced even more surveillance and danger when accompanying his father, who fixed houses for a living, in so-called safe neighborhoods in Los Angeles. Vincent had learned that police often patrolled these "rich" neighborhoods as soon as Vincent showed up. "This doesn't fly with me," Vincent said.

Several days before Vincent spoke with me, he had been helping his father complete a job in an affluent Los Angeles suburb. He was in the middle of unloading window blinds from his father's car when flashing red and blue lights caught his attention. "Apparently, someone called a cop on me," Vincent explained in a strained voice. "I didn't do anything wrong!" It was only after Vincent showed the officer the construction materials in the back of the truck that the officer let him go.

This wasn't the only time Vincent had been unfairly accused of doing something wrong in a predominately White and wealthy area of Los Angeles, however. When he was eleven years old, Vincent and his younger sister, who according to Vincent was faired-skinned and "nerdy looking," had accompanied their father to a job in Beverly Hills. After growing bored watching their father install new kitchen cabinets, the two siblings began walking aimlessly through the neighborhood.

Vincent, however, quickly realized that other residents were shooting him "dirty looks." He remembered one man shouting from a nearby car, "'There are five men in this van. You better let her go!'"

Vincent glared at the men but felt "intimidated." He recalled thinking to himself, "What are they talking about? Do they think I kidnapped her?" Vincent attempted to defuse the situation by walking in the other direction, but one man got out of the car and started approaching him.

His sister, however, intervened. She stepped in front of Vincent and said, "'This is my brother. You let him go!'"

Vincent's experiences of being surveilled by the police in both his own "dangerous" neighborhood and "safe" White neighborhoods were indicative of a broader pattern that sociologist Victor Rios calls "ubiquitous criminalization."[13] It is well documented that Black and Latinx boys are targeted by police and experience scrutiny in their everyday lives because they are seen as dangerous, threatening, and more adultlike than other youth.[14] Controlling images of Black and Latinx men as super-predators have also circulated widely in media, which fans long-standing racial hysteria that Black and Latinx boys pose a danger to White people, especially to White women.[15] For this reason, the police officers relaxed their guard only after Vincent had "proved" that he was in an affluent White neighborhood to work, as many Latinx people do. In the other incident, Vincent's sister's gender, light skin, and assertion that Vincent was her brother were required before the men in the van backed off.

Other people had also questioned Vincent's credibility during translation encounters. One "unforgettable" episode had occurred when his family was trying to move to a nicer apartment. Vincent said he had initially felt excited when he saw a big for-rent sign draped from the awning of his "dream home." Yet when Vincent and his parents arrived at the leasing office, the apartment manager, who had sounded welcoming when Vincent spoke with him on the phone several hours earlier, refused to show them the apartment. Suddenly, the unit was already occupied. Vincent's fury only grew stronger as he and his parents left the building. The "big-ass sign" seeking tenants was still displayed near the entrance.

Later that day, Vincent tried again. After scheduling several visits with prospective landlords over the phone, he suggested that his younger sister accompany his parents to the viewings while he remained at home. Although people often questioned Vincent's credibility during translation encounters, his sister did not encounter any problems. His parents signed a lease for a new apartment several days later.

"I don't want my look and tattoos to get in the way when I try to do my job. It's a waste of time to deal with people who tell my family that they don't have the apartment available, when I clearly see the sign [seeking tenants]," Vincent said. "Like I said, people think I am a cholo. But I don't sound like one. I sound American on the phone."

Navigating translation encounters made Vincent acutely aware of the way age, race, gender, and language shaped the forms of discrimination he experienced in face-to-face interactions. Born in the US, Vincent spoke English better than he spoke Spanish. With his deep and charming voice, it was easy for Vincent to speak like a White man, the kind of person who is often held in high regard during financial interactions.[16] However, he was often unable to activate the status conferred by his gender and English-speaking capabilities during face-to-face interactions. Instead, he was held accountable to racialized, controlling images that depicted Latinx boys and men as dangerous or violent criminals. Similar to the way that some Black people switch between so-called standard English and African American Vernacular English,[17] he devised a strategy to prevent his racialized masculinity from interfering with his ability to secure resources for his family. He had learned that he could pass as a White American adult when speaking to others over the phone.

Knowing and anticipating discrimination often means that individuals sometimes have to emulate "the language and manner of oppressor" in an attempt to protect themselves from the interlocking structure of race, class, and gender.[18] For this reason, research has demonstrated that many light-skinned Black people have secured resources that would otherwise have been withheld, including access to education, jobs, and housing, by passing as White.[19] Some LGBTQ people are also able to secure valuable resources by modifying their mannerisms, appearance, or attire at work or school or when they are with their family.[20] Similarly, children of immigrants—as outsiders-within—know that they risk having their competency as translators called into question during face-to-face interactions. However, speaking with others over the phone lowers the risk that they will be perceived as children or foreigners. Instead, their English fluency allows them to sound like a normative American adult over the phone, thereby challenging the inequality imposed by their race and age.

At the same time, this particular tactic of "doing American" over the phone does not always enable language brokers to avoid being racialized. For instance, when language brokers call state and local agencies, they often have to provide race-revealing information such as their parents' last names or their home address. Language brokers also cannot hide their gender behind the phone. Still, there are clear benefits of "doing American," or sounding like a White adult, especially when they are inquiring about an apartment, a car loan, or advertised goods. If they are successful at passing as an American adult on the phone, it is easier to connect their parents to crucial resources that provide their family a better standard of living. Ultimately, language brokers' conscientious decision to use the phone helps reveal how the adult-centric and racialized environments they navigate are also gendered. That is, the more different one is from an English-speaking White man, the more language brokers have to "do American" to avoid having their competency called into question as they attempt to help their family.

SHIELDING PARENTS FROM RACIALIZED NATIVISM: CENSORING AND FILTERING

At the beginning of their interview, many young language brokers said that they tried their best to translate everything verbatim when acting as a liaison between their parents and English-speaking monolingual adults. Indeed, when I asked whether they ever omitted information, many interpreted my question as an accusation. They thought I was asking whether they ever lied to their parents. For example, Christine, a Korean American, spoke in a polite but firm tone when she said, "Do you mean I lie to my parents? Actually, my friend asked me something similar before. He was asking me if I change my grade[s] or something. My parents are not that oblivious."

Still, as the interviews progressed, many language brokers described certain situations where they *did* deliberately censor or filter what English-speaking adults said. But rather than filtering messages to serve their own interests, language brokers used their bilingualism to contest and shield their parents from racialized nativism.

Jungsun, a fifteen-year-old Korean American, exemplified this trend. She had migrated to Los Angeles when she was five years old. She told me that she had always dreamed of living in a house with a swimming pool.

"Did your friends own a swimming pool?" I asked, thinking that might have been where she had first developed this idea.

"No, because in the movies, kids play in the swimming pool," she said. After a brief pause, she added in a softer voice, "And my dad paints houses and cleans pools for living."

I asked Jungsun, who often interpreted English-speaking clients' instructions, what it was like to accompany her father to work. She said that she met people "all the time" who made her job as a language broker difficult. "Some people just flat out disrespect my father," she explained.

"Why do you think that people disrespect your father?" I probed.

"I think it's because my dad works for them and because he can't speak English."

"Can you tell me more about these clients who disrespected your father?" I probed further.

After a brief pause, Jungsun began describing one client who stood out from the rest. "This client called me and said, 'Tell your dad that he needs to work faster. He is too lazy.'"

"Really? So did you tell your dad what she said?" I asked.

"Not everything," Jungsun said. "I didn't say that she said my dad is too lazy because he is not! I didn't want him to get upset."

"So what did you tell him instead?"

"I said, I think that customer is in a rush to finish the job."

When Jungsun said that the employer "disrespect[ed]" her father because he "works for them" and "can't speak English," she made it clear that she understood how power and status shape the range of emotions Americans can exhibit at work. Jungsun, like many other young language brokers, knew that Americans expect workers in low-status jobs to accommodate outlandish and, at times, abusive demands from their employers. After all, the media routinely depicts interns and assistants achieving upward mobility by maintaining a courteous and agreeable disposition while performing herculean feats on behalf of mercurial employers and customers. Those who become upset or who refuse to accommodate these demands are often fired.

Because her father's employer wielded a significant amount of power and the ability to worsen her family's already dire financial situation, Jungsun used her bilingual skills to "do" American. By shielding her father from his employer's racialized nativism, she ensured that he could maintain his composure and appear amiable. Jungsun, who also had to manage her own emotions, opted against telling her father that his employer had called him lazy.

Although many Korean American youth talked about translating for their parents' employers, Mexican American youth are far more likely to accompany their parents to jobs as housekeepers or maintenance workers in middle-class suburbs. In comparison to Korean Americans, Mexican American youth are also more likely to recall times when their parents had been perceived as "lazy" as a result of controlling images that depict Mexican immigrants as such. Mexican American youth work harder to "do American" by filtering racialized messages from White employers that call their parents' credibility as good workers into question. (I discuss Mexican American youths' perceptions of their parents' employers in greater detail in chapter 6.)

Antonio, a fifteen-year-old Mexican American youth, grew up in south Los Angeles, where almost two-thirds of the residents are Latinx. Since he lived less than a mile from the university I was attending at the time, we decided to meet at the front door of the building where my office was located.

"I never came into this school before," Antonio, dressed in a blue button-up dress shirt, said as I greeted him at the front entrance.

"Oh, really? It's your first time?" I asked.

He nodded and said, "I tried to check it out at night before, but a security guard said that I have to have a [student] ID."[21]

Walking across campus for the interview was a bittersweet experience for Antonio. Despite the close proximity to his neighborhood, the university seemed unreachable, much like other gated communities his parents remodeled and cleaned. It felt surreal to finally have a reason to enter the black wrought-iron fence that demarcated the campus's perimeter and walk down the main thoroughfare, which boasted perfectly manicured lawns and beautiful brick and cream-colored buildings. Yet as he walked across campus, Antonio recalled fearing how the campus security guards would treat him. Anticipating that he once again might be stopped at the gate, he said, "I was gonna tell them I have an interview today, but nobody was there."

As we continued talking, Antonio told me that he used to be "shy kid" who was always known for being creative, in part because he would create and read stories to his younger brother. Antonio beamed with pride as he talked about how his "hermanito" treated him like a rock star. It was also clear that Antonio deeply cared for his parents, whom he tried to "protect" from "feeling hurt." Only fifteen years old, Antonio had a lot to share about instances where his parents encountered "abusive people."

When Antonio was born, his mother was a nanny. He grew up knowing that his mother was taking care of other people's babies. "I wouldn't lie. I felt weird," he said. Yet Antonio eventually outgrew his discomfort. He understood that his mother had to work to support the family, and he had become proud of the fact that his mom "knows how to take care of babies" because she had "worked as a nanny for a long time."

"Did you meet any of the babies that your mom took care of?" I asked.

"I met one of them because my mom had to take the baby to the hospital. The baby girl had really bad stomach problems, but my mom could not get ahold of her mother."

Instead of thanking Antonio's mother for rushing the baby to the emergency room, the woman called his mother's credibility into question, behavior that aligns with the results of existing research, which shows that employers often question the competency of women, especially women of color.[22] Despite the fact that Antonio's mother had extensive experience working as a nanny, the employer automatically assumed that she, an immigrant woman of color, had fed the baby "the wrong food," a claim Antonio had to translate.

This incident had a lasting influence on Antonio. He had seen the lasting impact that these "mean" words had on his mother, who had been "very sad and angry" upon learning that her employer did not trust her ability to care for the baby. Although Antonio's mother ultimately quit her job after she found a cleaning position through a friend, Antonio said he was now "a lot more protective" of his mother's feelings when he translated "mean" comments other people said.

Antonio described one memorable event when he decided not to translate everything that was said by his mother's new manager, whom he "really hate[d]" because she acted like she "own[ed]" his mother. "My mom was just cleaning the apartment, and that crazy manager walks in and told her not to go up and down the stairs all crazy. But I didn't tell my mom that she called her crazy," he said. "I just told her that people downstairs can hear her walking so we should be quiet. My mom is doing this work to support me and my brother."

Antonio's voice was full of anger. "It's not okay to treat people like trash just because they can't speak English," he said.

"Can you tell me why you decided not to say that this person called your mom crazy?"

"Because my mom will get angry."

Although just thinking about this episode made Antonio angry, he hadn't expressed any anger toward the manager who had mistreated his mother. Instead, he had suppressed his feelings and contended with the racialized environment where emotional responses are highly racialized and gendered. [23]To ensure that his mother did not appear "crazy" and that she could continue supporting the family, he made a conscious decision to remain calm. Shielding his mother from gendered forms of racialized nativism helped ensure that his mother could maintain her composure.

Although many young language brokers talked about shielding their parents at workplaces, undocumented youth or youth with undocumented parents, who were hyperaware of their family's legal status, discussed censoring the content of messages in many other settings. For undocumented children of immigrants and for US citizens with undocumented family members I interviewed, their translation work involved gauging whether the other party had the authority to deport their parents or might report their parents to the authorities.[24] Fears that someone would call the police should their parents become "angry" were especially salient among Mexican American youth, who were cognizant of the fact that their families were racialized as "illegal."

For example, when I asked Jesus, a fourteen-year-old with undocumented Mexican parents, if there were people who made translation encounters difficult, he told me about the time an intoxicated driver crashed into his father's car. After the other driver attempted to flee the scene, Jesus's father sped after him. The man finally pulled over to the side of the road and stepped out of his car. Jesus, acting as his father's translator, told the man that his father would not report the incident to their insurance company and simply wanted payment for the damage. Jesus's fists were clenched as he recalled how the man began spewing xenophobic and racist remarks, which Jesus decided not to translate.

"I understood what my dad didn't understand. He was talking trash about Mexicans, like, 'Oh, you illegal. You wetback,' and all that. And he said he was gonna send my dad back to Mexico," Jesus said.

"Wow, that's crazy. So did you tell your dad what that drunken guy said?" I asked.

Judging by the way the man slurred his words, stumbled out of the car, and smelled like alcohol, Jesus knew that the man was inebriated. Yet Jesus did not even think about calling the police. Instead, he worried that the perpetrator, who almost killed Jesus and his father and could have been charged with a misdemeanor, was going to call the police on them. He decided against telling his dad what the other driver said out of fear that the man's comments "would anger" his dad and lead to an argument.

"I was thinking, 'What if this guy calls the police?' And my dad, he doesn't have proper documentation, he could easily be deported, and now I heard that the immigration people of the United States are actually harder on people without documentation now. Yeah, I didn't tell my dad because he doesn't have to listen to him."

Although Jesus said he wished his father, whom he described as a good fighter, could "beat up" this racist man, deportation is a state-initiated racial project.[25] This exclusionary practice, which fosters and normalizes racial violence that disproportionately targets Latinx immigrants, creates the conditions in which youth like Jesus have to manage their parents' emotions. As an outsider-within, Jesus was acutely aware of the way hostility, violence, and racialized nativism limited his family's access to critical resources. He knew better than to assume that law enforcement would protect the basic rights of people without documentation.[26] As a result, he managed his father's emotions by shielding him from the racist and xenophobic remarks the other driver made.

Although many children of immigrants censor some words to protect their parents from racialized nativism, others take advantage of English-speakers' inability to understand Spanish or Korean. In these cases, language brokers reported feeling powerful. Macarena, a nineteen-year-old Mexican American, translated for her mother as she cleaned clients' houses. Although most of the clients were friendly, Macarena said they occasionally dealt with unreasonably "demanding," "cheap," "angry," or "rude" clients who treated her mother like she was "dumb" and tried to get her mother to perform extra services for free. These encounters were annoying and infuriating, but Macarena, like other youth, rarely challenged or confronted these clients. For youth like Macarena, whose parents work in low-wage occupations, "doing American" involves avoiding outward expressions of anger. Instead, she did her best to appear calm and friendly to ensure that her mother didn't lose her job.

"I can't tell them that they are being abusive even though they are trying to take advantage of my mom," she said. "I just repress my anger, because they probably don't care about what I have to say anyways. I try to calm down and act friendly to them even though they are sometimes being racists towards my mom. Yeah, I just fake it."

Yet Macarena did not simply let these abusive employers take advantage of her mother. Instead, she used her bilingual skills to secretly charge more for undeserving clients. "There have been times where I have taken some stuff out [that my mom said] either because the people we've met didn't treat us nicely, or I just felt it would be best not to mention it," Macarena said. "For example, my mom says like, she'll clean the windows, like inside and out, for free, but sometimes I don't translate that, especially if clients are rude. So even though my mom says, 'It's free,' I just say that I will give them a discount."

Language brokers told me that it was difficult to remain calm when witnessing their parents experiencing racialized nativism and exploitation. This is especially the case for youth who translate for their parents at workplaces because their family survival is dependent on their parents' jobs. And because Mexican American youth are more likely to accompany parents who work in the informal economy, where employers sometimes withhold wages or refuse to pay, they are more likely to manage their emotions. This sense of needing to remain calm is also highly acute for youth who are undocumented or who have undocumented family members, because they live with fears of deportation. However, children and people of color are depicted as overly emotional even before they exhibit any emotions.[27] For this reason, "doing American" requires youth to manage their emotions. They attempt to appear calm, amiable, and friendly by shielding their parents from racialized nativism.

At the same time, youths' stories reveal how marginalized individuals are better at observing the dominant group than the dominant group is at observing them.[28] People living at the margins of society are positioned to experience what Du Bois called "double consciousness," which allows them to see inequality that often remains invisible to dominant groups.[29] Drawing on this double consciousness, children of immigrants find ways to subtly counter rude and racist English monolinguals. While affluent White English-speaking adults do not have the burden associated with experiencing the intersecting inequalities, they also lack the linguistic skills that bilingual children have. This allows youth of color, who are outsider-within, to devise a covert strategy to protect their parents from exploitative working conditions and racialized nativism. Ultimately, their outsider-within position allows youth to make creative use of their marginality as they attempt to change the harsh realities of their family's life.

POSING AS MIDDLE-CLASS ADULTS

As demonstrated, language brokers are cognizant of racial stereotypes associated with being a "submissive immigrant" or an "angry person of color." They also know that racialized nativism constrains their family's ability to access resources. While most language brokers try to manage their emotions to appear a calm and friendly American during translation interactions at their parents' workplaces, they also know that posing as normalized American adults requires them to appear more assertive by emulating middle-class behaviors in other settings. This display of professionalism is most often needed in educational settings like parent-teacher conferences, where parents have to be assertive if they want to change decisions made by educators. However, because youth often lack a full understanding of how social class intersects with race, age, and nativism to shape translation outcomes, posing is a strategy that often leaves working-class youth of color feeling powerless.

Sungmin, a sixteen-year-old Korean American, was one of many who attempted to pose as an American middle-class adult when translating for his mother. He immigrated to Los Angeles from Korea when he was eight years old. At the time of his interview, he had spent seven years attending schools in Los Angeles with mostly Black and Latinx children. A self-described introvert, Sungmin did not enjoy going to school, where he was regularly picked on by other boys for being thin and short.

Although he spoke with a flat affect throughout most of our conversation, his disposition changed as he began describing a "huge" fight he had gotten into in the cafeteria. He frowned and said, "I was just standing in line to get lunch. And Jose spit on me and was like, 'Hey chino, ching-chang, ching-chang.'"

Sungmin ran up the stairs and "beat up" Jose while other students watched and cheered. After administrators separated the two boys, the principal called Sungmin's mother to school for a meeting. His Korean monolingual mother asked Sungmin to say she was "very sorry" for his son's behavior. Upon hearing his mother's request, Sungmin felt angry. He was frustrated that his mother was acting like an immigrant instead of an American. "I was mad because I wanted my mom to be like other American parents. Defend me! Because my mom acts like an immigrant, [the principal] already had an upper hand on my mom," Sungmin said.

During the meeting, Sungmin convinced his mother that the decision was unfair. As soon as his mother agreed with Sungmin, he yelled at the principal.

"What did you say?" I asked.

"I said even though I broke the rule, making fun of someone and spitting is also bad. It's unfair. Jose has to get suspension, too. He made fun of me first."

Sungmin was one of the very few youth I interviewed who recalled openly expressing anger toward an adult authority. An Asian American boy like Sungmin, who was racialized as effeminate and bullied for his seemingly nonmasculine characteristics such as relatively small stature and introverted personality, was less concerned that appearing too aggressive would result in additional punishment from the principal or jeopardize his access to valuable opportunities in school. Instead, Sungmin was concerned by the way his educational trajectory would be affected if his mother, an Asian immigrant, came across as overly compliant in light of her son's unfair treatment at school.

Although Sungmin believed that acting like "American parents" would help persuade the principal, in reality, the interactional strategy he described did not fully align with the behavior and mannerisms of American parents who are able to change a decision made by the school authorities. Rather than yelling, most middle-class parents draw on other resources to ensure that the educational system accommodates their needs and concerns. For instance, rather than framing the authorities' decision as unfair, middle-class parents may escalate their concerns to the district or state level.[30] Middle-class parents also might criticize the broader problem at hand, such as the school's inability to address the racialized and gendered bullying Sungmin regularly encountered. They also might subtly communicate their social status to the principal, such as by dropping names of lawyers or reporters they know should their concerns go unaddressed.

Lacking the resources that many middle-class adults have, however, Sungmin's strategy of posing like an "American" was unsuccessful. In the end, Sungmin received a three-day suspension, which left him feeling frustrated and powerless.

Similar to Korean American youth, Mexican American youth also try during translation interactions to offset widespread stereotypes of immigrants as submissive. This is especially true when they translate on behalf of their mothers in educational settings. When it comes to the US public school system, mothers of color are keenly aware of the institutional scrutiny and punitive treatments their children experience.[31] Yet if they attempt to advocate for their children, Black and Latinx women are at a greater risk of being perceived as ill-tempered, illogical, or angry by teachers and administrators.[32] Mexican American youth, who are keenly aware of these stereotypes, describe putting more effort into attempting to present their mothers as middle-class American adults.

Carolina, an upbeat and energetic eighteen-year-old Mexican American high school student, was cognizant of how Latinx women are often seen as irrational. Although her parents had completed only middle school in Mexico, she was admitted to a magnet program in her high school, an academic track where White middle-class youth are often overrepresented. Carolina's mother had worked as a kitchen assistant for over ten years while her father suffered from sporadic employment working as a day laborer "here and there." Carolina described her mother as a strong woman who "would not let anyone disrespect [her] family."

After her younger sister, Lupe, was accused of smoking in the school's bathroom, Carolina witnessed her mother's strength firsthand while translating at a meeting her mother had with Lupe's teacher. "[My mom] was screaming and asking [Lupe's] teacher [in Spanish] if she saw Lupe smoking, because Lupe told us that she was just in the restroom when her friends were smoking. The teacher didn't see it. She told my mom that she heard this from other kids. And that was it. My mom totally lost it and started acting all ghetto."

Carolina recalled how the teacher rolled her eyes and shook her head. "My mom probably thought this teacher is not trusting what Lupe was saying. She wanted to defend her. I believed Lupe, too," Carolina said.

Because Carolina was enrolled in a magnet program, she frequently interacted with peers who came from middle-class backgrounds. These interactions had revealed differences between the way her mother and other parents interacted with school authorities. As an outsider-within, Carolina, perhaps correctly, feared that Lupe's teacher would judge her mother's behavior. Although Carolina understood why her mother was upset, she said she "got embarrassed" when her mother, who showed up in her dishwasher uniform, raised her voice at Lupe's teacher. Her mother was also speaking in Spanish, which her teacher could not understand.

"I didn't want the teacher to think that my mom is crazy and irrational," Carolina said.

Carolina responded by attempting to pose as a middle-class adult. Performing what she understood as American behaviors, she calmly told the teacher there was "not enough evidence" to discipline her sister. Nonetheless, Lupe ended up getting suspended from school. "I felt bad because I felt like I was not being professional enough," Carolina said. "You know, be firm with the teacher. I felt bad that I could not defend my sister."

Carolina was worried that the teacher might view her mother, a Spanish-speaking Mexican immigrant, as crazy and irrational. As mentioned in the case of Antonio in the previous section, Mexican American youth sometimes encounter people who use the word *crazy* to describe their mother's behavior. Indeed, Latinx women are often portrayed in the media as temperamental, crazy, loud, fiery, spicy, or overreacting. Not coincidentally, many of these media characters also have thick Spanish accents.[33] Consequently, Carolina, who knew that displays of anger put her mom at an increased risk of appearing incompetent, tried to act more "professional" and "firm." Still, as a young, working-class immigrant woman of color, Carolina was incapable of getting school authorities to take her seriously when she attempted to advocate for her sister.

It is tempting to believe that the outcomes that working-class children of immigrants face are the result of their or their family's behaviors. After all, unlike most youth and their parents, both Carolina's mother and Sungmin lost control and yelled at school authority figures. However, neither would have lost their temper had teachers and educators taken seriously the concerns of working-class immigrant youth of color in the first place. When Carolina told the teacher that there was not enough evidence to discipline her younger sister, she was right. When Sungmin said that a student who uttered a racial slur should also be penalized, he was right. Educators, moreover, did not take into account that Sungmin, an Asian immigrant youth, had been repeatedly picked on and bullied in school.

If Carolina's and Sungmin's mothers had the same resources, time, status, and social networks as middle-class professional adults have, they might have been more successful when negotiating with White middle-class educators. Alternatively, if institutions like schools had bilingual educators or provided language services that non-English speaking parents are entitled to, young people like Carolina and Sungmin would not have left feeling embarrassed, frustrated, and powerless. While it is possible that young immigrants of color may become better at deploying middle-class behaviors as they grow older, it is unlikely that institutional agents will ever see them as "true" Americans. In the end, "doing American" involves both recognized and rewarded displays of a dominant middle-class (and masculine) set of norms, which frame both working-class Asian and Latinx families as foreigners.

Ultimately, focusing on the behavior of Carolina's mother or Sungmin ignores the structural inequalities that working-class immigrants of color are up against during translation encounters. Institutions like schools are made up of middle-class White authority figures,[34] who often hold racist views about students and parents of color.[35] These educators also wield considerable power when it comes to shaping young people's academic trajectories.[36] In addition to disproportionately subjecting poor and working-class children of color, especially Black and Latinx youth, to exclusionary discipline,[37] educators are also less likely to recommend poor and working-class children of color, especially Black and Latinx youth, for Advanced Placement and college preparatory classes.[38] Although White and middle-class parents can, and often do, intervene when educators make decisions that could have lasting negative impacts on their children's academic trajectories, schools often fail to provide translation services or to hire bilingual educators, which makes it even more difficult, if not impossible, for immigrant parents to secure important educational resources for their children. In saying that they want to act like "American" adults, young people like Carolina and Sungmin are letting us know that institutional authorities treat those who they perceive as foreigners differently. They are also letting us know that institutions listen to and accommodate the needs of only "American" (i.e., White middle-class) adults who have the resources to defend their children.

INTERSECTIONALITY IN INTERACTIONS

To a certain degree, we all perform to ensure that we appear normal during social interactions. Some men attempt to appear sufficiently masculine by talking about sports or bragging about their sexual conquests around other men.[39] Some women attempt to appear desirable by putting on makeup and tight clothing before going to parties with their friends.[40] Job candidates also "do" professionalism by following the rules of the interview, which require firm, full-palm handshakes and direct eye contact, all while looking confident and comfortable in clothing deemed appropriate for a business environment. And if the job requires that workers demonstrate femininized characteristics such as empathy or kindness, women sometimes amplify these characteristics to increase their chance of securing a job.[41]

Although most people attempt to come across as competent during different interactions, not everyone can, or even wants to, appear at ease in every setting. The amount of effort that goes into being perceived as normal varies tremendously depending on one's position in the social hierarchy.[42] These efforts also speak volumes about the broader structures that grant power and privilege to those who appear credible and normal in any given setting.[43] At an early age, being their family's language broker allows many working-class immigrant youth of color to understand that their families are not seen as "normal Americans."

Images of "normal" American families, consisting White, middle-class, heterosexual parents and children, are ubiquitous in popular culture and reinforce perceptions of how "American" families should look and act.[44] Media, including animations, use standard English to depict normal Americans and accents to depict bad or odd characters.[45] Due to the historical legacy of racism, White people, especially men, dominate the highest-status and highest-paying jobs and occupations in the US and accumulate greater amounts of wealth in comparison to people of color.[46] Partly for these reasons, working-class children of immigrants equate standard English with the language spoken by White people. They also used the term *American* as a stand-in for being White and middle-class.

Because young language brokers are knowledgeable about how age, race, gender, and language shape one's ability to access resources, they often end up "doing American," or engaging in covert forms of resistance to ensure that their parents appear credible in a given setting. These strategies, which include passing, shielding, and posing, help demonstrate how the margin can create moments of subversion, resistance, and empowerment. For instance, passing, or hiding one's age and race on the phone when seeking services, helps ensure youths' families have access to resources, such as housing, loans, and other goods, that their parents likely would be denied otherwise. Shielding, or filtering messages during translation encounters to manage their parents' emotions, protects their parents from some elements of racialized nativism, exploitation, deportation, and public abuse, especially at work. While posing, young people try to contest unjust circumstances in educational settings by adopting the language and mannerisms of White middle-class parents. In doing so, they try to offset the racial stereotypes associated with being an "angry person of color" or a "submissive immigrant" and attempt to secure educational resources for themselves and their siblings by presenting their parents as rational adults, an image that is often associated with White middle-class men.[47] When combined, these three covert forms of resistance often allow youth, who do not have other means to resist unequal power relations, to attempt to broker social citizenship, including security, respect, well-being, and ultimately belonging for their family.

Some of their strategies, however, are more successful than others. Specifically, their attempts at enacting middle-class professionals' behaviors rarely work, in part because of how social class intersects with other forms of inequality to shape translation outcomes in school settings. Middle-class parents have far more resources, including money, time, education, and status, to help ensure that the education system works in their children's favor.[48] This is especially true in the case of affluent White families, as they not only experience their class position through race but are also more likely to be in positions of power.[49]

Whereas institutions like schools accommodate the needs of affluent White families, language brokers in this study lacked the same resources and status that White middle-class families have at their disposal. Consequently, when posing, these young people were often left feeling powerless and inadequate and blamed themselves or their parents for failing to reverse unfair decisions.

Social class, in comparison to race, age, gender, and language, is an invisible social category. It becomes visible only when social actors activate their class position during interactions and use their resources and capital to accommodate their needs. At the same time, however, class intersects with race, language, age, and gender to shape people's access to social citizenship in various settings. That is, it is only when children of immigrants cover their race and age behind the phone and speak so-called standard English that they are somewhat successful in gaining crucial resources and services for their family. It is precisely because age intersects with racialized and gendered meanings of linguistic fluency, which equate Americans with Whiteness and English-speaking skills, that compels children of immigrants to "do" American, to act like middle-class White (men), when interacting with the institutional authorities.

SIX INCLUSION WORK

Jacob, a nineteen-year-old Mexican American, grew up translating for his parents "everywhere." Although he never enjoyed talking to strangers, he wanted to be interviewed when he heard that I was studying immigrant youth's translation experiences. "Yes, people should know about this," he thought.

Jacob migrated to the US with his parents and younger sister when he was nine years old. "This was the time when the borders were more accessible and easier to cross than now." Jacob's memory resurfaced in vivid detail, taking him back to those early mornings when his parents roused him from slumber well before the break of dawn to meet the "coyote" and the rest of their group. He said, "As a kid, I was excited, but I was also so scared to see so many people there. The coyote told us to get in the car, and we were all on top of each other basically."

The coyote had promised a lot: they would arrive in the US within a few days. For the price of one thousand extra dollars—which Jacob's father paid—Jacob and his siblings would not have to walk as much as the adults. The coyote also reassured his father that everyone would get enough food and water while travelling.

The coyote shattered every one of these promises. Jacob's father, in frustration, confronted the coyote, and the coyote's response lingered vividly in Jacob's memory: "There's no special treatment for nobody." In the end, the coyote abandoned the group, leaving them "stranded in the middle of nowhere." Days stretched into an agonizing wait, and then, by what Jacob could only describe as a stroke of luck, his family stumbled upon another group of people.

It was an arduous journey, but after a relentless month of hardship, they finally arrived at his uncle's house.

Despite having such a "horrible experience" immigrating to the US, Jacob was not critical of his father. His father was a "brave man" who "took the risk" and "left everything he knew and cared for behind." He "made the decision to cross the border" to "prosper," "find freedom," and "to have a chance at a new start in the land of opportunity."

Throughout his interview, Jacob spoke about the deep bond he shared with his father, who worked as a gardener at his brother's landscaping business. Jacob and his father spent a great deal of time driving through the sprawling streets of Beverly Hills in his dad's pickup truck. Together, they mowed lawns, trimmed bushes, and blew leaves into large piles that Jacob, who often operated the leaf blower, transferred into green yard-waste bins. Although his father was often "close to broke," Jacob seemed proud to be the "ayudante," or helper, as the job required him to shoulder physically demanding work that "probably kept [him] away from troubles." His face radiated as he continued describing the gardening business his father—who he described "hardworking," a "family man" and a "breadwinner"—would open someday.

However, the fleeting spark of emotion that briefly animated Jacob's face quickly settled into a stoic neutrality as he talked about the "racist people" he and his father frequently encountered. His voice carried the weight of his experiences as he lamented, "People don't respect us."

Jacob then pointed at his hunter green T-shirt, which was embellished with the logo of his uncle's landscaping business. Speaking in a firm tone, he said, "You see this? This is our uniform. It's like telling people we are here to work. You know what I am saying?" Jacob vividly remembered how his uncle, a shrewd and savvy businessman, told him that the first thing he thought was "This is a nice way to advertise the business." His second thought was "'People won't bother us, like wondering why we were in their neighborhoods.'"

The "uniform" was not the only thing that separated Jacob's family from other people in Beverly Hills. Plenty of people in the affluent, predominately White neighborhoods where Jacob and his father worked spent their days sunbathing by their swimming pools or lounging around in athleisure wear inside their temperature-controlled, multi-million-dollar mansions. Jacob, who worked outside in the relentless heat, hardly saw these people. Nor did they acknowledge Jacob and his father's presence, except when they came out to pay their monthly bill, to complain about a hedge trimming, or to ask for help setting up lawn tables and chairs for a birthday party or baby shower in their backyard.

Considering that our conversation had already spanned forty-five minutes and Jacob had yet to broach the subject of his language-brokering experiences, I prompted him to share his interactions with his father's clientele. Jacob hesitated for a moment and then released a deep, weighty sigh. While interaction with "picky customers" was a routine aspect of their work, there was one encounter with "one crazy White dude" that remained etched in his memory with remarkable clarity. The passage of more than three years had done little to erode the vividness of that recollection.

"I think we woke this guy up because blower and mower can make loud noise. He came out wearing pajama and started cursing at my dad, asking him to fuck off." Jacob paused again before he continued. "I think he was still drunk or something, so he wanted us to come back in the late afternoon."

Jacob's first impulse was to yell, "No!" Today was his mother's birthday, and they still had five more yards to go before returning home to celebrate.

Yet, in contrast to Jacob's growing frustration, his father maintained a composed demeanor. He quietly instructed Jacob to inform the customer that they would be back later in the day. Without uttering another word, his father packed up the equipment and they left the property. Once they were seated in the truck, Jacob recounted how his father proceeded to explain his reasoning for complying with the customer's request. This man's parents owned an additional three properties, which they also mowed. Saying no could have meant losing "major businesses."

Although Jacob began telling this story in a calm and matter-of-fact manner, his simmering anger became palpable as he continued speaking: "You know, it was like ten in the morning and this dude was sleeping!"

Over the years, Jacob had learned to accommodate "crazy" and "picky" customers' requests. He realized that White people—who often "order[ed]" his dad around and complained about the quality of his work—were "spoiled" and "lazy" in comparison to Mexican Americans. "[White people] think that we are supposed to do everything they told us to do," Jacob said.

The frustration in his voice resonated deeply as he shifted the conversation to criticize how White parents raise their kids:

> White people teach their kids just study and let Mexicans cut your grass. . . . I mean everything is given to White kids. Their parents have a certain amount of money in their bank account, and they drive classic cars and they give that to their kids—like everything is passed down from generation to generation. They get pampered, so they don't have to pay rent, they don't have to translate for their parents and do chores like us. . . . White kids have it so easy, but that's gonna hurt them in the long run. They are gonna grow up thinking that things would fall into place for them.

Jacob was not wrong in perceiving White families in Los Angeles as being wealthier than Latinx families are. As a result of the historical legacy of racism, White families do average higher levels of wealth than Lainx people.[1] Middle- and upper-middle-class parents are also able to provide their children with far more resources and time than working-class parents are able to.[2] However, it is important to note that the White people Jacob was referring to had extreme amounts of wealth, even compared to the typical White person in the US. The census indicates that median home price in Beverly Hills was $2 million in 2019, which was far greater than $500,000 median home price in California as a whole.

Despite the very real differences Jacob observed, criticizing White families served a specific purpose. In a society where Mexican immigrants are portrayed as "illegal," "free-riders," "lazy" and "uneducated,"[3] Jacob flipped the stereotype about "real Americans" on its head. Drawing from the routine interactions with wealthy White people in Beverley Hills, he instead described White children as the ones who lacked the work ethic that "Mexicans" possessed.

Indeed, Jacob's negative perceptions of White people were clearly illustrated when I asked him if he would have preferred to have been born a White person. Vigorously shaking his head, he turned his marginality into an asset. He said, "I would much rather be full-on Hispanic and not be so spoiled. . . .

My parents are teaching me like, I can be rich on my own and still be a His-panic. . . . If anything, [White] people provoke me to become a strong individual," Jacob said.

Controlling images, or dominant groups' representations of people of color, have long constructed people of color as inferior to White people. Embedded within the discourses of politicians, social commentators, and popular media, these images play a crucial role in legitimizing people of color's access to full citizenship rights. As demonstrated throughout this book, the working-class Korean and Mexican American youth in this study regularly came across controlling images that construct them as perpetual foreigners or burdens. Yet, in comparison to Korean Americans, Mexican Americans were far more likely to report being stereotyped as lazy, criminal, and low-educated. Mexican Americans also recalled interactions where they or their parents were treated as illegal immigrants, regardless of their immigration status. These experiences of confronting different controlling images during translation encounters left youth feeling angry and sad, which in turn formed the basis for them to claim membership in American society.

To challenge the various forms of exclusion they have experienced in the US, youth like Jacob mobilize widely available cultural repertoires about "good" immigrants to claim membership in the larger society—a process I refer to as "inclusion work."⁴ In other words, youth put culture to use to validate their family's presence in the US when describing their past, present, and future experiences. They (1) "Americanize" their family's migration journey, (2) use "tradition" to construct their family as collective and hardworking, and (3) present themselves as "productive" citizens ready to achieve upward mobility. Furthermore, in light of contemporary racial images depicting Mexican immigrants as a problematic underclass, Mexican American youth deploy a wider range of cultural repertoires than Korean American youth, thereby revealing how inclusion work is shaped by youth's positionality within contemporary racial hierarchies.

Marginalized youths' attempts at normalizing their family's experiences speak to the ubiquity of controlling images that construct their families as a burden or perpetual foreigners in the US. Inclusion work, I argue, is a response to exclusion work.

AMERICANIZING PARENTS' MIGRATION JOURNEYS

The first inclusion work children of immigrants engaged in involves "Americanizing" their parents' immigration journeys. Regardless of when respondents or their parents had migrated to the US or the degree of poverty their parents experienced before and after migration, respondents deployed cultural repertoires about the American Dream to describe their parents' migration experiences around two main themes: escaping hardships and searching for opportunity in the "land of the free."[5]

When asked to explain why their parents moved to the United States, Korean and Mexican American youth drew upon what sociologist Lisa Sun-Hee Park calls the American myth of national origins.[6] In other words, youth construct their parents as "poor peasants who come to the 'land of opportunity' with nothing but their determination and hard work."[7]

Jinho, a seventeen-year-old working-class Korean American youth, described his parents' migration journey in a way that was representative of language brokers' responses. On a scorching day in the middle of August, I met Jinho, a seventeen-year-old Korean American, at a local coffee shop where the air conditioning roared at full blast. Jinho stretched out his arms as he entered the coffee shop to embrace the temperature-controlled air that greeted him. As we spoke, I learned that Jinho had been only six years old when he migrated to the US, but he told me he tried to stay up to date with Korean pop culture. Still, his memories about Korea seemed limited.

When asked about his childhood in Korea, he mentioned a river, a road, and snow and named the city he grew up in. "All I remember is playing with my brother on this small street and going to Hangang [river in Seoul] with my family, and oh, I remember seeing snow for the first time when I was kid, which was pretty exciting," he said with a grin.

"Do you know why your parents decided to come to the US?" I asked.

"Honestly, I have no recollection of what Korea was back then and why my parents came here. It wasn't a place where my future would be bright," he said his parents often told him.

Despite saying that he did not know why his parents migrated to the US, Jinho's response did not stop there. "All I know is that my parents came from a poor background. They weren't born with a silver spoon in their mouths. They never had that glamorous life, you know. They were raised in post–Korean

War, where hardship, hunger, and death were all around them. It was a real deal," Jinho continued. "When the whole economy was turning into a shit hole, they did not remain depressed or look back. They left behind their home and their family to come to the land of the free with just four very big suitcases of clothes. They wanted to pursue the American Dream."

"How old are your parents?"

"My mom is forty-two and my dad is forty-three."

"Did your parents tell you about the Korean War?"

"No, I learned it from . . . what's that famous Korean movie called?"

The movie he was referring to was *The Brotherhood of War*, a popular Korean film that indeed highlighted the hardship, which included hunger and death of family members, during the post–Korean War. However, considering that Jinho's parents were in their mid-forties, they had been born more than twenty years after the Korean War had ended. Rather than being raised in the aftermath of the Korean War, the poverty his parents had experienced was likely related to a major financial crisis in South Korea in the late 1990s, which prompted mass migration due to the country's high unemployment rate, currency devaluation, and the failure of major conglomerates. However, Jinho pieced together the limited information that he had heard from his parents with the battlefields, death, and hunger imagery he had seen in movies to describe his parents as individuals striving to achieve the American Dream in the "land of free."

Working-class Mexican Americans also mobilized publicly shared cultural repertoires to describe their parents as "good" immigrants who were escaping hardships and searching for opportunity in the US. For example, Christine, a US-born, fifteen-year-old working-class Mexican American, described Mexico as a "poor" country with a "bad" school system, where her parents "could not go to college." Mexico also had "a lot of problems involving the economy and crime," she said.

Despite portraying Mexico as "poor" and "dangerous," Christine said that she didn't "really know what exactly was going on in Mexico" before her parents migrated to the US because she was "born here." Christine, however, continued to speak about the conditions in Mexico without any prompting: "In Mexico, wages are low. It's pretty bad. I can't really explain it, but basically like you know, sewage systems don't work and there are just a lot of people living on the street. Kids are homeless and running around. And you know they do a bunch of criminal activities just to survive. My parents were trying to live on those harsh conditions."

Christine, like many other young people I interviewed, painted Mexico as an impoverished county that her parents had to flee. But like Jinho, her parents were not the source of her information. In addition to repeatedly saying she had limited information about Mexico's actual conditions, Christine said that her parents didn't "share details about their migration journey" with her "because it can be a sensitive topic for them." In fact, contrary to her characterization, she said they often told her how "wonderful Mexico was" and how much they missed the food and their family. Instead, Christine's perceptions of Mexico had largely been informed by televised images of gang violence and poverty in Mexico—which routinely depict Mexico as a dangerous and impoverished country.

Christine supplemented the imagery she saw on TV with language that closely paralleled rhetoric about the American Dream, explaining that all Mexican people migrated to the US for the same reason: to seek a stable and better life than Mexico could offer. "Whether they are escaping violence, . . . whether they come single or come with significant other, or immediate family, their reasons are all the same. No matter where they come from, they strive for better life, a stable home, and [the] American Dream," she said.

Christine then compared those who make it to the United States with those who fail. She said, "It is truly sad to learn that some people strive for the American Dream but never actually make it over to our country, land of the free. They get arrested or sometimes die." After pausing for a bit, Christine continued, "But my parents made it."

Even young people whose parents came from relatively affluent backgrounds emphasized the hardships their parents faced prior to migration. For example, Suejin, a fifteen-year-old Korean American who migrated to the US at age eleven, drew on her childhood memories when constructing her parents as immigrants escaping hardship in search of the "American Dream." Although Suejin recalled that her father had run a business for many years with the help of her "wealthy grandpa," her language shifted when describing her parents' migration journey. She said her parents moved to the US after defaulting on a business loan. They were "running away from loan sharks, those people who come to collect debts." Although it is possible that Suejin's parents had been experiencing downward mobility in Korea, she downplayed her family's affluence. She said her "poor" parents were escaping a society where they would be "looked down upon" in hopes of "find[ing] the American Dream here."

Mexican American youth whose parents came from relatively affluent backgrounds also emphasized the fact that their parents lacked opportunity and migrated in hopes of seeking the American Dream. For example, Fernando, an eighteen-year-old who migrated to the US at age nine, was one of the few respondents to counter the dominant rhetoric that painted Mexico as "dangerous." When asked about Mexico, he drew on his childhood memories and said, "Mexico is a beautiful country where kids have freedom to play anywhere." He also countered the assumption that Mexican families were poor. "I know that my mom was not poor. She lived a pretty good life in Mexico City because my grandparents were doing well," he said.

Yet, Fernando too drew upon the familiar story about "good" immigrants searching for better opportunities when explaining why his parents moved to the US. He presented his mother as an immigrant who migrated to escape gender inequality and patriarchal family dynamics. "My grandpa was a cop, and he was like a dictator, you know. America has always been seen as a country full of opportunities," he said. "So, my mom wanted to search for freedom here."

Drawing on his limited knowledge of his family in Mexico, Fernando characterized his grandfather as "a dictator"—which aligns with US representations of Mexican men as "macho."[8] In emphasizing how his mother lacked opportunities due to her subordinate status as a woman, Fernando—like many other interviewees—drew on rhetoric that helped present his parents as "good" immigrants. He said, "My parents were too ambitious to stay in Mexico. They wanted more opportunities to expand and grow. They wanted a better life in the land of opportunities."

Based on the results of existing research,[9] it is likely that most youths' parents faced economic or other hardships before migrating. Although seeking additional opportunities in the US likely played a role in shaping their parents' decisions to migrate, the young people I interviewed selectively used their knowledge, experiences, memories, media images, or other resources to construct their parents as "good immigrants." Indeed, the idea that immigrants escape hardships and find the American Dream in the land of opportunity is the quintessential American tale that predominates in US culture.[10] Knowing that their working-class immigrant parents were perceived as a burden or perpetual foreigners in the US, Korean and Mexican American youth made use of such cultural repertoires to validate their parents' presence in the US. While the causes of migration or the level of detail they knew about their parents' experiences varied, they drew on these repertoires to describe migration as a way for their parents to realize the American Dream.

There is, however, a key difference in how Mexican and Korean American youth mobilize "good" immigrant repertoires. More prevalent among working-class Mexican American youths' narratives is the assertion that their parents were "risk-takers." For example, Janet, a sixteen-year-old Mexican American, whose parents were lawful permanent US residents at the time of our interview, remarked, "My parents risked everything for a new life here. They were striving for the American Dream. . . . Not many people are capable of doing that. . . . They had a lot of courage to leave their home country to come here and go through many hardships."

Hector, a nineteen-year-old son of undocumented Mexican parents, also painted his parents as risk-takers. As a self-identified first-generation college student, Hector told me he was proud of having been accepted to one of the most competitive four-year universities in California. Indeed, he asked if I could meet him at a room in his university's library where he was studying for final exams.

Hector was waiting for me outside the library when I arrived, but I had to wave to get his attention. He had his nose buried in one of his biology textbooks. Since it was the beginning of finals week, the library was bustling with students. Hector, unfazed by the crowded atmosphere, told me he spent a lot of time there during finals week. In addition to allowing him to easily access books and a computer, the library environment helped him concentrate late into the night. Hector knew that his parents were very proud of him. He too was proud of his "courageous" parents.

Yet, Hector had heard other people refer to his parents as "illegal aliens" all the time. "You hear this in the news, movies, TV shows, just everywhere," he recounted sorrowfully.

However, he returned to speaking in his cheerful tone when I asked about his parents' migration journey. Unlike the vast majority of youth—who repeatedly said that their parents rarely spoke about their experiences migrating to the US—Hector had previously interviewed his mother for a school project that he had titled "My Mother's Journey to the North." "This was my favorite school project," he said, because it had allowed him to learn a lot about his mother's life.

"My parents came over illegally and undocumented. I heard that borders were more accessible and easier to cross twenty years ago. My dad paid someone to pass the border and they actually walked. My mom said that she was very excited to go to the North. She was wearing her best clothing and brought expensive things with her."

The "exciting" trip, however, turned out to be more difficult than his mother had planned. Their bags were stolen along the way. After that, his mother started "hid[ing] behind some bushes at night. Then she ran in the morning without eating or drinking."

"Once they got to San Ysidro, our uncle picked them up," he said. "There were five people total: my parents, my sister, and my two brothers. I was not born yet."

As he retold his mother's migration experiences, Hector refused to subscribe to the popular notion that she was a "criminal" or an "illegal alien." Instead, he reinterpreted her experience as an achievement by emphasizing how risky it had been for her to cross the border. After describing his mother's journey to the "North," he said, "I realized that she was a risk-taker. She faced her fears and took the chances."

Although Hector presented his mother as a risk-taker—perhaps because he had interviewed her—it was more common for Mexican American respondents to present their fathers as brave immigrants for having risked their lives to provide their families a better life. Similar to the way Latinx immigrant men retell their migration journeys as a "male quest story,"[11] Mexican American youth often attribute masculine characteristics—such as bravery, strength, and fortitude—to their father's act of crossing the border. This was clearly suggested by Rodrigo, a fifteen-year-old Mexican American who framed his undocumented father's migration journey as a "risk." He said, "My dad took the risk of crossing the border. He tried multiple times and got thrown back, but then he did not give up. He tried again and made it all the way."

Enrique, an eighteen-year-old Mexican American, whose father was a lawful permanent resident, also asserted that his father was a "very courageous family man" because "he crossed over to the United States to change our lives in a positive way and to provide a better life for his family."

Victoria, sixteen-year-old Mexican American whose parents later became US citizens, described her dad as a "brave man" for making the conscious decision to change his destiny. She claimed, "I am very proud of my dad. He is a brave man and I look up to him. He made the decision to cross the border. He had nothing but his clothes on his back and struggled to become something in life."

Perhaps because Mexican men are more likely be criminalized in the US,[12] the majority of working-class Mexican American youth I interviewed pieced together bits of information to present their parents, especially their fathers, as courageous. Conscious of controlling images that criminalize Mexican Americans as "illegal" border crossers, this form of inclusion work enables Mexican American youth to deploy the idea of the American Dream to present their parents as "good" immigrants who migrated to the United States in hopes of finding better opportunities for their family.

CONSTRUCTING IMMIGRANT FAMILIES AS COLLECTIVE AND HARDWORKING

The second way immigrant youth presented their families as "good" immigrants was by selectively drawing on rhetoric about collectivity and hard work. By claiming such characteristics—which are highly praised in the US—as their own "culture," respondents disputed the idea that their families were a burden or a threat. Instead, they presented their family as superior to the "typical" American family.

Korean Americans: "White Kids Are Selfish"
When describing their families, working-class Korean American youth drew on widely shared rhetoric about immigrant families to construct Asian families as "collective."

Yoon, who migrated to US when she was ten years old, spoke about her family in a way that was representative of Korean American youth. When I interviewed her, she met me in a park near her apartment, wearing a distressed, oversized denim jacket.

"We match," Yoon, who was nineteen at the time, said as she pointed at my denim jacket. A big smile spread across her face. She plopped down on the bench next to me and proclaimed, "We are twins." She gestured to our feet, pointing out that we were both wearing black boots as well.

With her upbeat and bubbly personality, I was surprised by how Yoon described herself. "I used to be shy," she said.

"Really?" I stared at her for a few seconds in utter disbelief.

"Well, I became shy when I came here," she clarified.

Prior to migrating to the US, Yoon used to be "outgoing" and always took the lead in her classes. Her charisma was evident, so much so that her first-grade teacher had told her parents that she was "very articulate" for her age.

Her father shared a similar trait. He exuded an "approachable" and "laid-back" demeanor, but he knew when to voice his opinion and "fight" for his family in Korea. What had changed, however, was her father's ability to take care of his family. Because Yoon's father worked "days and nights" as a parking lot attendant, he was "not really around." In addition, since he could not speak English, he often relied on Yoon—who was the oldest sibling in her family—to translate for him.

Indeed, it was through assisting her father that Yoon—who had been a leader in Korea but grown "shy" after moving to the US—gradually began to "get [her] personality back."

Describing how she had interacted with their previous landlord after he refused to return her family's security deposit back in full, she said, "You have to be friendly to get people's attention" and make them "listen to you." "You basically have to act like a White girl," she said. She rolled her eyes and smiled.

Although Yoon knew acting "like a White girl" could serve her family's interests when she translated for her parents, she made it very clear that her life was very different from that of White people. "White kids are selfish," she said.

When asked to elaborate, she began describing one of her "self-centered" White high school friends. "Her name was Amber, and oh my gosh, her parents were loaded, like millionaires. And she lived in this gigantic house."

Amber's place was just one of the many "gigantic" houses Yoon had been in over the years. She had other "rich" friends, both Asian Americans and Whites, and often went to their houses for sleepovers and to work on group projects for school.

In contrast to her friends, Yoon told me she wished her family didn't have to "worry about money all the time." She also wished they lived in a two-story house with a nice backyard, so she could have her own room. "I always shared a room with my sisters," she said.

Despite her longing, however, she was adamant that she didn't want to be more like Amber, who—despite shopping all the time with her parents' credit card—had weak family ties. In fact, Amber had rarely seen her family since leaving for college, which Yoon said was typical for White kids. They "leave home right when they turn eighteen" and go to "college with their parents' money." They only show up to "Thanksgiving dinner once a year."[13]

Contrasting herself to her White peers, she said, "I am helping my parents because that's what family members are supposed to do in Asian families. But Americans don't get it because they are too individualistic."

When speaking about her family, it was clear that Yoon was aware of how her family differed from the typical "American" family. After all, Yoon's father—unlike her upper-middle-class White friends' parents—had neither a "gigantic" suburban house nor English skills. Her father also probably did not have the time and resources to closely monitor his child's educational journey like some of the more well-off parents in her neighborhood did. In other words, Yoon—keenly aware of her family's position in society—knew she and her parents were excluded from the norm. Yoon's criticism of selective White middle-class children's and parents' behaviors thus reveals the pain of the race and class "injuries" that she encountered.[14]

But Yoon—like many Korean American youth I talked to—engaged in inclusion work not only to preserve her sense of self-worth but also to present her family as "good" immigrants. She drew on the notion of family collectivity—a highly praised characteristic in the US—to emphasize how her "culture" made her superior to the "typical" American family. Unlike "individualistic" Americans, she was "helping" her parents because "that's what family members are supposed to do in Asian families."

Nonetheless, to present her family in a positive light, Yoon drew on gendered, racialized, and classed notions of morality to depict her White friend as selfish. By singling out a White woman—which was common among youth who mentioned White people they knew—Yoon implied that White women are morally deviant for failing to fulfill the feminized expectation that women should care for their family. Yoon's assessment of White, or "American," families also overlooked the diversity of White American family forms.

By positioning their families as superior to White families, however, youths' responses served as a form of inclusion work. They drew upon widely shared cultural repertoires about immigrants' filial obligations and strong work ethic to reposition their families as "good" immigrants who were worthy of inclusion in American society.

Do-hyeon, who also attended schools with White middle-class youth, struggled to make sense of his seemingly different childhood, too. Like many other working-class Korean American youth, Do-hyeon—who was born and raised in Los Angeles—often witnessed his White peers' parents spending more time and energy on their children's education than his working-class parents were able to.

During his interview, he stated that he used to envy White peers because his parents, a taxi driver and a restaurant server, were "absent for the most part." He perceived White parents, when compared to his family, as being "a lot more involved" in their children's lives, which was evidenced by his parents rarely coming to his school events.

Do-hyeon's experience of observing White peers initially created a sense of inadequacy and influenced how he evaluated his own parents in comparison to his peers. The contrast between his "unorthodox" family and others at his school once made him think his mother and father were "bad." And yet, he told me he "grew out of" this belief. As Do-hyeon got "older and wiser," he realized his parents "did everything they could to provide for our family."

"They are actually very traditional, what you can call old-school Korean," he said. His "strict" father is "the rock of the family." Do-hyeon's mom is "an extremely sharp-witted, yet caring woman who balances out [his] father."

Although Do-hyeon shared a stronger bond with his mother, he dedicated a considerable amount of time to describing his father. By the time his father returned home from a grueling twelve-hour taxi shift, Do-hyeon explained that he was utterly drained. He would often collapse on the couch, occasionally drifting off to sleep with the television still on. He didn't engage in conversation with his children. Nor did he like asking others for help. Circling back to Korean tradition, Do-hyeon reiterated that his father was simply a "typical Korean man."

I pressed Do-hyeon on this point. "He doesn't ask you to translate for him?" I asked.

"He does, sometimes. But, he hates it. He usually tells my mom what he needs."

When he was "a little child," he did not like his father. On top of being reserved and strict, he said his father often grew angry when Do-hyeon or his brother got in trouble or performed poorly at school.

"Now, looking back, I think it is better this way," he said. "White parents provide comfort for their children. They are given too much freedom and find strictness as a form of abuse. Children of Asian immigrants are held to higher expectations and have more family responsibilities. I came to truly accept and appreciate my parents. My dad sacrificed everything for the family."

"If you could be born again, would you want to be Korean?" I asked Do-hyeon.

"Yes, I would rather be who I am today because if I say that I wish I were White because they have everything, I feel like I would be selling my soul," he said.

Yoon and Do-hyeon were different in many ways. In addition to having different gender identities, Yoon was the oldest child and Do-hyeon was the youngest. Yoon had lived in South Korea for ten years before migrating to the US; Do-hyeon, born in the US, had never been to Korea. They also grew up in different parts of Los Angeles and had different relationships with their fathers. Yoon described her working-class Korean immigrant father as "very approachable," "laid back," and "easy-going." Do-hyeon, on the other hand, described his father as "the rock of the family" and "strict."

In spite of all their differences, both Yoon and Do-hyeon wished their fathers had been more actively involved in their lives when they were young. Structural inequality embedded in people's workplace largely determines whether parents can actively get involved in their children's lives.[15] That is, the reason why Yoon's and Do-hyeon's fathers could not participate in their school lives was likely the result of institutional racism, language discrimination, and subordinated masculinity. They were constrained into working long hours in low-paying, low-status, and physically taxing dead-end jobs. And even if their monolingual immigrant parents had time to become more involved in their children's lives, schools rarely provide parents with sufficient translation support (see chapters 2 and 3 for more on this topic).

But rather than feeling disappointed in their fathers, Do-hyeon and Yoon both learned to characterize their families as superior to White families. Do-hyeon, for example, said he had "grown out" of the belief that his parents were "bad." Instead, he emphasized that his father was a "good" immigrant who subscribed to "typical" notions of Korean manhood: his father was a breadwinner who—despite being strict—put his family above his own interest. Furthermore, by highlighting how "children of Asian immigrants are held to higher expectations and have more family responsibilities," Do-hyeon implied that "Asian" parenting practices are better than the ways White parents raise their children.

When Do-hyeon said that his father was always exhausted after coming home from work, he seemed to recognize various structural hurdles that his father had endured as a working-class immigrant man. He also seemed to recognize that English-speaking, White, middle-class parents often had more flexible and less demanding work schedules, which enabled them to actively "get involved" in their children's school lives. Yet, instead of blaming broader structural conditions, Korean culture once again became the source of his father's emotionally distant behaviors. Do-hyeon characterized "Korean" parents—regardless of their social class and generational status—as a monolithic entity. They were inherently more strict, emotionally distant, and authoritarian than American ones.

In contrast to Do-hyeon's description, Korean culture—like US culture—is constantly shifting. Images of Korean family men in popular media have rapidly changed from the strict patriarch to the caring father. Partly due to globalization and Western imperialism, the image of emotionally affectionate fathers is also becoming increasingly popular in South Korea.[16] While there maybe more similarities than differences, Do-hyeon characterized the two cultures as being starkly different.

Do-hyeon's use of Korean culture, however, makes sense given that working-class immigrant fathers of color are constructed as inferior, unloving, controlling, and threatening in relation to middle-class White fathers.[17] Dubbed "new men" or "new fathers," the images of emotionally expressive, gender progressive, and highly involved family men have become ubiquitous in the US. This imagery glorifies a version of masculinity that is associated with successful White men who have professional-class jobs, which offer more flexible work schedules and sufficient time and resources to be nurturing. Not coincidentally, this imagery is cast in opposition to the hyper-masculinity that is often projected onto working-class men and men of color, thereby helping to obscure the institutional practices that prevent marginalized fathers from actively partaking in family activities.[18]

In this context, Do-hyeon defended "Korean" fatherhood. By arguing that White parents are overly indulgent with their children, he refuted the idea that his father's child-rearing practices were inferior to those of White parents. Instead, Do-hyeon used Korean culture to present his father as a "family man," or a breadwinner who also instilled family collectivity and responsibility in his sons. In doing so, Do-hyeon simultaneously constructed White childhood as deviant.

Not all Korean youth live in neighborhoods where they regularly interact with White families. In this case, they often referred to White families they had seen in TV shows or movies. For example, Sam, a sixteen-year-old, rarely interacted with White youth. He grew up in a neighborhood where the vast majority of residents are Latinx. Unlike the majority of Korean youth I interviewed, he compared his life to that of his best friend, Pedro, who is Mexican American. "His parents are just like my parents," he told me with a big smile.

Like Sam, Pedro has "friendly" parents. And Pedro's mom, just like Sam's mom, is an excellent cook. She makes "the best tamale in the world." And just like Sam, Pedro is close to his parents and translates for them, too.

Despite having a close friend with similar family circumstances, Sam still described his family as being different from the typical "American family." Sam, like many of my interviewees, spoke about "White" and "American" families as if they were interchangeable.

"Do you have any White friends?" I asked.

"Not really. No. Oh, I had one White friend in elementary school, but that was it. We were not that close. We never kept in touch once we went to middle school."

"Do you think you have a family life similar to White families?

"No."

"Why not?"

"You know, American parents." He gave me a pointed look.

I shrugged back and waited for him to elaborate.

"They always give, give, give, and children never give back. They soak up all their parents' money and send them to senior housing," Sam explained. Unlike "American families," Sam said that Korean "culture" places more importance on collectivity and filial obligation. "We don't do that. Koreans value family ties because we are very collective . . . so there are a lot of Korean morals and values that this translating reminds me of like respecting our parents, and prioritizing family."

Considering that Sam hardly interacted with White families, his reference to White families may seem puzzling. Yet, the imagery of affluent, "giving" White parents is everywhere. It's on social media and in children's books, television shows, movies, the news, and magazines. The idea of weakening family ties and the abandonment of elderly in today's American families is also pervasive in the US and often buttressed by references to the ethnic filial commitment of the Asian "model minority families."[19] Such widespread repertoires provide a powerful basis for Korean American youth like Sam to construct their families as "normal," if not superior, to "American families," who they view as too individualistic or selfish.

In sum, Korean Americans draw upon widely available meanings about "Americans" and "Asians/Koreans" to contest controlling images that depict their families as unfit to be citizens. Clearly, my interviewees' responses do not reflect the lives of all White American families. Not only do parenting practices differ based on social class in the US,[20] but many White women shoulder a disproportionate amount of household work—including childcare and eldercare—on behalf of their families.[21] Nonetheless, by positioning their families as superior to White families, young language brokers engage in inclusion work. They draw upon widely shared cultural repertoires about immigrants' family obligations to reposition their families as "good" immigrants who are worthy of inclusion in American society.

Mexican Americans: "White Kids Are Lazy"

Many Mexican Americans also refer to the presumed "collectivity" of Mexican American families when constructing "American" families as deviant. Unlike Korean Americans, however, Mexican Americans pair their argument about Mexican collectivity with discussions about how hard their parents work.

Nikki, a seventeen-year-old "proud Mexican American," had thick, curly, jet-black hair. During our interview, her oversized gold hoop earrings coordinated perfectly with the trio of gleaming gold chains gracing her neck. Her index and middle fingers, adorned with an assortment of golden rings, sparkled in the sun as she spoke about being born and raised in Los Angeles.

Although Nikki "learned to speak Spanish and English fluently" as a young child, her teacher in elementary school put her "in these English-learning classes that were practically a waste of time." "They just assumed I didn't know English," she said.

Nikki contrasted her experiences in school with those of her younger sister, who "always fit in" because "she has light skin and green eyes."

In comparison to her sister, Nikki described herself as "Black." She said that some people didn't even think that she was a "full Mexican."

"Was your sister also enrolled in ESL class?"

"No. She was not. Looking back at it now, it was pretty offensive. But I didn't know any better," she said.

Growing up, Nikki had always felt "different" especially when her family went out in public. People constantly stared at her, which caused her to become a "very insecure and shy girl."

Despite the racism and colorism she encountered, Nikki said learning Spanish and translating for her parents helped her "prove her Mexican side" and "appreciate Mexican culture." "I am Latina, hundred percent Mexican American. I grew up in a Mexican household, speak Spanish. I am hardworking and love to party," she proudly proclaimed.

Without my probing, Nikki then began describing stereotypical views about Mexicans that she knew many "Americans" subscribed to. "Americans might have a negative view on how we raise our kids, like we have too many kids and we don't give them the right education. We lack ambition, blah blah blah."

"Why do you think other people say that about Mexicans?" I asked.

"Because they don't know about us. They are wrong and stupid."

After a brief pause, she continued speaking in a louder voice: "They already judge us with our looks, and sometimes people might look at me and because I am Latina, they think I don't speak English. When I translate for my mom, they are like, 'Oh you speak English?' Yeah, I do speak English. Hello!"

"Who are they?" I asked.

"White people. Like, when I went to clean the house with my mom, one of the guys there, the owner was a White guy and he was like, 'Your English is good. Do you always work for your mom?' I said, 'No, I go to school.' And then he was like, 'What?' 'Yes, I go to school.' 'Oh really?' 'Yes.' Why are you surprised? I go to school."

"Did you say that to him?"

"No. These people are ignorant. They just think that White is better and that we are just wetbacks. You know what that is?"

I nodded and asked, "How did that make you feel?"

"I was angry. I wanted to hit him with the broom. It's so annoying. The fact that people jump to the conclusion and assume in their own way because I am Mexican."

At this point, I asked a question I asked all my interviewees: "If you were to be born again, would you want to be Mexican American?"

"Yes," she nodded reassuringly.

"Not White?"

"Hell no. Not White."

"Why not?"

"They think they are all that. They are lazy. They are boring. They don't have a culture. They grab it from other cultures and make it theirs. Like burritos. What the hell? I mean there's no such thing as burrito in Mexico. What's that shit? No. That's Americanized."

"I've heard this a lot. White kids are lazy. Can you tell me why you think that way?"

"Because they are! I think it's because White parents don't discipline their kids. They let their kids do whatever they want. American parents spoil their children. Sometimes, I see White kids running around in the restaurants and their parents don't even say anything. They just eat there, and their Mexican nannies are the ones who are chasing after them. We are the ones who clean up after them."

Her tone switched from being upbeat and cheerful to firm and serious. "Yeah, I'm proud. We work hard. We value family. To other people, we may seem weird and different, but I'm fine with it."

Her smile gradually returned as she continued speaking about Mexican families. "We raise our kids in a traditional way, like spanking them when we need to and pulling their ears. But that's how Americans should raise their kids. Like, like they have to discipline their kids. My parents taught and raised their daughters this way."

Research has demonstrated that structural inequality, including racial segregation and controlling images depicting Black and Latinx children as "dangerous" troublemakers, helps generate distinctive parenting practices.

Low-income parents of color, for example, are more likely to closely super-vise their children and are quicker to discipline them because they are aware that their children's behaviors can be adultified and criminalized in public spaces.[22] Furthermore, Black and Latinx parents are aware of the controlling images that depict them as neglectful or "bad" parents, which can in turn compel them to act strict.[23] Indeed, this was what Nikki pointed out when she said that "Americans have a negative view on how we raise our kids, like we have too many kids and we don't give them the right education."

Although parenting practices are not fixed but context-specific, Mexi-can youth like Nikki use descriptions about "Mexican culture" to explain why their family is different than "American" families by emphasizing their strict parenting, family collectivity, and hard work. In doing so, they position their families as superior to "Americans," who they characterize as "lazy" or "spoiled."

This pattern occurs partly because of the type of contact Mexican Ameri-cans have with White families. Many of the working-class Mexican Americans I interviewed attended schools in high-poverty, Latinx-majority neighbor-hoods. Consequently, their primary interactions with White people occurred during translation encounters when, as previously mentioned, their parents were working in middle-class, White-majority suburbs, which in turn made racial and socioeconomic inequalities visible to Mexican American youth.

For example, Francisca, a nineteen-year-old Mexican American accom-panied her mother to translate and clean houses in wealthy, predominantly White neighborhoods.[24] Because of her limited yet often unequal interactions with White middle-class adults who employed her mom, the defining feature of the "American" family for Francisca was wealth.

"Most of these rich American people I have encountered while translating have been very patient and kind," she said. "But there was this one White lady who was very impatient."[25] "Every time my mom didn't understand anything, she would yell and hit the wall. She was the reason I hated translating. She had no patience with me. She always cut me off and yelled at me if I told her to slow down a bit."

The experience of translating for this White woman was so stressful that Francisca began to lose sleep the night before she would accompany her mother to this house. "I was so stressed out. You know it's really difficult to translate especially when time is against you. I had to be precise and fast!"

In fact, it was through these translation experiences that Francisca began to perceive that "American" children were too "sheltered" and "pampered." Although she had grown up thinking White kids didn't "have any difficulties," she realized that "American children never have to work hard." "They have everything," she said, "That's not very good. Then they don't develop any motivation to succeed in life."

She then compared the "American" family with the "Mexican family." "Mexican family are different. In my culture, kids grow up with pressure from family to be a good kid."

"What do you mean by 'a good kid'?" I asked.

"Not spoiled. Put effort into everything. In my family, there are a lot of expectations with that. My parents put us all before themselves and work day in and day out, long nights to maintain us and keep a roof over our head. We were brought up to work hard and make our family priority."

Advocates often draw on the notion that immigrants are "family-oriented" and "hardworking" to offset the controlling images and to promote immigrant rights.[26] By drawing on these repertoires, young Mexican Americans like Francisca challenge the negative stereotypes about Mexican families and position themselves as "good" immigrants who value a strong work ethic. Their families appear superior in comparison to "lazy" or "spoiled" White children.

EMPHASIZING INTERGENERATIONAL MOBILITY

The third form of inclusion work involves immigrant youth using their upbringing to present themselves as upwardly mobile, second-generation immigrants who are ready to contribute to mainstream society. In contrast to the first two forms of inclusion work, which involve retelling their past and present family experiences, this form of inclusion work is future-oriented and centered on the themes of productivity and consumption. This strategy, however, remains interconnected with the first and second strategies youth employ. Given that the parents migrated to the "land of opportunity" and teach their children about collectivity and hard work, it has become the second generation's obligation to achieve the American Dream. By presenting themselves as upwardly mobile, youth attempt to offset the anti-immigrant discourses characterizing immigrants of color as a public burden in favor of presenting their families as good immigrants.

I interviewed Katie, a sixteen-year-old, at the two-bedroom apartment her parents were renting. This was the cheapest two-bedroom apartment they had been able to find when they moved to Los Angeles. Katie had helped her parents fill out numerous rental applications before they had found this one. She said it had been difficult for them to find an affordable apartment because landlords usually don't like having five people in a two-bedroom apartment.

Katie led me to her bedroom, which she shared with her two sisters. Numerous colorful Post-it notes dotted the wall close to her bed. Some of the notes contained logistical reminders: "$ for gas company," "BOA fees," and "Sign up by 7/10." Others contained motivation phrases. A yellow Post-it note read, "You can do it!" in Korean. A green one said, "Your future is created by what you do today." A bright pink one read, "Be like Annette," who, as I later learned, was the "most compassionate and wise Christian" Katie had ever met, while working in a part-time job at Target.

When I praised Katie for having a spotless and organized room, she credited her mother. After finishing a ten-hour shift at a Korean grocery store, she would clean their entire house top to bottom. "All she does is clean," Katie said.

After settling in Los Angeles, Katie's parents had opened a small "food court–like" restaurant, where they sold Korean bulgogi (beef) bowls in Koreatown. Katie used to "help out" after school, taking orders from customers. She was known as a "cutie" by some of their older regular Korean customers.

That business, however, had "miserably failed." It left her parents with a large amount of debt. Recounting the times when her dad urgently asked her to call credit companies, Katie said that she saw "a lot of mistakes" that her parents had made. She was shocked to see the amount of interest they were paying every month. "I know they were struggling, but I was thinking, 'What were they thinking?'" she incredulously asked.

At the time of our interview, Katie's father was still looking for a job. But she told me that there weren't many options for a fifty-year-old Korean immigrant man who can't speak English. Katie's mother was working as a cashier in a Korean grocery store, but they kept falling behind and accumulating debt.

Even though Katie's parents were in a tough financial spot, she described translating for her parents in positive ways. Over the years, she had learned to "look forward." She was "learning things through [her] parents' mistakes so much faster" than she otherwise would have. Nor did Katie blame her parents for their financial difficulties. They tried to "make it here" to provide a better life for their family. They were "just unfortunate."

Katie also credited her family's experiences for influencing her career interests. Speaking in a more upbeat tone than before, she told me she wanted to become a bilingual lawyer. "I can't believe I want to be a lawyer after dealing with my parents' debts and credit card companies," she said. "But I realized that my upbringing forced me to be very independent and competent."

These skills were assets that can potentially help her obtain intergenerational mobility and make her parents "happy." "So why not use these skills, succeed in life, and get respect for what I do?"

Notions of self-reliance, productivity, and independence are considered quintessentially American traits.[27] This is particularly true for immigrants, who are regularly evaluated in terms of their potential contribution to the US economy. Because many respondents knew these traits are paramount to being a "good" immigrant, they often described their language-brokering work like Katie did. They were learning valuable skills that would be beneficial in the future.

Similar to Katie, Chulmin described himself as efficient and responsible. Unlike most language brokers, however, Chulmin described his father as "really demanding." His father would tell him, "We are going to DMV after school and that's it." Although Chulmin didn't mind helping his father, he wished his father would ask him nicely and be more "emotionally affectionate" overall.

However, Chulmin presented his father in an honorable light by using Korean "culture" to account for his father's demeanor. "My grandpa was demanding," he said. In Korea, "children obey their parents."

Although Chulmin said that fathers in Korea are respected, he had multiple translation interactions where his parents were "looked down upon." Moreover, Chulmin said that his father was literally and figuratively a "big" person in the family, which made him stand out in public spaces. He said, "They are probably thinking, why are you relying on a kid?"

Despite having encounters that sometime made him "sad," he claimed that his language-brokering experiences would help him in the future. Through interacting with his father, he had learned to be "responsible" and "efficient."

"I don't think people realize that translation will benefit me in the future. The fact that I had a lot of stuff on my shoulder, to translate and to make sure everything was done correctly, it made me more responsible and efficient."

Both Chulmin and Katie found mainstream American society to be largely unwelcoming to their non-English-speaking, working-class immigrant parents. But rather than being critical of the US, they both reported having learned valuable skills such as competence, efficiency, and self-reliance. They used these highly regarded traits, moreover, to offset negative perceptions about their families. Rather than being a burden, Chulmin and Katie claimed that the positive traits they learned while serving as their family's language broker would help them be successful, earn respect, and enter mainstream American society.

Like working-class Korean Americans, most Mexican Americans I interviewed also claimed that growing up in working-class immigrant households allowed them to cultivate socially valued skills such as competency and self-reliance. However, unlike Korean Americans, Mexican Americans offered another reason they wanted to achieve success in the US: Mexican Americans repeatedly said they were going to obtain social mobility to prove "racist" people wrong.

Gloria, the nineteen-year-old Mexican American college student whom I introduced in chapter 2, frequently found herself facing individuals she described as "racist." These people expressed their astonishment upon learning that "Mexicans actually go to college." Although these negative interactions made her realize that Mexicans are seen as "stupid," she countered such controlling images by arguing that having language-brokering responsibilities allowed her to be self-sufficient. She anticipated that these skills would help her "contribute to the workforce in the future."

But in addition to gaining these socially valued skills, she described feeling motivated for a second reason. She also wanted to prove people wrong. "The best way to respond to these racist people is to show them that I can overcome hardships," she said. "Little do they know is that I am in school to be a teacher. One day, I am going to tell them, 'Look, thanks to my immigrant parents' struggles, I am now a Mexican teacher.'"

Alejandro, a Mexican American, was nineteen years old. Deep frown lines framed the bottom half of his face. When paired with his shaved head and thin moustache, his appearance gave the impression that he was much older than he was. During his interview, he repeatedly told me he was an American because he was "born here." [28]

There were few things that frustrated Alejandro more than the police officers who patrolled his neighborhood, however. When they were not stopping and searching Alejandro and his friends, they were harassing others.

Alejandro's experiences left him with the impression that people think "Latino parents just let their kids be out in the street and that their parents don't raise them right. They think all Mexicans turn out to be gangs and smoking because their mom has no control of them and that they don't have a dad in their life."

Negative stereotypes about Latinx families were particularly acute for Alejandro, who was raised by a "struggling" single immigrant mother. "Sometimes it is discouraging when people say that I will not be anyone important because my mom is poor, and she can't speak English." But rather than letting other people's negative opinions "get [him] down," he told me he didn't "agree with this statement." He loved his "strict" but "caring" mother. He didn't think "helping out" by translating for her was a "big deal."

"Yes, they struggle to live up to that American fame, and yes I had to help my mom with everything," he said. Speaking in a louder voice, he added, "But, I did not control her or anything, because she is still strict with me."

Indeed, the "small act" of giving back to his mom had a big result in Alejandro's life. He said, "I am more independent than other people because I helped my mom ever since I was young. Translating thing is good thing because I had to help my mom instead of hanging out with the wrong friends and end up going down the wrong path."

The rhetoric that Black and Latinx boys are "at risk" of joining gangs and doing drugs because their parents don't give them enough supervision is prevalent in the US.[29] Alejandro was aware of such rhetoric and deployed it when crediting language brokering as having a positive impact on his life. During all those years living in what he considered a "dangerous" neighborhood, Alejandro managed to stay away from drugs, he told me. He saw how drugs could make people forget about "what is important in life"—including one of his good friends, who went to prison for being in possession of an illegal substance. "Just because I came from a low-income home, I mean these factors like being poor and helping parents should be overall reason for not giving up in becoming someone," he said forcefully.

Alejandro paused and continued, "I feel that all that racism me and my mom experienced in life gave me a better motivation to make something of myself and level up in life. I don't want to be known as that minority. . . . I want to prove to people and show them that my mom's struggles as an immigrant made an impact on my life. . . . and that I have a lot to offer here."

Like many Mexican American youth, eighteen-year Gael was very cognizant about the "negative Mexican stereotypes" that cast all "Mexicans as poor, low-educated wetback, who have ten kids." Because of such stereotypes, Gael seemed a bit hesitant and uncomfortable when describing his family's financial situation in detail, especially issues related to welfare. When I asked him what type of documents he translated for his family, he said that he "just translate[s] medical related documents for his grandmother," but after a pause, he added, "and some welfare stuff for my mom." Speaking quickly in his soft voice, Gael said that his single mother, a domestic worker with three children, "worked all the time but was still struggling. She had no choice but to depend on government."

Although Gael, for the most part, kept his answers short, perhaps implying that he did not want to talk about his family's tenuous economic position, he spoke at great length about the lessons he learned from being a language broker. "If I never helped my mom and grandma, I don't think I would be as disciplined as I am today. I think having a huge responsibility on my shoulders kind of molded me into an independent person at a young age but that has worked to my advantage in areas such as getting through school."

Although Gael said that his mother was always busy, he attempted to present his mother as someone who passed down the important qualities necessary and praised in the US. He said, "My mom wasn't a person I would go to for help with my homework like maybe some other American kids can do. She never really pushed me to do well because she is so busy. Well, she did, but only by saying I need to work hard. But I think in the long run, I know that it's only going to help me when I get a job. I already have all these skills that companies look for."

Despite their tenuous economic circumstances, the youth I interviewed argued that the skills they learned in childhood would allow them to become productive members of US society. In a society where the success and contributions of children of immigrants are narrowly evaluated in economic terms, they presented themselves as upwardly mobile and productive, which provided these second-generation immigrants a rebuttal to the forms of exclusion their families routinely faced. This form of inclusion work, moreover, is especially salient for working-class Mexican Americans. To offset the alarmist images of uneducated, burdensome immigrants, Mexican Americans attempted to transform their family's perceived deficits into socially valued American characteristics.

CLAIMING MEMBERSHIP IN EVERYDAY LIFE

Inclusion work is a response to exclusion work. Racialization—the recursive process of ascribing racial meanings to human bodies and groups' practices— has profoundly shaped the distribution of and access to material resources and power in the US.[30] In a society where biological bases for racial disparities have lost their explanatory power, culture has become a powerful means through which dominant groups, including politicians, social commentators and moral leaders, justify racial inequality.[31] Through the concept of inclusion work, I have demonstrated in this chapter how immigrant youth of color— who are cognizant of how their family deviates from the hegemonic representations of "American" families—use culture to claim membership.

To resist controlling images, children of immigrants in this study selectively deployed cultural repertoires about "good" immigrants. That is, rather than passively absorbing cultural values, they made use of available cultural repertoires that are highly idealized in the US. First, they "Americanized" their parents' journey to the US to present their parents as heroic immigrants who left their homelands to achieve the American Dream in the land of opportunity. Second, these respondents made use of seemingly positive repertoires regarding their ethnic culture to construct their families as "good" immigrants who are collective and hardworking. Third, when discussing their future, these young people drew upon the language of independence, efficiency, and self-discipline to present themselves as productive citizens, as opposed to "bad" immigrants who are a burden on society. Such inclusion work enabled them to present their family as "good" immigrants and prove their family's belonging. Their inclusion work thus testifies to their probationary status as racialized "foreigners," which plays a key role in prompting them to engage in inclusion work in the first place.[32] Through this process, they attempted to turn marginality—or growing up in Mexican or Korean working-class immigrant households—into perceived assets.

The fact that children of immigrants supplement their limited knowledge about their parents' migration journeys with repertoires about "good" immigrants that are often celebrated in the US illustrates the importance of reexamining how culture is theorized within the sociology of immigration. That is, culture is not a set of uniform entities that individuals are passively socialized into.[33] Instead, examining what children of immigrants do with culture reveals that young people can put culture to use for strategic ends. Although the respondents' responses were not wholly consistent across contexts—precisely because culture is not always cohesive[34]—young people, as active social actors, mobilize the coexisting cultural repertoires they encounter in different institutions to claim inclusion in a society that excludes immigrants of color from achiving full citizenship.

The fact that young people use evidently free-market or capitalistic language that emphasizes efficiency, productivity, and competency is seemingly contradictory when paired with their narratives about prioritizing their filial obligations. Indeed, as I demonstrated, they highlight their commitment to family collectivity to condemn White middle-class families, who they perceived as overly individualistic and materialistic. Their response thus shows how ethnocentric images of White middle-class families can serve as a default standard through which children of immigrants interpret their own family lives and defend their family practices in the first place. Moreover, the notion that workers exhibit discipline and efficiency has long been celebrated under capitalism and remains important within today's economy.[35] As a result, children of immigrants selectively made use of these seemingly contradictory cultural repertoires in different contexts to present their families as "good" immigrants who are worthy of belonging in the US.

Using comparative analysis of two differently racialized groups, this chapter also revealed how inclusion work takes different forms based on immigrants' race. Mexican Americans—who are far more likely to be racialized as illegal and uneducated than are Korean Americans—put more discursive effort into validating their family's presence in the US. For example, although both groups construct their parents as heroic immigrants who escaped poverty in search of the American Dream in the land of opportunity, Mexican Americans are more likely to construct their parents as courageous risk-takers in an attempt to redefine the meanings of border crossing. Mexican Americans are also more likely to argue that achieving intergenerational mobility would enable them to "prove" racist people wrong. When taken together, these findings reveal how young people's group position in the contemporary US racial hierarchy shapes their inclusion work.

This comparative analysis also demonstrates how different racialization processes embedded in various institutions shape the ways in which youth rearticulate their group's position. The working-class Korean American youth I interviewed were more likely to interact with middle-class White families at school. By virtue of their peers' class background, Korean American youth often observe White parents devoting significantly more energy and time to their children's education than their own parents can. To make sense of their different family lives, working-class Korean Americans construct "American" children as "selfish" in relation to "collective" and "family-oriented" Asian/Korean Americans. By comparison, working-class Mexican Americans are more likely to live in Latinx-majority neighborhoods with high concentrations of poverty. Their interactions with White people often occur when they are helping their parents, who tend to work in the informal service sector in middle-class suburbs.[36] Cognizant of the broader racial meanings depicting Mexican immigrants as belonging to a "lazy underclass" and witnessing stark differences between the lives of their family and the families of their parents' White employers, working-class Mexican Americans construct "American" children as lazier than "hardworking" Mexicans. Thus, this chapter clarifies the ways in which neighborhood and school segregation,[37] the racialized division of labor,[38] and controlling images[39] can generate distinct experiences of exclusion and form a powerful basis for divergent forms of inclusion work for immigrants of color.

Although inclusion work demonstrates youths' ability to put culture to use when confronted with ideological assaults on their worth, their efforts inadvertently shift focus away from more systemic and pervasive patterns of inequality. That is, by presenting their families as groups that have the potential to overcome institutional inequality through family ties, hard work, and self-sufficiency, their efforts help reinforce the myth of the American Dream, as well as the moral boundary between "good" and the "bad" immigrants. Moreover, despite their efforts to challenge the prevailing images that depict their families as perpetual foreigners, respondents reified the boundary between "real" Americans and foreigners when drawing upon "ethnic" culture to distinguish their family practices from those of White families. Paradoxically, then, when youth at the margin attempt to challenge controlling images, they divert attention from the very structures responsible for producing their daily struggles in the first place—including class disparities, racial discrimination, and a lack of institutional translation support. In short, because inclusion work is constrained within the confines of existing cultural repertoires, as well as a group's position in the contemporary racial hierarchy, young people's narratives must be understood as structurally reproductive—rather than transformative—agency.[40]

In this light, it is crucial to create alternative cultural repertoires that marginalized immigrants can draw upon when claiming membership in the larger society.[41] In contrast to this country's founding myths, immigrants are not simply pushed to migrate because of devastating conditions in their home country nor is it possible for all immigrants to achieve the American Dream in the land of opportunity. Migration is a historical process in which larger forces like colonialism, imperialism, global capitalism, and military occupations are responsible for the displacement of migrants from their homelands.[42] Indeed, as illustrated throughout this book, the reason why children of immigrants engage in language-brokering work is that institutional inequalities have systematically marginalized their families and denied them access to fundamental social citizenship rights in the United States. Because culture is an imperative site of struggle, bringing counter-hegemonic narratives into their toolkits remains an important first step in promoting the full inclusion of marginalized immigrants.

SEVEN LEARNING FROM CHILDREN LANGUAGE BROKERS

It is a peculiar sensation, this double-consciousness, this sense of always looking at one's Self through the eyes of others, of measuring one's soul by the tape of a world that looks on in amused contempt and pity. One ever feels his twoness—an American, a Negro, two souls, two thoughts, two unreconciled strivings, two warring ideals in one dark body, whose dogged strength alone keeps from torn asunder.

—W. E. B. Du Bois *The Souls of Black Folk*[1]

I know that they are going to treat us like we are illegal aliens, like trash. . . . People think that American means White, but I am an American. I am also Mexican. I am bilingual . . . I hear everything they say, but I don't have to translate everything.

—Antonio, fifteen-year-old

My mother's English has remained rudimentary during her forty-plus years living in the United States. When she speaks Korean, my mother speaks her mind. She is sharp, witty, and judgmental, if rather self-preening. But her English is a crush of piano keys that used to make me cringe whenever she spoke to a white person. As my mother spoke, I watched the white person, oftentimes a woman, put on a fright mask of strained tolerance: wide eyes frozen in trapped patience, smile widened in condescension. As she began responding to my mother in a voice reserved for toddler, I stepped in. From a young age, I learned to speak for my mother as authoritatively as I could. Not only did I want to dispel the derision I saw behind that woman's eyes, I wanted to shame her with my sobering fluency for thinking what she was thinking. I have been partly drawn to writing, I realize, to judge those who have unfairly judged my family; to prove that I've been watching this whole time.

— Cathy Park Hong, *Minor Feelings: An Asian American Reckoning*[2]

At the turn of the twentieth century, Du Bois powerfully theorized unequal power structures and institutional arrangements between White and Black people, which instilled what he called a "double consciousness" in Black people. As Du Bois argued in his sociological masterpiece *Souls of Black Folk*, Black people feel their "twoness" as an objectified other and a subjective self. Twoness, Du Bois argues, paradoxically fosters creativity. Encountering systemic forms of inequality allows Black people to see beyond the "veil," which is a "peculiar sensation" or a "second sight" that enables Black people to have more awareness of systemic forms of racism that are often invisible to White people.

More than a century later, a lot has changed. Antonio, quoted at the opening of this chapter, grew up during a time when many of the explicit forms of racial discrimination Du Bois identified have been outlawed. Furthermore, now that large-scale immigration to the US is mostly from Latin American and Asian countries, the demographic composition of the United States has shifted dramatically. In Los Angeles, where I interviewed children of immigrants, Latinx people are the majority, constituting 49 percent of residents. Asian Americans are approximately 15 percent of the population. Only 25 percent of Angelenos are White. While shifting demographics in Los Angeles and other US cities have prompted discussions about the "Browning of America" or a "minority majority" country, many of the unequal power structures and institutional arrangements that Du Bois identified more than a hundred years ago persist. And as a result, many youth continue to feel a double consciousness in a nation where—to paraphrase Antonio—American still means White.

The twoness that Latinx and Asian Americans experience, however, is different than the twoness that Black people feel. In a society where Latinx and Asian Americans are frequently the target of racialized nativism, Mexican American language brokers like Antonio look at themselves through "the eyes of others" to find that people treat his family like "illegal," "aliens," and "trash." Navigating multiple forms of inequality in the US can have a lasting impact on the sense of twoness immigrant youth of color develop. Indeed, while growing up in Los Angeles, Cathy Hong Park, a Korean American poet, noticed "amused contempt and pity" coming from White people who infantilized her Korean immigrant mother based on her perceived foreignness. Much like the youth I interviewed, Cathy Park Hong views translation as an opportunity to dispel derision. Becoming adept at speaking and writing English was a way for her to prove Americans wrong.

While much has been written about the forms of racism immigrant youth of color encounter in the US, existing scholarship has largely overlooked the possibility that children of immigrants, who are active social agents, use their "twoness" to negotiate the dominant ideologies pertaining to what it means to be an American and an immigrant of color. Yet as this book has revealed, children of immigrants are far from passive recipients of "American" values. They actively enact or "do American" in their everyday lives to secure resources for their families. They also selectively deploy widely cultural repertoires about "good" immigrants to claim membership and present their parents and their future selves as hardworking and family-oriented immigrants pursuing the American Dream. Resisting controlling images about "bad" immigrants allows them to broker belonging and claim full citizenship rights for themselves and their families. After unpacking the theoretical significance of these findings within this concluding chapter, I end by offering potential solutions to address the structural problems that children of immigrants face.

POLITICS OF EXCLUSION AND SECURING FULL CITIZENSHIP RIGHTS

When I speak about my research with English-speaking adults who are outside immigrant communities, they regularly echo the sentiments often reported by mainstream journalists. They express concern that translating for one's family forces children to grow up too fast, jeopardizes children's psychological development, and causes parents to lose authority over their children. The solution to these problems, some have told me, is to prevent what they perceive as role reversal from happening in the first place. If immigrant parents learned English and assimilated into the mainstream, they could protect their children from the "dangers" of the adult world.

Assuming that adult immigrants need to master the English language and assimilate into the mainstream encompasses a wide spectrum of views that includes, on one end, efforts to frame immigrants as a major "problem" and drain on institutional resources. On the other end, this rhetoric encapsulates a fear of difference, which positions immigrants of color as "threatening" to challenge the idealized notion of what an American family is supposed to be.

That is, the controversy over children's language-brokering work is a controversy over what constitutes a good family, a good childhood, a good immigrant, and a good citizen—a controversy that helps reveal long-standing and largely unexamined assumptions about which people are deserving of being treated fairly and receiving full rights in American society.

Full citizenship rights in the United States have historically been reserved for White, heterosexual, landowning men. By comparison, White women, people of color, and children have historically been afforded far fewer citizenship rights.[3] Because citizenship status—or recognition as a full member of a society—has been deeply connected to one's ability to own property, vote, obtain paid employment, maintain a family, and receive a formal education, those who lacked citizenship rights have often been relegated to the bottom of the societal hierarchy under the assumption that they are less "civilized," "rational," and "independent" than those at the top.[4]

Although important legal gains have been made over time, systemic forms of inequality continue to prevent many people from having access to safe, secure, and dignified lives. Extensive research has shown that one's ability to obtain full citizenship rights differs based on gender, race, and nationality. For instance, due to limited state-sanctioned forms of family support, including federally funded parental leave and childcare, women today spend significant amount of time engaging in housework, emotional work, and care work, which in turn can leave many women feeling conflicted about work and family commitments.[5] At the same time, because institutional racism has historically prevented men of color from earning a family wage, women of color have performed labor-intensive, low-paying jobs even when White middle-class women have been subjected to a cult of domesticity.[6]

This trend persists in the contemporary US. Privileged women often manage their "second shift" by hiring babysitters, live-in caregivers, house cleaners, and gardeners.[7] Privileged women also rely on others for food preparation and cosmetic treatments such as hairdressing, waxing, manicures, spa treatments, and skin care.[8] At the same time, because housework and care work have historically been feminized, devalued, and deemed low-skill, women of color often work long hours in these low-status jobs. In addition to lacking benefits and paid leave, they often face exploitation as a result of their working conditions.[9]

This is particularly true for low-income immigrants of color, as they are

largely excluded from "mainstream" workplaces that require English proficiency. And partly because low-income immigrant women of color are grossly
underpaid and live and work in areas that are highly segregated by race, class,
and language, they have difficulty obtaining the education, credentials, or English proficiency needed to leave these jobs.[10] Instead, they remain in positions
where they have few choices other than taking jobs that other "Americans"
refuse to—or have little time to—perform.

What existing research has largely undertheorized, however, is how language intersects with other forms of inequality to shape people's ability to
achieve full citizenship rights. Because non-English-speakers of color are
often seen as "undeserving foreigners," English fluency is more than a simple
requirement to access high-paying jobs. It is interpreted as a sign that someone is willing to assimilate into the mainstream—which is presumed to be a
requirement for securing full access to other basic rights, including the rights
to safety and health. In a society where self-sufficiency and individual responsibility are highly valued, non-English-speaking immigrants of color are
portrayed as a group that drain health, education, and other social services
reserved for "real" Americans.[11]

And as I have demonstrated, language becomes a crucial marker through
which immigrants of color became walking targets of racialized nativism.
Indeed, the English-speaking healthcare providers and police officers in this
study often acted as if immigrants with limited English proficiency failed to
meet the requirements for basic human rights, such as inquiring about their
own well-being, security, and protection—rights that are afforded to immigrants in the state of California. Working in overcrowded and underfunded
institutions, agents are encouraged to prioritize efficiency over equal access.
Rather than using interpretation services, institutional agents regularly rely
on stopgap measures to communicate with non-English-speaking clientele,
such as translation from their bilingual coworkers or clients' family members.
Other times, institutional agents rely on body language or a mixture of Spanish and English to carry on conversations. Despite condemning "foreigners"
for speaking with accents, these agents often speak with heavy English accents
when attempting to communicate in "broken" Spanish or Korean. My findings demonstrate how English-speaking institutions can become, as a result, a
site of discipline where unequal power relations are reproduced. Rather than
ensuring equal access, institutional agents expect non-English-speaking im-

migrants to be grateful for whatever services they receive. This is especially the case when they interact with immigrant women of color, whose gender, race, and lack of English fluency contribute to institutional agents' impression that they are "docile" and "submissive." Ultimately, language intersects with other forms of inequality to shape people's access to full citizenship rights.

Many institutional agents—like the broader public—believe the simplest solution is for immigrants to learn the language and assimilate into the US. In actuality, the assumption that immigrants need to assimilate into the mainstream and learn the language of their new country helps to justify their exclusion. Their perceived foreignness encourages local agents to shift the institutional responsibility of providing translation services onto immigrants themselves. Consequently, the young people in this study repeatedly said that their parents were afraid to speak with monolingual English speakers. They also repeatedly said that their parents, especially their mothers, were treated like a "kid," "stupid," or an "alien" for not speaking English. Furthermore, considering that Mexican Americans are racialized as belonging to a problematic underclass,[12] many Mexican American youth also recalled situations where their families were perceived as "lazy," "criminal," "uneducated," "wetback," or "illegal." In other words, monolingual immigrants of color become a target for what historian George Sanchez calls racialized nativism, or antagonism and hostility aimed at racially identifiable immigrants.[13] And as I discuss in greater detail next, it also compels immigrant youth of color to step in and attempt to broker citizenship and belonging for their parents.

FAMILY SURVIVAL STRATEGIES AND THE ROLE OF CHILDREN

Although institutions in the US often fail to provide people at the margin with full citizenship rights, social actors regularly develop creative solutions to the barriers they encounter. For example, research has found that women of color—who often lack the resources to outsource domestic labor like middle-class, White, heterosexual women often do—have developed survival strategies such as extended family kinships, fictive kin, and split households to secure resources in the face of lack of citizenship rights.[14]

Whereas existing research has largely focused on the work of adults, *Language Brokers* demonstrates that children in working-class immigrant households also secure resources to obtain citizenship rights for their families. Even when they had friends and adult family members to rely on, working-class immigrant youth often told me their parents' unpredictable work schedules makes it difficult for them to coordinate with other adults. Arranging for a friend or family member to translate is even more difficult in urgent situations, such as when parents need to speak with doctors, police officers, teachers, landlords, or utility companies. Finding an adult to translate is often a challenge, but children—who have had more opportunities to learn English in school than their immigrant parents have—are often already at home. Due to their presumed dependency, young people also have less control over their schedules and often tag along as their parents complete errands anyway.

Despite being poised to step in, young people initially reported that their interpretation work was difficult—especially when they were still in the process of learning a different language themselves. Although the level of language comprehension they need as a language broker is far above their "grade level" in school, they rarely gave up. Instead, they consult dictionaries and online resources to learn the vocabulary and terminology they need. As their capabilities increased, they receive responsibilities and rights that other children are regularly denied by default of their age. The more they translate, the more time they spend with their parents.

The young people I interviewed regularly recalled how satisfying it was to help their parents earn money and other financial rewards. Along the way, they visited their parents' workplaces, spoke with their parents' employers, and interacted with other institutional agents. Other rewards were less tangible but bolstered their self-esteem, pride, and satisfaction, such as when adults, including their parents, deemed them mature, reliable, competent, responsible, and intelligent. This is especially true for elder siblings and daughters of immigrants, who shoulder a disproportionate amount of the language-brokering work and are often prevented from having freedom outside the household.

Indeed, the way they are treated and the rewards they reap likely stand in sharp contrast to their daily experiences in school, where working-class children of color are often perceived as academically inferior and expected to learn a curriculum that is devoid of applicability to their everyday lives.[15] Unlike in school, young language brokers know that the stakes of their translation work are real and high—especially when they speak with employers, health-care providers, police officers, or landlords. Because young people's skills are needed, valued, and rewarded, the circumstances encourage language brokers to take their work seriously and their ability to translate quickly progresses.

As young people become their parents' "mouths" and "ears," their family responsibilities often expand to encompass far more than translation. Because the children of immigrants in this study grew up in working-class households, their language-brokering work revealed their parents' hardships, including their parents' precarious financial situations and issues related to unemployment, lost wages, and landlord-tenant disputes. Learning about their immigrant parents' harsh realities compelled them to take their translation responsibilities even more seriously. They began anticipating their family's needs. Without needing to be asked, they started taking care of their younger siblings, completing additional chores, making important decisions around the house, and advocating for their parents.

Rather than being developmentally limited by their age, language brokers' circumstances—and the trust they receive from their parents and other adults—enable their language-brokering capabilities to flourish. Rather than passively absorbing an ethnic culture that supposedly values familialism, structural circumstances encourage children to view their language-brokering responsibilities as "normal." The survival strategies working-class immigrant youth enact while attempting to ensure their family's survival help to promote intergenerational relationships and a strong sense of reciprocity with their parents.

Ultimately, by bringing young people's experiences to the center of my analysis, this research sheds light on the pivotal role children of immigrants play in compensating for the absence of a robust safety net within the US. The survival strategies employed by these children of immigrants are a direct response to the lack of adequate social citizenship rights granted to working-class immigrant families of color.

Despite being active social agents who develop creative solutions to the forms of inequality their families encounter, young people's ability to enact survival strategies on behalf of their parents is limited because of age-based inequality they experience. Children—even those engaged in "productive" activities—lack full citizenship rights in comparison to adults due to long-standing assumptions about young people's developmental inferiority.[16] Although they often rely on young language brokers to communicate with immigrants of color, English-speaking adults in this study often assumed that children lack the necessary knowledge and capabilities to translate for their families. Indeed, the youth I interviewed often reported that adults spoke to them in a condescending or belittling way, which made them feel as though they were not being taken seriously.

In addition to translating within adult-centric institutions that devalue their skills, youths' language-brokering responsibilities often run counter to age-based expectations of a "normative" childhood that are embedded in—and regularly enforced by—schools. Schools, for example, operate under the assumption that childhood is a time when children need to be protected from the "real" world and "adult" responsibilities.[17] Schools also assume that young people have sufficient free time and resources to complete homework and study for tests after school. Moreover, schools reinforce age expectations by enforcing mandatory attendance policies that penalize children for missing school unless a parent writes a note in English to legitimize the child's absence.

Although children of immigrants are keenly aware of their teachers' expectations and exhibit a strong commitment to obtaining upward mobility, it is difficult for them to prioritize school over family responsibilities. This is especially the case during crisis situations, which require the young people to "drop everything" to help their parents navigate issues such as housing instability, legal problems, and medical emergencies. Because these situations often generate a domino effect that requires the young people to engage in a chain of successive situations, they often have to miss school and have difficulty completing their homework and studying for tests. Without an English-speaking parent who could excuse their absence or speak with their teachers, many working-class immigrant youth of color face a difficult double bind. They are left feeling inadequate about their inability to juggle both their school and family responsibilities.

Both Mexican and Korean Americans experience this double bind, but their inability to balance school and family responsibilities engenders different feelings of disappointment. Because educators often racialize Mexican American families as "deviant,"[18] Mexican American youth often report feeling angry at teachers who harshly judge their parents for presumably failing to provide their children with a "normal" childhood. In contrast, consistent with existing research that demonstrates how educators racialize Asian parents as middle-class minorities who offer significant parental support,[19]

Korean American youth report feeling inadequate for not living up to educators' assumptions that their families are "model minorities." Instead of criticizing the educational system for failing to provide adequate resources for working-class children of immigrants, the model-minority stereotype makes many working-class Korean Americans feel as if their family is responsible for structural problems embedded in school. Ultimately, age intersects with race and class to shape immigrant children's understanding of family and school responsibilities.

Despite accumulating negotiation skills by speaking and advocating for their family in various institutions, age-based inequalities prevent language brokers from drawing on this embodied capital in school. Instead, they are held accountable to ethnocentric and classed expectations about their capabilities. The young people I interviewed, for example, repeatedly said that their teachers expected parents to be the ones taking care of their children. They were also keenly aware that schools expect "students" to prioritize their schoolwork instead of family work. Because schools overlook and stigmatize the realities of working-class immigrant families' lives, the children of immigrants often felt that they have to keep their family lives private from their teachers when crisis situations occur. Considering that school officials often accommodate requests made by White middle-class parents and children,[20] these findings highlight the importance of critically examining how taken-for-granted school policies—which are based on White middle-class values about an "ideal" childhood—help produce and reproduce inequality.

SECURING CITIZENSHIP RIGHTS

Although US institutions fail to provide working-class immigrant youth of color and their families full citizenship rights, the young people develop various strategies when attempting to broker belonging. One such strategy is "doing American," meaning that they use their simultaneously elevated and subordinated status as "outsiders-within"—a place of strength and creativity—to change their family's social and economic realities. For example, because their outsider-within position as working-class bilingual immigrant youth of color enables them to see how age and race hinder their ability to gain resources for their family, they opt to speak "standard English" over the phone whenever possible to increase the likelihood they can pass as "American adults." Furthermore, as bilingual youth, they take advantage of English speakers' inability to speak Spanish or Korean when translating for their parents. That is, young language brokers censor and omit parts of conversations to shield their parents from racialized nativism.

This shielding strategy—which goes unnoticed by English-speaking adults—enables youth to covertly contest those who treat their parents with disrespect. And because omitting parts of the conversation often prevents their parents from feeling angry, it also helps ensure that their parents, especially their dads, come across as amiable "Americans" instead of "angry" people of color—crucial to remaining on good terms with their employers, keeping their jobs, and accessing crucial social services. However, young language brokers also know it is important to appear assertive in some circumstances, such as educational settings when attempting to challenge school authorities' decisions. As a result, they attempt to emulate middle-class behaviors like acting firmly to avoid having their parents, especially their moms, viewed as "submissive" immigrants.

Doing American from an outsider-within position enables children of immigrants—who have limited power and resources—to secure safety, dignity, and welfare for their families. And yet, not all of their strategies are equally successful. Notably, their attempts at posing like rational middle-class American adults in school settings rarely enabled them to change the decisions made by school authorities. Lacking the same resources and forms of social capital that middle-class American parents often possess, the children of immigrants often feel powerless when attempting to counteract racial stereotypes associated with being an "angry person of color" or a "submissive immigrant." However, the young people I interviewed often recalled feeling empowered and proud at their ability to use their bilingual skills to covertly manipulate conversations and shield their parents from racialized nativism, exploitation, and public abuse. When combined with the relatively successful strategy of using the phone to sound like an "American" adult—which was particularly beneficial for Mexican American boys—doing American illustrates the multiple inequalities that marginalized youth must navigate in the attempt to secure citizenship for their family.

In addition to performing American, immigrant youth of color also engage in three forms of "inclusion work" to mobilize culture to present their families as worthy of belonging in a society that excludes them. Because immigrant youth of color are cognizant of how their family deviates from hegemonic representations of "American" families, they mobilize seemingly positive cultural repertoires about "good" immigrants to offset the risk they perceive as "bad" immigrants whose families are a burden on society. To do so, they "Americanize" their parents' journey to the US by presenting their parents as heroic immigrants who left their homelands to achieve the American Dream in the land of opportunity. They also construct their families as collective and hardworking by making use of seemingly positive repertoires about their ethnic cultures. Third, when discussing their imagined futures, youth present themselves as productive citizens by drawing on rhetoric about independence, efficiency, and self-discipline.

The forms of inclusion work youth draw upon, however, vary based on their race. In light of contemporary racial images depicting Mexican immigrants as a problematic underclass, Mexican American youth deploy a wider range of repertoires than Korean American youth when attempting to depict their families as worthy of inclusion. Not only are Mexican Americans more likely to redefine border crossing by constructing their parents as brave risk-takers, but they also claim that obtaining intergenerational mobility is a way they can prove racist people wrong. Furthermore, whereas Korean Americans are more likely to construct "American" children as selfish, Mexican Americans are more likely to construct "American" children as lazy. These differences occur as a result of patterns of racial segregation and meanings embedded in schools, workplaces, and neighborhoods, thus illustrating how young people's positionality within contemporary racial hierarchies inform their attempts at validating their family's presence in the US.

Rather than passively internalizing American values and assimilating into mainstream, children of immigrants—as a less powerful group—strategically put language and culture to use. Regardless of whether they embrace American values, children of immigrants respond to hegemonic meanings of Americanness when attempting to present themselves and their parents as "good" immigrants who are courageous, collective, diligent, and hardworking. For this reason, their strategies should be understood as everyday acts of resistance. It is only because of their position as outsiders-within that they are able to devise strategies that anticipate and help them navigate racialized nativism and adult-centric, White, and English-speaking spaces. My findings thus demonstrate that margin can create moments of subversion, resistance, and potential for empowerment. "Doing American" and "inclusion work" are creative ways for youth to challenge harmful controlling images, maintain their sense of dignity, and gain important resources for their families.

Still, institutional hierarchies that deny social citizenship rights to immigrants make it difficult for children of immigrants to craft strategies that do not involve some aspect of compliance. Regardless of whether they entirely embrace "American" values, their situated performance and discursive strategies of brokering belonging unwittingly reproduce the dominant meanings of Americanness that serve to exclude their families from full citizenship rights in the first place. In a nation where pro-immigrant rhetoric depicting "good" immigrants as hardworking "Americans-in-waiting" coexists with racialized nativism representing immigrants of color as a drain on public resources, children of immigrants attempt to prove their belonging by distancing themselves from "bad" immigrants, who presumably remain less deserving of these same rights. The ways that children of immigrants "perform American" during interactions, as well as how they rearticulate their family's position in society, illustrate how their lives are shaped by the hegemonic meanings of "American" as well as the racialized dichotomy between "good" and "bad" immigrants. In short, while citizenship is "a privilege or assumed right for some," it remains an "allusive status that requires continuous effort to establish oneself as deserving of equal rights and opportunities" for those who are marginalized by race, class, and language.[21]

To the extent that the nation affords people differing amount of citizenship rights based on race, class, gender, language ability, and age, working-class children of immigrants will continue to face difficult double binds. They will also "do American" and engage in inclusion work in an attempt to broker belonging and ensure their family's survival. However, there are ways to increase social and institutional support for language brokers—a topic I discuss next, when suggesting ways to resolve this difficult double bind.

MOVING BEYOND DICHOTOMOUS THINKING AND INCREASING SOCIAL SUPPORT

The solution to resolving the double bind that working-class immigrant youth encounter might seem simple. Perhaps children should just say no to their parents. Indeed, this is what adults, especially educators, often suggest when

I share results from this study. More often than not, they tell me that children should focus on school, not their families.

However, it is difficult to imagine these same people expecting adults, especially mothers, to say no to their children or elderly parents. To the contrary, people often criticize mothers who prioritize their own work and social mobility over their family and childcare responsibilities. Rather than assuming that mothers need to choose between work and their families, research has identified best practices designed to allow women to better navigate this difficult double bind.[22] In this sense, the children of immigrants I interviewed have much in common with the "typical" American adult. It is unlikely they would ever say no to their parents, especially when their parents' or siblings' health is at stake, their families are about to get evicted or deported, or their parents have been in a major car accident. The children of immigrants I interviewed are deeply invested in their "family work" because it helps their parents—who lack full citizenship rights—access crucial institutional resources that are otherwise reserved for English-speaking, middle-class White American adults.

Rather than assuming that children should tell their parents no, it is crucial to move beyond dichotomous understandings of childhood and adulthood altogether. This binary largely overlooks the fact that everyone—regardless of their age, gender, class, and race—is interdependent on others. For instance, White, landowning men initially became "independent" and "rational" citizens by heavily depending on the labor of women and people of color, who were seen too "needy," "childlike," and "uncivilized" to receive full citizenship rights.[23] The impact of this legacy continues today. Because the labor market is stratified by race and gender,[24] so-called self-determined people in high-power careers and positions—especially upper-class White men—regularly rely on free or subsidized labor. This subsidized labor includes unpaid interns, underpaid and overworked employees, nannies, housekeepers, gardeners, repair people, and restaurant staff who play a critical role in shaping the perception that privileged people in positions of power are self-sufficient and independent. Not coincidentally, people of color—who comprise the majority of the current immigrant population—are concentrated in many of these low-paying jobs and occupations.

And yet, as I have demonstrated, the "affordable" and "easy" solutions that those at the top of the social hierarchy rely on to manage work and family commitments exacerbate the double bind that families in more marginalized positions face. Working-class immigrants of color—perceived as "undeserving foreigners"—have few choices other than working in presumably "low-skill" jobs and occupations, where they often face under- or unemployment, exploitation, and work-related injuries. Without access to affordable and safe housing, universal healthcare, paid family and medical leave, adequate translation services, and a living wage, working-class immigrant parents of color have limited time and resources to juggle their family and work commitments. Instead, they come to rely on their children, who activate their double consciousness and bilingual skills in an attempt to resolve systematic issues related to race, gender, and language-based discrimination that their families encounter. Navigating flawed institutions on their parents' behalf while lacking full citizenship rights themselves places working-class children of immigrants in an impossible situation. Given this reality, it is crucial to move beyond the dichotomous thinking that naturalizes the broader system of stratification in work and families. Instead of assuming that "independent" people are the most deserving of full citizenship rights, it is crucial to recognize that people at the top of social hierarchy are dependent on people at the margin to maintain their wealth and status.

There are also practical steps we can take to improve language brokers' lives. Rather than expecting working-class children of immigrants to shoulder more "responsibilities," institutions and policies need to increase social support for language brokering. A necessary first step is raising awareness that immigrants, by law, are entitled to language access. Title VI of the Civil Rights Acts of 1964 mandates language access for federally funded programs, and California's Dymally-Alatorre Bilingual Service Act pertains to state and local agencies that providing public services. Within healthcare contexts in California, Senate Bill 853 mandates that health plans provide interpretation and translation services, while the Kopp Act requires language access in acute care hospitals. However, perhaps because these services are limited or insufficiently advertised, the children of immigrants I interviewed were largely unaware of their family's rights. As a result, they rarely requested an interpreter or encouraged their parents to ask for one.

We also need to shift the way service providers routinely attempt to communicate with others. Although many social service providers I spoke with knew that non-English speakers are entitled to language support, they rarely use California's telephone interpreter services. Instead, they rely on the already overburdened bilingual social service providers, especially when they are pressed for time. Nevertheless, bilingual employees often find it challenging to juggle interpreting tasks alongside their regular job responsibilities. This is particularly taxing because their language proficiency is frequently undervalued and inadequately rewarded within their workplaces. Furthermore, English monolinguals often rely on institutional agents of color who "look" Asian or Latinx even though they are not fully fluent in Spanish or Asian languages. In the event that these bilingual agents are unavailable, some English-speaking agents may rely on their "broken" English or limited vocabularies to communicate with non-English speakers.

The police station where I observed attempted to resolve these issues by seeking help from unpaid volunteers such as myself. On a number of occasions, Korean-speaking immigrants expressed gratitude and reported that they were relieved to talk with someone who was fluent in Korean. Clearly, having bilingual volunteers on site helps improve communication between institutional agents and non-English speakers. However, it is also problematic to rely on volunteers for translation services. Although it became easier for me to translate what the police officers were saying as I became familiar with the staff, the station, and their routines, volunteers are unpaid and susceptible to experiencing burnout. Indeed, it is perhaps for this reason that many police officers perceive volunteers as "unreliable" and often resort to relying on family members or coworkers instead.

For this reason, it remains important to shift the responsibility for providing "free" translation services from non-English speakers, volunteers, and child language brokers to English-speaking institutions. Unlike bilingual institutional agents who translate on an ad hoc basis, interpreters are not distracted by other jobs. The credentialing process also ensures that interpreters are fluent in the language and the terminology needed to discuss the task at hand. Given social service providers' preference for in-person providers, institutions should hire a sufficient number of certified bilingual staff who can speak the most popular languages in the region, especially institutions like hospitals and police stations where emergency situations frequently occur. Alternatively, these institutions could also pay bilingual staff who regularly perform extra work.

It is equally important for schools and teachers to alleviate the double bind working-class immigrant youth experience. Considering that White middle-class children are the ones who come closest to meeting the age-based standards embedded in schools, educators should rethink taken-for-granted school practices like assigning homework, expecting youth to spend hours studying for tests, or enforcing mandatory attendance policies. These practices overlook the realities of children who are marginalized by race, class, and nationality. Not all teenagers have "free" time to complete homework or a dedicated place to study for the tests after school. Nor do all teenagers have parents who can easily communicate with school officials to "excuse" their absence when a family crisis occurs. Reconfiguring age-based expectations embedded in schools is important because many young people in the US, especially those who are marginalized by multiple inequalities, do not follow the "normalized" chronological life stages where one moves from being a "dependent" child to an "independent" adult.

In addition to seeking institutional change, it remains imperative to recognize and respect children's brokering work as real work. Although state policymakers have attempted to prevent children from interpreting in public spaces, children are knowing and reflexive social actors. As my results make clear, they are able to connect their immigrant families to a wide range of institutional resources and information. Because immigrant parents trust their children, they might feel more comfortable speaking with them than with designated translators. Especially in times of crisis or emergency, young people might be the most knowledgeable and best equipped to strategize within their family's constraints. However, many children of immigrants in this study reported having negative interactions with social service providers. Because frontline social service providers possess a large measure of control over the distribution of institutional resources, it is critical to raise service providers' awareness of the importance of treating child language brokers like social agents who are providing a valuable service. Instead of condemning the work of these children as a form of exploitation or demanding that they perform language-brokering work, institutional agents must learn to respect children's experiences and knowledge. This can be as simple as waiting for children to finish interpreting, talking more slowly, explaining complex terms, encouraging them to ask questions, and trying to accommodate their schedules.

Importantly, although children of immigrants frame language-brokering work as "family responsibilities," their work and the subsequent double bind they experience must be understood as the consequences of institutional failures. If we truly care about the well-being of American children, including children of immigrants, the state must be held responsible for resolving the structural problems language brokers are currently attempting to resolve. This means providing better access to social provisions such as healthcare, safe and affordable housing, childcare, livable wages, and paid sick leave for all. It also means reexamining the tax breaks and benefits that disproportionately benefit wealthy people who are perceived to be "independent" and "self-sufficient." Social citizenship is not "charity" or a "handout." Security, protection, well-being, and dignity are basic rights for all people.

MEASURING DIFFERENT OUTCOMES

When I present my research, audience members often ask, "What will happen to these kids when they grow up?" Although I did not conduct a longitudinal study, nearly all my respondents stated that growing up in a working-class immigrant household and shouldering translation responsibilities will help them obtain social mobility. Indeed, it was clear that they had gained a tremendous amount of knowledge and skills from performing language-brokering work. Such work enhances children's ability to solve problems and build their vocabularies. They learn how to manage time, multitask, be responsible, and find information that is not readily available. They also learn how to negotiate as they speak to their parents' clients, employers, landlords, and healthcare providers. Because they care deeply about their parents, they refuse to give up when tasks seemed daunting or time-consuming. Along the way, they learn to persevere—arguably one of the most important qualities to achieving social mobility.

At the same time, the immigrant youth I interviewed came of age during a time of rapid economic, cultural, and social transformations—including growing levels of income and wealth inequality, a rise in anti-immigrant policies, declining social mobility, and the weakening of affirmative action.[25] Indeed, studies have consistently demonstrated that institutional racism and classism make it difficult for upwardly mobile working-class youth of color to translate their aspirations into reality.[26] Having to balance family responsibilities and schoolwork can also negatively affect working-class children's academic performance and life outcomes.[27] Even if they attend and graduate from college, the youth I interviewed—who are largely without the resources, networks, and support that middle-class, White young adults often have access to—may have difficulty translating their degrees to professional-class careers.[28] When paired with the routine forms of social exclusion they experience while brokering and defending their family's belonging in the US, their—especially Mexican Americans'—optimism about their futures may erode over time. Consequently, working-class immigrant youth of color may reevaluate the idea of American Dream as they grow older, especially if they cannot justify their family's presence by achieving intergenerational mobility. In the end, middle-class White children—the group that respondents in this study constructed as lazy and spoiled—are far more likely to obtain social mobility with the help of their parents' networks, resources, and transmittable cultural knowledge, which are highly valued in "mainstream" society.[29]

Still, language brokering offers working-class children of immigrants an opportunity to developed embodied knowledge and skills that more privileged youth often lack. For example, as youth gradually accumulate experiences of interacting with adults, they acquire "people skills." That is, witnessing their parents' struggles leads children to develop a sense of empathy toward other marginalized groups, which can serve as an asset in the future.[30] They become effective and empathetic communicators who know how to ask the right questions in the right way, which might help improve their relationships with family, friends, acquaintances, and coworkers down the line. Importantly, similar to young people who travel long distances to go to school outside their neighborhood,[31] language brokers often develop what W. E. B. Du Bois calls a "double consciousness," meaning they are able to "see" inequality that often remains invisible to people who stay within racially segregated spaces.[32]

Because language brokering is an asset that has the potential to make a significant difference in youth's communities and beyond, I propose changing the evaluative criteria used to measure success in the US. Instead of using White middle-class parameters to evaluate children's academic outcomes, we should strive to create institutions that include language brokers' embodied knowledge. For example, although educators generally recognize the importance of problem solving and communication skills as critical parts of youth development, the classroom is often identified as the main place where learning takes place. However, this study demonstrates that powerful learning experiences can and do occur outside classrooms as well. In acknowledging that language brokers are already engaging in different forms of experiential learning, teachers could begin incorporating students' everyday experiences into the curriculum. One way to do so is by creating more flexible and open-ended homework assignments that privilege helping others and solving problems in everyday life. In this way, language brokers could readily apply their bilingual skills and everyday experiences to different contexts while getting "credit" for doing the work that they are already performing out of necessity. Furthermore, making the curriculum relevant to students' lives would have the added bonus of combating the assumption that immigrant youths' childhoods are inferior to the "typical" White, middle-class childhood. Valuing and normalizing diverse family structures within school classrooms would, in turn, ensure that all students have the opportunity to learn from and reap the benefits of language brokers' valuable skills and expertise.

Finally, we must treat language brokers' social location at the margin of language, race and class as a special place of strength. Similar to the ways that people "undo" gender at the interactional level,[33] marginalized youths' worldviews, derived from their particular social location, can potentially effect change beyond their families when they, for example, become teachers,[34] social workers, [35] healthcare providers,[36] or activists.[37] In fact, it was from her own outsider-within status that Patricia Hill Collins produced Black feminist thought—a theoretical framework that has profoundly shaped the study of sociology as a discipline.[38] Furthermore, as the historical changes of the 1960s and 1970s suggest, the boundaries of what seems possible can expand when the "right" historical circumstances provide people at the margin with greater opportunities to join larger movements. In short, outsider-within ways of seeing the world can "reaffirm human subjectivity and intentionality" and produce cumulative effects on power relations and inform organized movements.[39] When combined with their simultaneously elevated and subordinated status as outsiders-within, the specialized form of knowledge that language brokers accrue while brokering belonging can create moments of resistance and empowerment that reverberate far beyond their own family's lives.

There is much that adults can learn from children's experiences of translating multiple and intersecting forms of inequality. Their attempts at securing citizenship for their families not only illuminate the contradictions that undergird our national identity but also the disjuncture between our nation's beliefs in equality and its actual practices of exclusion. Translating their experiences into lasting change requires us to look not at individuals or families but at broader systems, institutions, and interactions in which all groups are embedded but have particular ramifications for those living at the margins. It will also require us to imagine new possibilities for inclusion and metrics for "success," where belonging is measured by how empathetic, compassionate, and conscious "Americans" become.

APPENDIX

Language Brokers primarily draws from eighty in-depth interviews with working-class Mexican and Korean American language brokers who grew up translating for their immigrant parents. Interviews are well suited for interrogating people's deeply held perceptions, experiences, and desires, including their "honorable" or idealized expectations.[1] Interviews also allow researchers to compare the salience of different types of narratives across groups.[2] When combined with the additional twenty interviews I conducted with healthcare providers and my six months of participant observation research at a Southern California police station, this methodological approach allowed me to compare how institutionalized inequality shapes working-class Korean and Mexican American young people's perceptions of their language-brokering work.

GATHERING RESPONSES FROM LANGUAGE BROKERS

I recruited most language brokers from various community-based organizations serving low-income youth in Los Angeles. During the recruitment process, I shared my own experiences of growing up in an immigrant household, including the translation responsibilities I shouldered for my working-class immigrant parents. I also posted recruitment flyers in front of high schools, churches, and parks in Los Angeles neighborhoods with high percentages of low-income immigrants of color. The recruitment flyer, which asked young people to share their experience of translating for their parents, also indicated that interview participants would receive a $20 gift card for their participation in my study.

Although I initially worried that youth might not want to speak about language-brokering experiences with a stranger, having a similar upbringing appeared to reduce the power imbalance between an adult researcher and young people; more than one hundred potential respondents contacted me during subsequent weeks. Many told me they were surprised—but excited—that a researcher was writing about their family's experiences, and the vast majority of youth I spoke with expressed a sense of enthusiasm about the project. Jonathan, a seventeen-year-old Mexican American, articulated a perspective that many young people shared when initially speaking with me. He said, "The public should know about our experiences—why we need to and want to help our parents. They are my parents, not just dumb Mexicans who can't speak English." This desire to "be heard" by "the public" ultimately became a central theme of my analysis.

To select youth from low-income families, I surveyed potential respondents about their parents' level of education and occupation, family home ownership, and eligibility for free or reduced lunches, which is the federal marker of experiencing poverty in childhood. While college degree attainment often serves as a proxy for being middle-class in the United States, existing literature has demonstrated that having a college degree does not fully account for immigrants' postmigration socioeconomic status. Not only does college completion take on different meanings in other countries,[3] but racial and linguistic discrimination also makes it difficult for immigrants to translate their educational credential into favorable occupations in the United States.[4] As a result, I interviewed young people whose parents had graduated from college in Mexico or Korea only if they qualified for free or reduced-price lunches and had parents who worked low-wage jobs in the United States.

Table 1 includes more detailed demographic information about my interviewees. Respondents (n = 80) consisted of 37 Korean Americans (22 girls, 15 boys) and 43 Mexican Americans (25 girls, 18 boys). When making comparisons among respondents, 30 percent of Korean mothers and 35 percent of

Korean fathers had graduated from college. Seven percent of Mexican mothers and 9 percent of Mexican fathers had a college degree. Although interviewees' ages ranged from 12 to 23, 90 percent of respondents were high school students, with an average age of 17 years. Respondents were either born in the US (n = 32) or immigrated to the US prior to turning 12 (n = 48). Only 6 participants were only children. Among respondents who had siblings, the majority (n = 60) were the eldest child, which is in line with existing work suggesting that gender and birth order affects siblings' participation in language-brokering work.[5] Furthermore, 23 percent of respondents were undocumented immigrants, and 26 percent had at least one undocumented parent.

While speaking with youth, I collected detailed information about their experiences by asking follow-up questions to probe for details about specific translation encounters they described. The recollections I solicited are what

TABLE 1.   Characteristics of Young People Sampled for Interviews

	MEXICAN (%)	KOREAN (%)	TOTAL (%)
GENDER			
Male	42	41	41
Female	58	59	58
GENERATION STATUS			
1.5 generation	67	70	69
2nd generation	33	30	31
SOCIOECONOMIC BACKGROUND			
Single-parent household	39	27	34
Free or reduced-priced lunch	93	92	93
Mother graduated from college	8	32	19
Father graduated from college	9	35	22
At least one parent working in low-wage job	93	92	93
At least one parent owns a house	0	0	0
IMMIGRATION STATUS			
US citizen	42	43	43
Lawful permanent resident	26	46	34
Undocumented	32	11	23
At least one undocumented parent	40	11	26
	N=43	N=37	N=80

Arlie Hochschild calls "magnified moments," or "episodes of heightened importance, either epiphanies, moments of intense glee or unusual insight, or moments in which thing go intensely but meaningfully wrong."[6] Because asking respondents to reflect on their emotions often yields rich data, I asked youth to describe their "meta-feelings," or how they felt about their feelings.[7] Throughout each interview, I remained alert to respondents' nonverbal cues, including their use of metaphors and jokes, with the intention of moving beyond respondents' tendency to present the most "honorable" description of their lives.[8] Taken together, these interview strategies allowed me to capture what behaviors and desires youth perceived as admirable, while also identifying how social forces shaped their ability to navigate different institutions and spaces and claim belonging.

Interviews were semi-structured, lasted between one to three hours, and took place at a location chosen by the interviewee. Discussions centered on four general topics: (1) knowledge of their parents' immigration experiences; (2) relationship with their parents; (3) understanding of family labor, including language-brokering experiences; and (4) experience with school and peers, including any future life plans. I conducted interviews until I reached a point of saturation, as indicated by encountering repeated themes in new interviews.[9] Interviews were audio-recorded, transcribed with the interviewee's permission, and conducted in accordance with Institutional Review Board protocols. Minors received permission from their parents before participating in the interview. The names of all my interviewees have been changed in this book to protect their confidentiality.

When analyzing data, I used an inductive analytic approach and initially read transcripts line by line to generate emergent trends from the data.[10] One initial emergent theme revolved around a lack of translation services, which compelled youth to begin "helping" their parents. Although youth were committed to shouldering what they considered "family" responsibilities, their narratives also reveal how certain school practices—such as mandatory attendance, significant study time for exams, and assigned homework—overlooked the realities of working-class children of immigrants' lives. As a result, many youth felt torn between their desire to "help" their families and succeed in school. Moreover, another initial recurring theme was the experience of encountering English-speaking adults who enforced racial, language, and age inequalities during translation interactions. Therefore, I analyzed the strategies these language brokers use to confront these inequalities in translation interactions. In the process, I identified the subtle tactics that they use to secure vital resources for their families. I also identified the recurring cultural repertoires they employ to portray their parents in the most honorable manner during the interview process.

It's important to note that their narratives are not simply recounted events. When discussing their family lives, youth in this study selectively employed specific past events and supplemented their knowledge with language that closely aligned with the commonly shared repertoires about "good" immigrants. Through this approach, these youth endeavored to portray their family's migration history, present actions, and future aspirations in a positive light. When coupled with the various forms of racialized nativism their families face in the US, this process illustrates how children of immigrants can harness culture as a toolkit, strategically employing it to shape a narrative that might challenge the prevailing stereotypes. Consequently, their collective narratives serve as a form of resistance as these youth endeavor to redefine their social identities in relation to other people, particularly those holding more power.

After establishing the main themes, I further divided the responses into thematic categories to compare how their responses varied across contexts and situations. Finally, I stratified my data by respondents' race to identify whether and how Korean American and Mexican American youths differently experienced and responded to the racialized nativism they encountered. Based on the analysis of the similarities and differences in respondents' accounts, I developed a new theoretical understanding of how lack of citizenship shapes working-class youth's subjective realities, as well as how their racialized experiences shape the ways youth enact Americanness and claim membership in the larger society.

GATHERING RESPONSES FROM HEALTHCARE PROVIDERS AND POLICE OFFICERS

When I spoke with language brokers, they repeatedly said that translating was especially difficult when their parents needed to speak with healthcare providers and police officers. As a result, I supplemented the interviews I conducted with youth with twenty interviews with healthcare workers and six months of ethnographic research at a police department in Southern California. Although I interviewed two White doctors (one man and one woman), almost all healthcare workers that I targeted were nurses. I focused on nurses because language brokers were far more likely to talk about their interactions with nurses than other healthcare providers. Indeed, because nurses are the ones that conduct intake exams, care for patients, administer medications, and explain follow-up care instructions, nurses' job responsibilities position them to have the most interactions with language brokers. Respondents were recruited through snowball sampling, meaning that I asked each interviewed respondent for referrals to their coworkers. Among the 18 nurses that I interviewed, 16 were women (7 White, 2 Black, 4 Asian American, 3 Latinx) and 2 were men (1 White and 1 Latinx). Interviews with healthcare providers lasted between fifty minutes and two hours and were conducted in their homes, hospitals, or coffee shops. Interviews focused on three areas: (1) their daily routines; (2) their experience of working with diverse patients, including non-English-speaking immigrants of color; and (3) their perspectives about and encounters with child language brokers.

Initially, I attempted to interview police officers to get their perspectives and experience of interacting with children of immigrants who serve as language brokers for their parents. Upon attempting to interview the first police officer, however, it became clear that it would be difficult to gather rich data from interviews alone. For example, when I asked about the racial composition of his workplace, he said, "You tricked me. I thought you were gonna ask me about kids. You didn't tell me this project was going to be about race. I can't answer that kind of stuff." The interview ended shortly thereafter.

Although I contemplated giving up on this aspect of my project, I came across an advertisement seeking a bilingual volunteer to interpret at a police station in Southern California that was situated in a low-income community that served a racially diverse population. I immediately contacted the officer in charge. During my brief screening interview—which was conducted in English and did not include an evaluation of my ability to speak Korean—I explained the purpose of my research and was granted permission to gather data. Their pressing need for an interpreter who spoke Korean appeared to outweigh any concerns they might have had about my research. I conducted participant observation at least once a week for approximately two hours per visit. I also visited the police station at different days and times in an attempt to observe and interact with different police officers. Although my responsibility was to interpret for Korean immigrants, I was able to observe and document the activities of police officers when they were interacting with non-Korean speakers. When I was interpreting for Korean speakers, I made mental notes and subsequently jotted them down. After my visit, I expanded my handwritten notes into detailed fieldnotes in which I reconstructed conversations and interactions that I had observed.

On most days, the station was extremely crowded, but I used occasional lulls in activity to have informal conversations with officers, all of whom knew I was conducting research about the experiences of language brokers. During these conversations, I asked clarifying questions about events I observed. Perhaps because I was volunteering alongside them, most police officers were far more willing to speak openly about their experiences than the officer I had attempted to formally interview.

Because young people's voices are rarely included in sociological research, I primarily draw from the interviews with language brokers in this book. However, the supplemental data I gathered with nurses and police officers was critical in allowing me to more fully understand how language is used to exclude immigrants of color and why youth feel compelled to translate for their parents in the first place. The tendency to prioritize efficiency over equality in crowded and underfunded institutions ultimately compels language brokers to broker belonging on behalf of their family members.

NOTES

Chapter 1

1. This information is outdated; the COVID reinfection rate has gone up since 2022. At the same time, the question demonstrates how people, especially immigrant families, tried to keep track of shifting information as the pandemic unfolded.

2. Foner and Dreby 2011.

3. Katz 2014.

4. Author's calculations using US Census Bureau 2010 American Community Survey 1-year estimates.

5. Scholars have employed various terms such as "family interpreters" (Valdés, 2003), "advocates" (Abel Valenzuela, 1999), "problem solvers" (Park, 2005), and "para"-phrasers (Orellana, Dorner, and Pulido 2003) to describe young people who utilize their bilingual skills to speak, listen, read, write, and represent their immigrant family members. Here, I use the widely accepted term "language broker" to underscore how children act as agents when mediating conversations, using their bilingualism with the clear intent to serve the interests of their family. While I interchangeably use *interpreting* or *translating* throughout this book, what bilingual children of immigrants ultimately do is much more than explaining words. Despite the unequal power dynamic they have to navigate, they broker belonging using their bilingual abilities.

6. Orellana 2009.

7. For instance, see Associated Press 1991; Flores 1993; Gold 1999; Hedges 2000; Kratochvil 2001; Nissman 2004; Romney 2003.

8. Hedges 2000.

9. Orellana 2009.

10. Fueled by the surge in European immigration into the US at the turn of the twentieth century, early assimilation theorists hypothesized that children of immi-

grants would eventually integrate into the "mainstream" as they shed their ethnic culture and absorbed "American" culture and values (Gordon 1964; Park 1950; Warner and Srole 1945). However, as increasing numbers of immigrants of color began migrating from Asia and Latin America after 1965, scholars began to challenge the one-dimensional "straight-line" approach of classical assimilation theory.

11. For example, introduced by sociologists Alejandro Portes and Min Zhou (1993), "segmented assimilation theory" attempted to account for the experiences of immigrants of color in the US, who are less likely to experience the upward mobility that earlier waves of European children of immigrants experienced. Portes and Zhou argued that instead of following one pathway to assimilation and absorbing White, middle-class values, nonwhite children of immigrants would experience downward mobility if they absorbed the "underclass" values that other residents in "inner city" neighborhoods were presumed to possess. Nonetheless, it was assumed that immigrant parents could buffer their children from absorbing the so-called deleterious values of those around them if they successfully passed down their "ethnic" cultural values. In recent years, neoclassical assimilation theorists project more optimistic outcomes for children of immigrants. According to Richard Alba and Victor Nee (2003), institutional changes brought about by the civil rights movement have dismantled many overt forms of racial discrimination that once prevented immigrants of color from experiencing upward mobility. With the "declining significance of race" in the US, neoclassical assimilation theorists assume that nonwhite immigrants can now join the mainstream (Alba and Nee 2003).

12. Other sociologists have explored assimilation patterns among children of immigrants. Drawing from interviews with young adults of immigrant parents in New York, sociologist Philip Kasinitz and his colleagues (2008) discovered that these young individuals are increasingly integrating into the American mainstream, often outperforming "native-born" groups. While I am referring to some of the most influential research in the field of sociology, this body of literature primarily revolves around whether and how children are assimilating into the mainstream society.

13. Indeed, race scholars have criticized the "rebirth" of assimilation theory, showing how assimilation theories fail to fully account for structural forms of racial inequalities in the US (Jung 2009; Kim 2008a; Omi and Winant 2014; Park 2005; Treitler 2015). For example, in his thorough assessment of segmented assimilation theory, Moon-Kie Jung (2009) argued that segmented assimilation theory depicts the American "underclass" as "a cauldron of contagious social ills" (387), while uncritically celebrating the cultural values immigrants presumably possess. In this process, segmented assimilation theory also reinforces existing racial stereotypes: Asian immigrants are inevitably depicted as "model minorities," whereas Mexican immigrants are racialized as a problematic "underclass" (Kwon 2015). Additionally, because this line of scholarship tends to theorize culture as a set of static values internalized by individuals, it risks perpetuating essentialist and overly deterministic understandings of culture that leave little room for human agency (Jung 2009; Kwon 2022; Lamont and Mizrachi 2012).

14. Apart from mainstream journalists who have posited that language brokering

leads to a familial role reversal, scholars have also contended that the tendency of children of immigrants to acquire English at a faster pace than their parents can disrupt intergenerational relationships.

According to sociologist Alejandro Portes and Ruben Rumbaut (2001), children of immigrants, who have greater acculturative opportunities—including the opportunity to learn English—through school, peers, and the media, often internalize "American" values faster than their parents. They argue that this acculturative gap can create familial role reversal and undermine immigrant parents' authority—an outcome termed "dissonant acculturation." Additionally, as Marjorie Orellana (2009) has documented, numerous early studies on children's caregiving practices in their households have portrayed their labor contribution as a manifestation of "parentification." However, scholars focusing on young language brokers argue that such perspectives not only imply an overly static power dynamic between parents and children (Crafter and Iqbal 2021) but also overlook the collaborative efforts that immigrant families invest in navigating various institutions (Valdés, 2003) and the forms of care work that children manage to facilitate immigrant settlement processes (García-Sánchez, 2018; Orellana 2009). In this book, I expand upon these arguments to underscore how racialized nativism and other structural inequalities experienced by immigrants of color in the US compel young people to act as brokers of belonging or social citizenship for their families.

15. Marshall 1950.

16. Glenn 2002, 19.

17. Fraser and Gordon 1992.

18. Bloemraad, Korteweg, and Yurdakul 2008.

19. For instance, in 1790, Congress determined that full citizenship rights—including the right to vote—should exclusively be reserved for White men who owned property. Their ability to "own" property in the US was achieved through the enslavement, genocide, and conquest of people of color, but this unequal distribution of rights was justified through racialized, classed, gendered, and nativist imagery (Glenn 2002; Lopez 2006; Ong 2003). This imagery depicted White landowning men as "civilized" and therefore superior to all other people on the basis of their "fitness of self-government" and perceived ability to fight the "Indians" and prevent enslaved Black people from revolting (Jacobson 1999, 19).

20. For example, despite gaining recognition as a separate quasi-sovereign nation in 1786, the US government prevented Indigenous peoples from obtaining full citizenship rights. Instead, they were often forced to sign treaties and relocate to reservations (Almaguer 2008; Lopez 2006). Even as Black people and Indigenous peoples ostensibly gained access to certain political and civil rights through the passage of the Thirteenth Amendment, both groups were denied access to citizenship rights through the mid-twentieth century through policies and practices like racial covenants, poll taxes, and Jim Crow laws that legalized racial segregation (Jacobson 1999; Lopez 2006). The abolition of slavery also set the stage for the recruitment of low-wage Asian laborers to the US, most of whom were men from China and Japan. And yet, federal laws prevented Asian immigrant men from becoming naturalized citizens. Racialized as "coo-

lies" or "yellow peril," Asians—deemed "aliens ineligible for citizenship"—were also prevented from owning and leasing land (Glenn 2002; Molina 2006; Saxton 1971; Takaki 1989). As the number of Asian men in Western states grew, lawmakers eventually restricted immigration from Asian countries through the passage of immigration laws such as the Chinese Exclusion Act of 1882, the Gentlemen's Agreement of 1907, and the Immigration Act of 1917, which caused major labor shortages in sectors like railroads, agriculture, mining, and construction (Espiritu 1997; Takaki 1989). To resolve this labor shortage, desperate US employers hired contractors to recruit Mexican workers by any means necessary (Massey, Durand, and Malone 2002). For this reason, the era of Asian exclusion coincided with the era of the enganche (the hook or indentured), and Mexican laborers started migrating to the US in large numbers at the beginning of the twentieth century (Massey et al. 2002). However, Mexican American men's relatively higher status as "loyal" workers in relation to Asian and Black men was short lived. Repatriation programs replaced previous "assimilation" programs, and Mexican immigrants who remained in the US were racialized as threats, thus subjecting Mexican immigrants to nativism and racist politics that had previously been reserved for Asian immigrant groups (Molina 2006).

21. As the number of people of color living within US states and territories rapidly increased throughout the early to mid-1900s, the citizenship rights once reserved for White men gradually expanded to include other groups of people. For example, much like Asian and Mexican immigrations, Southern and Eastern European immigrants who arrived in the US between 1880 and 1920 also lacked basic rights, including access to education, equal employment opportunities, and safe and affordable housing. However, casting oppositional and seemingly negative qualities—such as dependency and unproductivity—onto people of color allowed people who belonged to these immigrant groups to claim Whiteness and gain access to better institutional resources (Guglielmo 2003; Jacobson 1999; Roediger 1991; Saxton 1971). Furthermore, the passage of the Nineteenth Amendment in 1920, which granted political citizenship to White women, was largely based on the racist assumptions that White women deserved to vote because they were responsible for birthing and raising the next generation of "citizens" (Glenn 2002). Indeed, some of the leading advocates of women's rights argued that US-born White women's fecundity would protect the nation from those who were seen as less "civilized"—especially Black, Indigenous, and Chinese people (Glenn 2002). Because European immigrants' and White women's inclusion was defined in relation to the exclusion of others, the category of citizenship expanded in ways that continued to prevent people of color—including Mexican and Asian immigrants—from obtaining full citizenship rights.

22. Although the civil rights movement successfully outlawed many de jure forms of inequality in the 1950s and 1960s, systemic forms of inequality continue to prevent people of color from accessing many of the civil, political, and social dimensions of citizenship that are necessary for ensuring full access to safe, secure, and dignified lives. For example, scholars and politicians attributed the poverty that many Black people experienced after the civil rights movement to their "dysfunctional" and "morally inferior" values and attitudes (Bonilla-Silva 2017; Omi and Winant 2014). Dubbed

the "culture of poverty" in the 1960s—and embedded within policies, institutional practices, and everyday discourses—this racialized logic depicted Black people as undeserving of full citizenship rights due to their presumed inability to pull themselves up by their bootstraps (Bonilla-Silva 2017; Omi and Winant 2014). Indeed, in the 1980s, Ronald Reagan deployed racialized and gendered rhetoric that depicted Black mothers as "welfare queens" to justify the government's decision to slash funding of social welfare programs (Collins 2002). These controlling images legitimized inequality by constructing poor people—especially poor women of color—as "undeserving" of governmental "handouts" because they were "getting something for nothing" (Fraser and Gordon 1992, 50), thereby obfuscating the ways that systemic forms of inequality have historically prevented Black people from accessing jobs and occupations that pay a living wage.

23. Bonilla-Silva 2017; Feagin 1991; Lipsitz 2006; Rothenberg 2016.

24. Feagin 1991; Rothenberg 2016.

25. Many social welfare policies have been enacted to ensure White men's social citizenship rights, especially in the times of economic upheaval. For example, after the collapse of housing markets during the Great Depression, the government passed numerous policies under the New Deal to support the poor. And yet, policies such as the Wagner Act and the Social Security Act denied benefits to farm workers and domestics, thus ultimately excluding many women and people of color from receiving the protection afforded to White men (Lipsitz 2006). The Federal Housing Administration and the Veterans Administration also provided substantial subsidies for potential homeowners. However, the major beneficiaries of these government benefits were White men as numerous racists practices such as "confidential" city surveys and appraisers' manuals ensured that funding was not distributed among people of color (Lipsitz 2006). Instead of fighting for universal healthcare and pensions for all, trade unions in the post–World War II period further protected the citizenship rights of White unionized workers by providing them with pensions, private health insurance, and job security. While people often perceive these social policies as important means to helping ensure intergenerational mobility for many families, White men have accrued the most wealth and safety from these government benefits.

26. Charles and Grusky 2005; Collins 2019; Glass, Simon, and Andersson 2016; Gornick and Meyers 2003.

27. Gerstel 2011; Swartz 2009.

28. Expectations that family members will care for one another are activated and intensified in times of crisis, such as when families experience economic hardship, illness, or problems with work (Gerstel 2011; Swartz 2009).

29. Hochschild and Machung 1989; also see Budig and England 2001; Damaske 2011; DeVault 1999; Fuwa 2004; Hays 1996.

30. Hochschild 2012; Parreñas 2015.

31. Glenn 2002; Hondagneu-Sotelo 2007.

32. Because women of color have often worked outside their home to offset the poverty brought about by institutional racism, they have often viewed work outside their own home as integral to their family's survival and have developed strategies to

balance work and family responsibilities (Collins 2002; Dow 2019; Espiritu 1997; Glenn 1992). For example, Black women have historically relied on "othermothers," or relatives or close friends who share child-rearing responsibilities with biological mothers (Collins 2002). Similarly, a system known as *compadrazgo*, or godparenting, helps ensure Mexican Americans are able to rely on extended family networks for financial and child-rearing support (Thornton Dill 1988). Furthermore, Chinese immigrants who were unable to form nuclear families due to racist and sexist immigration policies that excluded Asian women from migrating to the US developed family-type relationships with close friends or "fictive" kindships to balance work and family responsibilities (Glenn 1983; Takaki 1989).

33. Van Hook and Glick 2007.

34. Abrego 2014; Dreby 2010; Glenn 1983; Parreñas 2015.

35. Kibria 1993.

36. Elliott, Powell, and Brenton 2015.

37. Pugh 2014; also see Corsaro 1992; García-Sánchez 2018.

38. Estrada 2019; Lopez 2003.

39. Antonini 2010; Chung 2016; Crafter and Iqbal 2022; Delgado 2020; García-Sánchez 2014, 2018; Katz 2014; Kwon 2013, 2015; Orellana 2009; Tse 1995; Valdés, 2003.

40. Estrada 2019; Park 2005; Song 1999.

41. Omi and Winant 2014.

42. Collins 2002.

43. Patricia Hill Collins (2002) originally developed the concept of controlling images to understand the gendered forms of racism that Black Americans face in the US. She argued that racialized and gendered imagery has historically helped legitimize Black people's limited access to full citizenship rights. For instance, Black women were racialized as "mammies"—or loyal, submissive servants or "surrogate mothers in Black face"—to justify the system of slavery, but controlling images have shifted throughout history to justify Black people's social position in the racial hierarchy. In more recent years, this mammy image reconfigured into the "matriarch" image, which has helped to confine Black women to "mummified professions" in low-paid services long after the abolition of slavery. A growing body of research has extended Collins's concept to identify how different racialization processes reinforce racial domination (Kim 1999; Gold 2004; Saito 2009; Xu and Lee 2013).

44. Kim 1999; Kim 2008b; Sanchez 1997.

45. Chavez 2013; Espiritu 2003; Park 2011.

46. Calavita 1996, 300.

47. Calavita 1996; Chavez 2013.

48. This image emerged around the time when the Immigration Act of 1965 abolished national-origin quotas and allowed family members to migrate to the US. The policy, however, was not expected to produce a drastic change in the number of Asian immigrants since only a very small number of Asian Americans were qualified at the time to bring their families to the US. Initially, Korean immigrants took advantage of the provision designed to recruit "professionals" and persons with "exceptional ability

in the sciences and arts." Because this wave of Korean immigrants was selected along the lines of education and class, Korean Americans in the US today are largely middle class (Min 1998), although social class background has become more diversified with the increasing number of Koreans migrating under the category of family reunification (Lew 2006).

49. Partly due to the selective nature of the Immigration and Nationality Act of 1965, Asian Americans tend to display relatively higher academic and career outcomes (Lee and Zhou 2015).

50. Chung 2016; Kim 1999; Lew 2006; Louie 2004; Park 2008.

51. Chung 2016; Kim 1999; Park 2008; Pyke 2000.

52. Espiritu 2003; Kim 2008b; Park 2005; Tuan 1998.

53. Kibria 2002; Kim 2008b; Kwon 2014; Lew 2006; Louie 2004.

54. The booming economy of the Roaring Twenties and the labor shortages during WWI temporarily shielded Mexican Americans from the harsh exclusionary practices that had targeted Asian Americans. Various Americanization programs attempted to foster patriotism among Mexican Americans (Massey et al. 2002; Molina 2006).

55. Calavita 1996; Chavez 2013; Massey et al. 2002.

56. Chavez 2013; Park 2011; Reese 2005.

57. Calavita 1996; Chavez 2013; Park 2011.

58. Golash-Boza and Hondagneu-Sotelo 2013; Menjívar and Abrego 2012.

59. De Genova 2002; Dreby 2015; Gonzales 2016.

60. Kim 1999; Molina 2006; Saito 1998.

61. For exceptions to this trend, see Lee 2015; Lew 2006; Valdez 2011; Vallejo 2012.

62. Du Bois 1903, 1920.

63. hooks 1984, vii.

64. hooks 1984, vii.

65. The term "outsider-within" denotes a distinct viewpoint arising from the social position of marginalized individuals. While Collins (1986) originally coined this term to capture the unique perspective that Black women develop due to their multiple marginalized identities, I adopt this term in my book to illustrate how children of immigrants employ their "in-between" status as a means of navigating intersecting inequalities and striving to secure citizenship rights for their families. Their position as an outsider-within often subjects them to oppression, yet it also provides an avenue for empowerment, enabling them to counter this oppression by creatively employing their status as working-class bilingual youth of color.

66. Corsaro 1992; Pugh 2014; Thorne 1993.

67. Corsaro 1992; Pugh 2014; Thorne 1993.

68. Solberg 1997; Taft 2019.

69. Pugh 2014; Taft 2019.

70. Zelizer 1985.

71. Rorabaugh 1988.

72. Mintz 2004.

73. In the 1820s, religious leaders began advocating for public education as a way to instill self-discipline, respect, time management, and literacy in young people between the ages of six and fourteen.

74. Kett 1977.

75. Peavy and Smith 1999.

76. Zelizer 1985.

77. Mintz 2004, 2831–32.

78. Clement 1997.

79. There were other factors that accounted for this shift. In the late nineteenth century, labor unions demanded a "family wage" that would allow male breadwinners to provide for the entire family alone (Mintz 2004). At the beginning of the twentieth century, psychologists also started to depict adolescence as a unique stage in which young people experience emotional instability (Mintz 2004). Convinced that the proper adult supervision is essential during this state of hormonal transition, many psychologists argued that all adolescents needed to spend time in high schools (Mintz 2004).

80. Zelizer 1985.

81. García-Sánchez 2018; Lesko 2012.

82. Orellana 2009; García-Sánchez 2018.

83. As Marjorie Orellana points out (2009), even some scholarly accounts depict the rapidly increasing number of immigrants and their children in the US as a major problem with which key institutions like the educational system must contend.

84. See https://obamawhitehouse.archives.gov/the-press-office/2012/06/15/remarks-president-immigration.

85. Shedd 2015.

86. Bettie 2014; Howell 1973.

87. Lew 2006.

88. Logan and Stults 2011.

89. Lichter, Parisi, and Taquino 2015; Logan and Stults 2011.

90. Hondagneu-Sotelo 2007; Ramirez 2011.

91. US Census Bureau 2020.

92. California Bilingual Services Act, Sec. 7290 et seq., 2010.

Chapter 2

1. Research focusing on the perspectives of young language brokers in healthcare facilities has highlighted the increased difficulty for children in mediating communication in these settings due to procedures that are not well-known, language that is specialized, and the urgency involved in such circumstances (Katz, 2014). Additionally, children often navigate tensions between differing opinions among their family members and healthcare providers regarding treatment, which can leave them feeling uncomfortable (García-Sánchez, 2014). I build on these studies to demonstrate how the institutional context and the English-speaking authorities' perceptions about low-income immigrants of color shape the ways in which young language brokers step in to resolve the structural problems.

2. Cohen, Moran-Ellis, Smaie. 1999; García-Sánchez 2018; Katz 2014; Orellana 2009.

3. For instance, Cohen et al. (1999), who explored the perspectives of doctors in the UK, discovered that they were more hesitant to disclose complicated and sensitive topics to child language brokers during consultations. This hesitancy was rooted in the perception that children should remain innocent or lack the knowledge to convey complex medical information. Similarly, Katz (2014), who interviewed healthcare providers in Los Angeles, found that they were reluctant to depend on young people for interpretation, as they believed that some of the information might be age-inappropriate for children. Despite this reluctance, these studies reveal that healthcare providers still rely on children and family members due to limited language support available within healthcare facilities.

4. Especially in times of crisis, many working-class women, lacking affordable and safe childcare options, have to bring children to social service agencies. These crowded institutions, however, are often hostile to children (Hays 2003). They frequently lack inviting decor, friendly staff, and age-appropriate books, toys, and games that would help keep children entertained. Often in my observations, there weren't enough seats for young children to sit quietly. All this likely further exacerbated working-class mothers' inability to access social services.

5. Studies have demonstrated that many immigrant women are afraid to report incidents of domestic violence to the police because of a lack of institutionalized language support, concerns about their legal status, social isolation, and economic instability (Menjívar and Salcido 2002).

6. Paik 2021.

7. Hays 2003; Paik 2021.

8. In fact, there are multiple 24/7 medical interpreter companies that provide language support in more than two hundred languages.

9. Wingfield 2019.

10. Previous studies have demonstrated that "equity work" is even more imposing for healthcare professionals at the bottom of occupational-status hierarchies, like nursing aides and health technicians (Wingfield 2019). Considering that patients often question nursing aides' competency, especially if they are women of color, healthcare providers' attempts to communicate with their patients by relying on these workers' unpaid labor likely redoubles the difficulties they face on the job.

11. Calarco 2020; Lareau 2011.

12. Cobas et al. 2022, 10.

13. Wingfield 2019.

Chapter 3

1. Research consistently finds that the work of actively facilitating the immigrant settlement process falls on the shoulders of immigrant women. After migrating to the US, immigrant men's earning capacity often declines, whereas the proliferation of feminized low-skill service jobs in the US increases immigrant women's earning potential. In the case of migrants from Asia and Latin America, for example, social net-

works channel women into low-wage service occupations (Hondagneu-Sotelo 2007; Kibria 1993). Despite immigrant women's greater rate of participation in the labor market, they also continue to perform unpaid "invisible" labor such as housework, care work, volunteer work, and the mediating work of navigating government bureaucracies (Kibria 1993).

2. Sanchez 1997.

3. Glenn 2010; Hondagneu-Sotelo 2007; Lew 2006; Park and Pellow 2013.

4. Glenn 2010; Hondagneu-Sotelo 2007; Park and Pellow 2013; Parreñas 2015.

5. Hondagneu-Sotelo 2007; Min 1996; Lee 2002; Lew 2006.

6. Glenn 1983; Hondagneu-Sotelo 2007; Kibria 1993; Lee 2002; Lew 2006; Min 1996; Park and Pellow 2013.

7. Espiritu 1999 ; Glenn 2002; Hondagneu-Sotelo 2007; Lew 2006; Zinn 1989.

8. This aligns with research that has explored how children of immigrants leverage their bilingual skills to facilitate their parents' interactions with various institutions. For instance, see Marjorie Orellana's (2009) groundbreaking studies on Latinx language brokers.

9. See Orellana, Dorner, and Pulido (2003) for an in-depth exploration of the diverse domains in which children of immigrants act as language brokers for their families.

10. Hochschild 2012.

11. In comparison to Mexican Americans, Korean Americans were more likely to recall times when they struggled to locate adult bilingual staff who could step into serve as translators.

12. Crozier and Davies 2007.

13. Song 1999; Abel Valenzuela 1999.

14. Kane 2012.

15. As indicated by Hemi's quote, language brokers' "family work" often involves "management activities" or "cognitive labor" that entails "anticipating needs, identifying options for filling them, making decisions, and monitoring progress" (Daminger 2019, 609).

16. In addition to challenging dominant understandings of children's capabilities, these young people's narratives also contradict the "typical" understanding of adolescents as rebelling against their parents.

17. Balsa and McGuire 2001.

18. Hoffmann and Tarzian 2001.

19. Wingfield 2010.

20. Werner and Malterud 2003.

21. Schnittker 2004.

22. Malat and Hamilton 2006.

23. Pugh 2015.

24. Smith, 1993.

25. Calarco 2020; DeVault 1999; Haley-Lock and Posey-Maddox 2016; Lareau 2011; Lewis-McCoy 2014.

26. Calarco 2020; Robinson 2014.

27. Kibria and Becerra 2020; Ong-Dean 2009; Traustadottir 1991.

28. Horvat, Weininger, and Lareau 2003; Kupchik 2010; Lareau 2011.

29. Blair-Loy 2003; Collins 2019; Elliott, Powell and Brenton 2015; Hays 1996.

30. Collins 2019; DeVault 1994; Elliott, Powell and Brenton 2015; Hays 1996.

31. Since girls have fewer opportunities to be perceived as competent than boys (Musto 2014, 2019), this finding likely helps explain greater gender disparities in language brokering that are well-documented by existing research.

32. Lippi-Green, 1997, 238–239.

Chapter 4

1. Although there was "far less concern with organizing experience by chronological age" two hundred years ago (Mintz 2004, 36), schools have historically played a central role in reproducing and solidifying the White, middle-class expectation that children are "proto-people," "adults-in-the-making," or "embodiment of the future" (Pugh 2014). Indeed, by labeling young people as "students," schools implicitly position young people as having identities and responsibilities that are different from those of adults, who are expected to work (Meyer 1977; Thorne 2009). In addition to homework expectations, states enforce compulsory school attendance policies while placing restrictions on young individuals seeking full-time employment outside the home or school (James and Prout 2015; Lesko 2012). These policies often make it difficult for youth to balance their family and school commitments.

2. The ways in which young people described their position in the family was gendered. Whereas Yolanda and other girls used the term *third parent*, boys often said that they were "the man of the house," as demonstrated in chapter 3. Both girls and boys used these terms to highlight that their responsibilities were seen as adult responsibilities.

3. Age likely shaped this interaction. Yolanda was likely "proud" in part because she had successfully shouldered an "adult" activity of negotiating for money. It is also possible that her mother's client, who was "impressed," responded more positively to an eight-year-old than she would have if an adult immigrant woman of color had tried to negotiate for a fair wage.

4. Indeed, research finds that Latinx immigrant women, who are overrepresented in low-paying domestic work in the informal economy, are often susceptible to exploitative work conditions. Their feminized labor is not considered "real" work and takes place inside other people's houses (Hondagneu-Sotelo 2007).

5. Smith 2006. Also see Dhingra 2020; Espiritu 2003; Katz 2014; Kibria 1993; Louie 2012; Park 2005.

6. Like other young people in this study, Yolanda's choice of occupation was gendered. Indeed, Latinx women are the fastest-growing non-White group that chooses a teaching career, which often provides a pathway to mobility (Flores 2017).

7. Some scholars have argued that familismo—ideals such as family cohesiveness, conformity, and the obligation to care for one another—characterize Latinx family relations (Desmond and López Turley 2009; Ovink 2018). Scholars have applied similar arguments about Asian American families and referred to Confucian cultural

ideals such as collectivism, filial piety, generational hierarchies, and family devotion to explain why Asian Americans maintain familial solidarity (Hardway and Fuligni 2006; Oxfeld 1993). As this research demonstrates, however, these analyses obscure the more complicated role migration plays in shaping family relations. Rather than simply prioritizing family interests over individual desires, this chapter reveals how young people experience the difficult double bind. And yet, as I detail in chapter 6, these seemingly positive cultural repertoires about Latinx and Asian American families serve as resources for marginalized youth to claim membership in the larger society.

8. Kibria 1993.

9. Partly because the media often sensationalizes poverty and portrays children as helpless victims in times of crisis, childhood scholars have urged researchers to use caution when writing about high-stakes crisis situations (Orellana 2009; Gárcia-Sánchez 2018). And yet, as sociologist Arlie Hochschild argues (2012), these "magnified moments" of high emotional intensity often provide a window into how people interpret the structural constraints they encountered. In the case of working-class immigrant youth of color, these moments also revealed how they attempted to fulfill their dual role as a language broker and a student."

10. Park 2011; Van Natta 2023.

11. The Emergency Medical and Treatment Labor Act of 1986 prohibits the refusal of care to anyone, including uninsured patients and patients who lack funds to pay for treatment. Hospitals, however, can attempt to collect from uninsured emergency patients.

12. Gordon 1999.

13. Lara-Millán 2014.

14. Dobransky 2011; Lara-Millán 2014.

15. Tamayo-Sarver et al. 2003.

16. Lara-Millán 2014; Lincoln 2006; Roth 1972; Spencer and Grace 2016.

17. Chung 2007; Min 1996; Lew 2006.

18. Bettie 2014; Musto 2019; Ochoa 2013; Angela Valenzuela 1999.

19. Camila's perspective on what constitutes a family aligns with public opinion. Despite a growing tendency among the public to adopt a broader definition of family, encompassing heterosexual couples with children, the prevailing benchmark for public notions of family remains a married, heterosexual couple with children (Powell et al., 2012). For working-class children of immigrants, this "standard" understanding of family acts as an interpretive framework, allowing them to juxtapose it against their own family life (Pyke 2000).

20. Pyke 2000; Smith 1993.

21. These ethnocentric and classed images of the "normal American family" are the result of—and help perpetuate—racial and socioeconomic segregation in housing, schools, and the workforce (Musto 2019; Ochoa 2013; Romero 2011).

22. Pyke 2000; Smith 1993; Zinn 1989.

23. Bettie 2014; Musto 2019; Ochoa 2013.

24. Musto 2019; Ochoa 2013.

25. Ochoa 2013; Posey-Maddox 2014; Angela Valenzuela 1999.

26. Ranita Ray (2022) has argued that schools can be a hostile institution for girls of color, where they frequently experience gendered racial harassment from teachers. These interactions not only lower their self-esteem but also creates a profound sense of disconnection from their immigrant backgrounds.

27. Research consistently shows that Latinx boys are hyper-criminalized in low-income urban areas like the neighborhoods where many of the youth I interviewed grew up (Rios 2011; Shedd 2015).

28. Ray 2022; Angela Valenzuela 1999.

29. Ray 2022.

30. It is important to note that the anger that young people experience toward teachers (or lack thereof) is part of the way they are racialized in schools. Latinx students are racialized as angry and violent (Rios 2011; Shedd 2015; Angela Valenzuela 1999), while Asian American students are racialized as docile (Kim 1999; Park 2005; Louie 2004). Yet the different racialization process is what contributes to these emotions in the first place.

31. Lesko 2012; Mintz 2004.

32. Part of the reason why students spend a significant amount of time studying is that admission requirements for higher education take their grades and SAT scores into account. And because schools rarely provide translation services for immigrant parents who are not familiar with the US education system, hiring private tutors or counselors can especially benefit children of immigrants (Lew 2006; Louie 2004).

33. Dhingra 2020; Lee and Zhou 2015; Lew 2006; Louie 2004.

34. Calarco 2020; Hamilton 2016.

35. Williams 1977, 132.

36. Dhingra 2020; Lee and Zhou 2015; Lew 2006; Louie 2004.

37. Ochoa 2013; Angela Valenzuela 1999.

38. Dhingra 2012; Kim 1999; Lew 2006; Louie 2004; Park 2008.

39. Lew 2006; Louie 2004.

40. Rios 2011.

41. Park 2008, 136.

Chapter 5

1. Goffman 1955; Goffman 1963; Ridgeway 2011; West and Zimmerman 1987.

2. In their influential work, sociologists Candace West and Don. H. Zimmerman (1987) developed a concept called "doing gender." In this view, individuals actively accomplish and produce gender in everyday interactions because they anticipate being held accountable to normative expectations of femininity and masculinity. Extending the concept of doing gender to account for other systems of inequality, Candace West and Sarah Fenstermaker (1995) later argued that people also "do difference" in situated interactions. Using a case of Black men, who often suffer from racial and gender profiling, they argue that Black men might react to unjust detention with extreme deference, knowing that indignation could generate hostility or brutality from police officers. Although Black men's expression of anger could serve the interests of White men, West and Fenstermaker (1995) contend that broader social forces inevitably

compel Black men to "do difference." Rather than merely "displaying" or suppressing their "differences," therefore, West and Zimmerman (1987, 126) argue that individuals' "competence as members of society is [held] hostage" to the production of unequal relations.

3. Collins 1986, 2002; Du Bois 1903; hooks 1984.

4. Collins 1986, 14.

5. Collins 1986; Du Bois 1903; Fanon 1963; hooks 1984; Kelley 1993; Rawick 1972.

6. West and Fenstermaker 1995.

7. Goffman 1955.

8. Bettie 2014.

9. Lippi-Green 1997, 45.

10. Morris 2012; Musto 2019.

11. Spencer, Steele and Quinn 1999; Steele 1997.

12. Ayres 1991; Bay Mia 2015.

13. Rios 2011.

14. Elliott and Reid 2019; Ferguson 2000; Rios 2011; Shedd 2015.

15. Elliott and Reid 2019.

16. Neely 2022.

17. Baugh 1992.

18. Lorde 1984, 114.

19. Daniel 2010; Kanuha 1999; Williamson 1980.

20. Connell 1987; Kanuha 1999; Schippers 2002.

21. This interview was conducted at a private and gated university, which requires people to show their ID to enter campus at night, a policy that was designed to ensure that students feel safe.

22. Wingfield 2010.

23. Evans and Moore 2015; Wingfield 2010.

24. I conducted interviews during a time when enforcement-driven police were deporting immigrants in record high numbers, which may have increased youths' concerns about the possibility of deportation.

25. De Genova 2002; Dreby 2015; Gonzales 2016; Menjívar and Abrego 2012.

26. Considering that the police often perceive Black and Brown men as being overly angry and violent (Rios 2011; Shedd 2015), Jesus's conscious decision to manage his father's and his own anger also may have been an attempt to protect both of them from potentially harmful interactions with law enforcement.

27. Kang 2010; Wingfield 2010.

28. Collins 1986, 2002; Du Bois 1903; hooks 1984; Kelley 1993.

29. Du Bois 1903.

30. Calarco 2018; Lareau 2011.

31. Dhingra 2020; Dow 2019; Elliott and Reid 2019; Espiritu 2003.

32. Dow 2019; Flores 2017; Lewis-McCoy 2014.

33. Berg 2002.

34. According to the National Center for Education Statistics, the majority of K–12 students in the US are now students of color. Teachers of color, however, make up of

only 20 percent of the K–12 workforce. Despite being two of the fastest growing populations in the US, only 8 percent of principals are Latinx, and a mere 1 percent are Asian American.

35. Downey and Pribesh 2004; Ferguson 2000.

36. Educators' widespread and racialized perceptions that youth of color, especially Latinx and Black youth, are at risk underlies their tendency to subject youth of color to heightened surveillance and harsh discipline (Musto 2019; Ochoa 2013; Rios 2011).

37. Ferguson 2000; Perry and Morris 2014.

38. Bettie 2014; Lewis and Diamond 2015; Ochoa 2013.

39. Grazian 2008; Pascoe 2007; Schippers 2002.

40. Hamilton 2007.

41. Hochschild 2012.

42. Dhingra 2007; Goffman 1963; West and Fenstermaker 1995; West and Zimmerman 1987.

43. Dhingra 2020; Kang 2010; Ridgeway 2011.

44. Pyke 2000; Smith 1993.

45. Lippi-Green 1997.

46. Charles and Grusky 2005; England 2010; Oliver and Shapiro 2013.

47. Neely 2022.

48. Calarco 2018; Lareau 2011.

49. As a sociologist Jessica Calarco argues (2020, 223), many institutions, including schools, are "privileged-dependent organizations, deriving social and economic status from that of the family families they serve."

Chapter 6

1. Keister, Vallejo, and Aronson 2016; Lipsitz 2006.

2. Calarco 2018; Hamilton 2016; Lareau 2011.

3. Chavez 2013; Ochoa 2013; Park 2011.

4. The very notion of work not only captures people's desire to be fully included in the larger society, but it also underscores efforts that may not always be effective because their attempts can unwittingly reproduce inequality. In the case of marginalized children of immigrants, their "work" also highlights the fact that young people put culture to use not only for themselves but also for members of their group and family who also face social exclusion.

5. Advocates, big businesses, and pro-immigrant politicians have fostered the narrative about good immigrants that counters the rhetoric depicting immigrants of color as a burden. These alternate narratives redefine immigrants of color as hardworking contributors who move to the land of opportunity to partake in the American Dream (Andrews 2017; Yukich 2013). Furthermore, the idea that the United States is a nation of immigrants and the national myth of the American Dream both act as cultural repertoires and resources for inclusion work.

6. Park 2008.

7. Park 2008, 136–137.

8. Smith 2006.

9. Kasinitz et al. 2008.

10. Park 2008.

11. Ruehs 2016.

12. Dreby 2012; Golash-Boza and Hondagneu-Sotelo 2013.

13. When discussing how White families were selfish and uncaring, some young people mentioned White people they knew. In these cases, they were more likely to name White women than White men. For example, when probed, Yoon referred to one of her "self-centered" White friends who used her "parents' credit card" and rarely visited her family after leaving home. Similar to the way other Asian American youth draw on gendered discourses of morality (Espiritu 2003), Yoon drew on gendered and racialized notions of morality when depicting her White friend as selfish. Implicit in her argument is that White women are morally deviant for failing to fulfill the feminized expectation that women should care for their family. Nonetheless, race was more salient than gender in Yoon's responses. She—like the vast majority of interviewees—did not explicitly discuss "uncaring" White people's gender. Instead, she and other interviewees tended to emphasize the seemingly different racial practices between Korean/Asian families and White families.

14. Bettie 2014; Sennett and Cobb 1972.

15. Calarco 2018; Hamilton 2016; Posey-Maddox 2014.

16. Kim and Pyke 2015.

17. Coltrane and Adams 2008; Hondagneu-Sotelo and Messner 1999.

18. Hondagneu-Sotelo and Messner 1999.

19. Pyke 2000.

20. Calarco 2018; Hamilton 2016; Lareau 2011.

21. Connidis and McMullin 2002.

22. Elliott and Reid 2019; Ferguson 2000.

23. Elliott and Reid 2019; Ochoa 2013.

24. Mexican American girls are more likely to accompany their mother to the suburbs, where their mother shoulders feminized work as a nanny or housekeeper in a wealthy White household. By comparison, Mexican American boys tend to accompany their father to the suburbs, where their father performs masculinized work doing construction or gardening in a wealthy White household.

25. When giving examples of these negative interactions, Mexican American language brokers typically referred to encounters their parents had with White women. Previous studies have demonstrated that Mexican immigrants who work as gardeners or housekeepers in Los Angeles suburbs are often disrespected by White women, who—as a result of the gendered division of labor in upper-middle- and upper-class families—are more likely to supervise their work (Hondagneu-Sotelo 2007; Ramirez 2011).

26. Andrews 2017; Yukich 2013.

27. Lamont 2009; Park 2005.

28. There is a difference in the way US-born youths and undocumented immigrants use legal status to define American identity. Whereas US-born youths point out that they are Americans by virtue of their birthplace, undocumented youths downplay legal status as a central marker of being American. However, consistent with the re-

sults of existing research (Espiritu 2003; Park 2005; Flores 2017; Warikoo and Bloem-raad 2018), regardless of birthplace and legal status, the respondents in my study recognized that their racial status is what precludes them from being seen as "real" Americans by the larger society.

29. Ferguson 2000; Rios 2011; Shedd 2015.

30. Bonilla-Silva 2017; Collins 2002; Feagin 1991; Lipsitz 2006; Omi and Winant 2014.

31. Bonilla-Silva 2017; Collins 2002; Feagin 1991; Omi and Winant 2014.

32. Kim 2008b; Park 2005; Sanchez 1997.

33. DiMaggio 1997; Lamont 2009; Swidler 1986.

34. DiMaggio 1997; Hallett 2010; Swidler 1986.

35. Neely 2020; Warikoo and Bloemraad 2018.

36. Hondagneu-Sotelo 2007; Ramirez 2011; Romero 2011.

37. Logan and Stults 2011; Musto 2019.

38. Espiritu 1997; Hondagneu-Sotelo 2007; Romero 2011.

39. Espiritu 1997; Vasquez-Tokos and Norton-Smith 2017.

40. Hays 1994. See also Bettie 2014; MacLeod 1987; Willis 1977.

41. As Swidler (1986) has argued, periods of social upheaval and disturbance can also give rise to new frameworks that enable people to reassess their social realities. Historically, these countercultural frameworks emerge alongside social movements and can serve as "cultural anchors," representing a set of core concerns that facilitate community building (Ghaziani and Baldassarri, 2011) and foster racial coalitions among marginalized groups (Jones, 2019; Escudero, 2020). For example, organizers from Asian and Latinx communities have deployed the cultural repertoires developed by the civil rights movement to resist controlling images and racial classifications imposed by the state (Okamoto 2014; Mora and Okamoto, 2020). Indeed, young people who participate in grassroots movements not only gain toolkits to address immigrant rights and social inequalities, but they also bring these resources into their homes, which can politicize their parents as well (Terriquez and Kwon 2015). Consequently, it is imperative to provide young people alternative cultural toolkits to push back against the country's founding myths, thus rendering larger structural forces like colonialism, racism, imperialism, and global capitalism visible (Espiritu 2003).

42. Espiritu 2003; Kim 2008b; Park 2008.

Chapter 7

1. Du Bois 1903, 2.

2. Hong 2021, 98–99.

3. Fraser and Gordon 1992; Glenn 2002; Molina 2006.

4. Glenn 2002; Molina 2006.

5. Bianchi et al. 2012; Budig and England 2001; Damaske 2011; Daminger 2019; DeVault 1994; Hays 1996; Hochschild and Machung 1989.

6. Collins 2002; Espiritu 1997; Glenn 2002, 2010; Zinn 1989.

7. Hondagneu-Sotelo 2007; Macdonald 2011; Parreñas 2015.

8. Kang 2010; Mears 2014.

9. Hondagneu-Sotelo 2007; Kang 2010; Macdonald 2011; Parreñas 2015.

10. Hondagneu-Sotelo 2007; Kang 2010.

11. Kibria and Becerra 2020; Lippi-Green 1997.

12. Calavita 1996; Chavez 2013; Ocampo 2022; Ochoa 2013; Angela Valenzuela 1999.

13. Sanchez 1997.

14. Abrego 2014; Collins 2002; Glenn 1983; Le Espiritu 1997; Thornton Dill 1988.

15. Musto 2019; Oakes 2005; Ochoa 2013; Angela Valenzuela 1999.

16. García-Sánchez 2018; Lesko 2012; Orellana 2009; Pugh 2014.

17. James and Prout 2015; Mintz 2004; Thorne 2009.

18. Bettie 2014; Musto 2019; Ochoa 2013; Angela Valenzuela 1999.

19. Dhingra 2020; Lee and Zhou 2015; Lee 2015; Lew 2006; Louie 2004,

20. Calarco 2011, 2020.

21. Park 2005, 6.

22. Blair-Loy 2003; C. Collins 2019; Damaske 2011; Elliott, Powell, and Brenton 2015; Hays 1996.

23. Glenn 2002; Molina 2006.

24. Ray 2019; Wingfield 2010,

25. Bettie 2014; Silva 2012.

26. Bettie 2014; MacLeod 1987; Ray 2017; Rendón 2019.

27. Katz 2014; López Turley, Desmond and Bruch 2010; Rendón 2019.

28. Ray 2017; Rendón 2019.

29. Calarco 2018; Hamilton 2016; Lareau 2011.

30. Estrada 2019.

31. Rendón 2019; Shedd 2015.

32. Du Bois 1903.

33. Butler 2004; Deutsch 2007.

34. Flores 2017.

35. Watkins-Hayes 2009.

36. Wingfield 2019.

37. Rios 2011.

38. Collins 1986, 2002.

39. Collins 1986, 28; also see Kelley 1993.

Appendix

1. Hays 1996; Lamont et al. 2016; Pugh 2013.

2. Lamont et al. 2016.

3. Feliciano and Lanuza 2017.

4. Min 1996; Lew 2006.

5. Song 1999; Abel Valenzuela 1999.

6. Hochschild 2012, 4.

7. Pugh 2013.

8. Pugh 2013.

9. Glaser and Straus 1967.

10. Glaser and Strauss 1967.

BIBLIOGRAPHY

Abrego, Leisy J. 2014. *Sacrificing Families: Navigating Laws, Labor, and Love across Borders*. Stanford, CA: Stanford University Press.

Alba, Richard D., and Victor Nee. 2003. *Remaking the American Mainstream: Assimilation and Contemporary Immigration*. Cambridge, MA: Harvard University Press.

Almaguer, Tomás. 2008. *Racial Fault Lines: The Historical Origins of White Supremacy in California*. Berkeley: University of California Press.

Andrews, Abigail L. 2017. "Moralizing Regulation: The Implications of Policing 'Good' versus 'Bad' Immigrants." *Ethnic and Racial Studies* 41(14):2485–503.

Antonini, Rachele. 2010. "Special Issue: Child Language Brokering: Trends and Patterns in Current Research." *Mediazioni* 2010(10).

———. 2016. "Caught in the Middle: Child Language Brokering as a Form of Unrecognised Language Service." *Journal of Multilingual and Multicultural Development* 37(7):710–25.

Associated Press. 1991. "For Immigrants' Children, An Adult Role." *New York Times*, August 15.

Ayres, Ian. 1991. "Fair Driving: Gender and Race Discrimination in Retail Car Negotiations." *Harvard Law Review* 104(4):817–72.

Balsa, Ana I., and Thomas G. McGuire. 2001. "Statistical Discrimination in Health Care." *Journal of Health Economics* 20(6):881–907.

Baugh, John. 1992. "Hypocorrection: Mistakes in Production of Vernacular African American English as a Second Dialect." *Language and Communication* 12:317–26.

Bay Mia, Fabian Ann. 2015. *Race and Retail: Consumption across the Color Line*. New Brunswick, NJ: Rutgers University Press.

Berg, Charles Ramírez. 2002. *Latino Images in Film: Stereotypes, Subversion, and Resistance*. Austin: University of Texas Press.

Bettie, Julie. 2014. *Women without Class: Girls, Race, and Identity*. Berkeley: University of California Press.

Bianchi, Suzanne M., Liana C. Sayer, Melissa A. Milkie, and John P. Robinson. 2012. "Housework: Who Did, Does or Will Do It, and How Much Does It Matter?" *Social Forces* 91(1):55–63.

Blair-Loy, Mary. 2003. *Competing Devotions: Career and Family among Women Executives*. Cambridge, MA: Harvard University Press.

Bloemraad, Irene, Anna Korteweg, and Gökçe Yurdakul. 2008. "Citizenship and Immigration: Multiculturalism, Assimilation, and Challenges to the Nation-State." *Annal Review of Sociology* 34(1):153–79.

Bonilla-Silva, Eduardo. 2017. *Racism without Racists: Color-blind Racism and the Persistence of Racial Inequality in America*. Lanham, MD: Rowman & Littlefield.

Budig, Michelle J., and Paula England. 2001. "The Wage Penalty for Motherhood." *American Sociological Review* 66(2):204–25.

Butler, Judith. 2004. *Undoing Gender*. New York: Routledge.

Cobas, José A., Bonnie Urciuoli, Joe Feagin, and Daniel J. Delgado. 2022. *The Spanish Language in the United States: Rootedness, Racialization, and Resistance*. New York: Routledge.

Cohen, Suzanne, Jo Moran-Ellis, and Chris Smaje. 1999. "Children as Informal Interpreters in GP Consultations: Pragmatics and Ideology." *Sociology of Health & Illness* 21(2):163–86.

Calarco, Jessica McCrory. 2018. *Negotiating Opportunities: How the Middle Class Secures Advantages in School*. New York: Oxford University Press.

———. 2020. "Avoiding Us vs. Them: How Schools' Dependence on Privileged 'Helicopter' Parents Influences Enforcement of Rules." *American Sociological Review* 85(2):223–46.

Calavita, Kitty. 1996. "The New Politics of Immigration: 'Balanced-Budget Conservatism' and the Symbolism of Proposition 187." *Social Problems* 43(3):284–305.

Charles, Maria, and David B. Grusky. 2005. *Occupational Ghettos: The Worldwide Segregation of Women and Men*. Stanford, CA: Stanford University Press.

Chavez, Leo. 2013. *The Latino Threat: Constructing Immigrants, Citizens, and the Nation*. Stanford, CA: Stanford University Press.

Chudacoff, Howard P. 1989. *How Old Are You? Age Consciousness in American Culture* Princeton, NJ: Princeton University Press

Chung, Angie. 2007. *Legacies of Struggle: Conflict and Cooperation in Korean American Politics*. Stanford, CA: Stanford University Press.

———. 2016. *Saving Face: The Emotional Costs of the Asian Immigrant Family Myth*. New Brunswick, NJ: Rutgers University Press.

Clement, Priscilla. 1997. *Growing Pains: Children in the Industrial Age, 1850–1890*. New York: Twayne.

Collins, Caitlyn. 2019. *Making Motherhood Work: How Women Manage Careers and Caregiving*. Princeton, NJ: Princeton University Press.

Collins, Patricia Hill. 1986. "Learning from the Outsider Within: The Sociological Significance of Black Feminist Thought." *Social Problems* 33(6):14–32.

———. 2002. *Black Feminist Thought: Knowledge, Consciousness, and the Politics of Empowerment*. New York: Routledge.

Coltrane, Scott, and Michele Adams. 2008. *Gender and Families*. Lanham, MD: Rowman & Littlefield.

Connell, Raewyn. 1987. *Gender and Power: Society, the Person, and Sexual Politics*. Stanford, CA: Stanford University Press.

Connidis, Ingrid Arnet, and Julie Ann McMullin. 2002. "Sociological Ambivalence and Family Ties: A Critical Perspective." *Journal of Marriage and Family* 64(3):558–67.

Corsaro, William A. 1992. "Interpretive Reproduction in Children's Peer Cultures." *Social Psychology Quarterly* 55(2):160–77.

Crafter, Sarah, and Humera Iqbal. 2021. "Child Language Brokering as a Family Care Practice: Reframing the 'Parentified Child Debate.'" *Children & Society* 36(3):400–14.

Crozier, Gill, and Jane Davies. 2007. "Hard to Reach Parents or Hard to Reach Schools? A Discussion of Home-School Relations, with Particular Reference to Bangladeshi and Pakistani Parents." *British Educational Research Journal* 33(3):295–313.

Damaske, Sarah. 2011. *For the Family?: How Class and Gender Shape Women's Work*. New York: Oxford University Press.

Daminger, Allison. 2019. "The Cognitive Dimension of Household Labor." *American Sociological Review* 84(4):609–33.

Daniel, G. Reginald. 2010. *More than Black: Multiracial Identity and New Racial Order*. Philadelphia: Temple University Press.

De Genova, Nicholas P. 2002. "Migrant 'Illegality' and Deportability in Everyday Life." *Annual Review of Anthropology*: 419–47.

Delgado, Vanessa. 2020. "'They Think I'm a Lawyer': Undocumented College Students as Legal Brokers for their Undocumented Parents." *Law & Policy* 43(3):261–83.

Desmond, Mathew, and Ruth N. López Turley. 2009. "The Role of Familism in Explaining the Hispanic-White College Application Gap." *Social Problems* 56(2):311–34.

Deutsch, Francine M. 2007. "Undoing Gender." *Gender & Society* 21(1):106–27.

DeVault, Marjorie L. 1994. *Feeding the Family: The Social Organization of Caring as Gendered Work*. Chicago: University of Chicago Press.

———. 1999. "Comfort and Struggle: Emotion Work in Family Life." *The ANNALS of the American Academy of Political and Social Science* 561(1):52–63.

Dhingra, Pawan. 2007. *Managing Multicultural Lives: Asian American Professionals and the Challenge of Multiple Identities*. Stanford, CA: Stanford University Press.

———. 2012. *Life behind the Lobby: Indian American Motel Owners and the American Dream*. Stanford, CA: Stanford University Press.

———. 2020. *Hyper Education: Why Good Schools, Good Grades, and Good Behavior Are Not Enough*. New York: New York University Press.

DiMaggio, Paul. 1997. "Culture and Cognition." *Annual Review of Sociology* 23(1):263–87.

Dobransky, Kerry. 2011. "Labeling, Looping, and Social Control: Contextualizing Diagnosis in Mental Health Care." *Advances in Medical Sociology* 12:111–31.

Dow, Dawn Marie. 2019. *Mothering while Black: Boundaries and Burdens of Middle-Class Parenthood*. Berkeley: University of California Press.

Downey, Douglas B, and Shana Pribesh. 2004. "When Race Matters: Teachers' Evaluations of Students' Classroom Behavior." *Sociology of Education* 77(4):267–82.

Dreby, Joanna. 2010. *Divided by Borders: Mexican Migrants and Their Children*. Berkeley: University of California Press.

———. 2012. "The Burden of Deportation on Children in Mexican Immigrant Families." *Journal of Marriage and Family* 74(4):829–45.

———. 2015. *Everyday Illegal: When Policies Undermine Immigrant Families*. Berkeley: University of California Press.

Du Bois, W. E. B. 1903. *The Souls of Black Folk*. New York: Bantam Classic.

———. 1920. *Darkwater: Voices from within the Veil*. New York: Harcourt, Brace, and Company.

Elliott, Sinikka, Rachel Powell, and Joslyn Brenton. 2015. "Being a Good Mom: Low-income, Black Single Mothers Negotiate Intensive Mothering." *Journal of Family Issues* 36(3):351–70.

Elliott, Sinikka, and Megan Reid. 2019. "Low-Income Black Mothers Parenting Adolescents in the Mass Incarceration Era: The Long Reach of Criminalization." *American Sociological Review* 84(2):197–219.

England, Paula. 2010. "The Gender Revolution: Uneven and Stalled." *Gender & Society* 24(2):149–66.

Escudero, Kevin. 2020. *Organizing While Undocumented: Immigrant Youth's Political Activism under the Law*. New York: New York University Press.

Espiritu, Yen Le. 1997. *Asian American Women and Men*. Thousand Oaks, CA: Sage.

———. 1999. "Gender and Labor in Asian Immigrant Families." *American Behavioral Scientist* 42(4):628–47.

———. 2003. *Home Bound: Filipino American Lives across Cultures, Communities, and Countries*. Berkeley: University of California Press.

Estrada, Emir. 2019. *Kids at Work: Latinx Families Selling Food on the Streets of Los Angeles*. New York: New York University Press.

Evans, Louwanda, and Wendy Leo Moore. 2015. "Impossible Burdens: White Institutions, Emotional Labor, and Micro-Resistance." *Social Problems* 62(3):439–54.

Fanon, Frantz. 1963. *The Wretched of the Earth*. New York: Grove Press.

Feagin, Joe R. 1991. "The Continuing Significance of Race: Antiblack Discrimination in Public Places." *American Sociological Review*:101–16.

Feliciano, Cynthia, and Yader R. Lanuza. 2017. "An Immigrant Paradox? Contextual Attainment and Intergenerational Educational Mobility." *American Sociological Review* 82(1):211–41.

Ferguson, Ann Arnett. 2000. *Bad Boys: Public Schools in the Making of Black Masculinity*. Ann Arbor: University of Michigan Press.

Flores, Glenda M. 2017. *Latina Teachers: Creating Careers and Guarding Culture*. New York: New York University Press.

Flores, Veronia. 1993. "Language Skills Translate to Major Duties for Kids." *Chicago Sun-Times,* April 4.

Foner, Nancy, and Joanna Dreby. 2011. "Relations between the Generations in Immigrant Families." *Annual Review of Sociology* 37:545–64.

Fraser, Nancy, and Linda Gordon. 1992. "Contract versus Charity: Why Is There No Social Citizenship in the United States?" *Socialist Review* 22:45–68.

García Valdivia, I. 2022. "Legal Power in Action: How Latinx Adult Children Mitigate the Effects of Parents' Legal Status through Brokering." *Social Problems* 69(2): 335–55.

García-Sánchez, Inmaculada M. 2014. *Language and Muslim Immigrant Childhoods: The Politics of Belonging.* Oxford, UK: Wiley-Blackwell.

———. 2018. "Children as Interactional Brokers of Care." *Annual Review of Anthropology* 47:167–84.

Gerstel, Naomi. 2011. "Rethinking Families and Community: The Color, Class, and Centrality of Extended Kin Ties." *Sociological Forum* 26(1):1–20.

Glaser, Barney, and Anselm Strauss. 1967. *The Discovery of Grounded Theory.* Chicago: Aldine.

Glass, Jennifer, Robin W. Simon, and Matthew A. Andersson. 2016. "Parenthood and Happiness: Effects of Work-Family Reconciliation Policies in 22 OECD Countries." *American Journal of Sociology* 122(3):886–929.

Glenn, Evelyn Nakano. 1983. "Split Household, Small Producer and Dual Wage Earner: An Analysis of Chinese-American Family Strategies." *Journal of Marriage and the Family* 45(1):35–46.

———. 1992. "From Servitude to Service Work: Historical Continuities in the Racial Division of Paid Reproductive Labor." *Signs: Journal of Women in Culture and Society* 18(1):1–43.

———. 2002. *Unequal Freedom: How Race and Gender Shaped American Citizenship and Labor.* Cambridge, MA: Harvard University Press.

———. 2010. *Forced to Care: Coercion and Caregiving in America.* Cambridge, MA: Harvard University Press.

Goffman, Erving. 1955. "On Face-Work: An Analysis of Ritual Elements in Social Interaction." *Psychiatry* 18(3):213–31.

———. 1963. *Stigma: Notes on the Management of Spoiled Identity.* New York: Touchstone.

Golash-Boza, Tanya, and Pierrette Hondagneu-Sotelo. 2013. "Latino Immigrant Men and the Deportation Crisis: A Gendered Racial Removal Program." *Latino Studies* 11(3):271–92.

Gold, Matea. 1999. "Small Voice for Her Parents." *Los Angeles Times,* May 24.

Gold, Steven J. 2004. "From Jim Crow to Racial Hegemony: Evolving Explanations of Racial Hierarchy." *Ethnic and Racial Studies* 27(6):951–68.

Gonzales, Roberto G. 2016. *Lives in Limbo: Undocumented and Coming of Age in America.* Berkeley: University of California Press.

Gordon, James A. 1999. "The Hospital Emergency Department as a Social Welfare Institution." *Annals of Emergency Medicine* 33(3):321–25.

Gordon, Milton M. 1964. *Assimilation in American Life: The Role of Race, Religion, and National Origins*. New York: Oxford University Press.

Gornick, Janet C., and Marcia K. Meyers. 2003. *Families That Work: Policies for Reconciling Parenthood and Employment*. New York: Russell Sage Foundation.

Grazian, David. 2008. *On the Make: The Hustle of Urban Nightlife*. Chicago: University of Chicago Press.

Guglielmo, Thomas A. 2003. *White on Arrival: Italians, Race, Color, and Power in Chicago, 1890–1945*. New York: Oxford University Press.

Haley-Lock, Anna, and Linn Posey-Maddox. 2016. "Fitting It All In: How Mothers' Employment Shapes Their School Engagement." *Community, Work & Family* 19(3):302–21.

Hallett, Tim. 2010. "The Myth Incarnate: Recoupling Processes, Turmoil, and Inhabited Institutions in an Urban Elementary School." *American Sociological Review* 75(1):52–74.

Hamilton, Laura T. 2007. "Trading on Heterosexuality: College Women's Gender Strategies and Homophobia." *Gender & Society* 21(2):145–72.

———. 2016. *Parenting to a Degree: How Family Matters for College Women's Success*. Chicago: University of Chicago Press.

Hardway, Christina, and Fuligni, Andrew J. 2006. "Dimensions of Family Connectedness among Adolescents with Mexican, Chinese, and European Backgrounds." *Developmental Psychology* 42(6):1246–1258.

Hays, Sharon. 1994. "Structure and Agency and the Sticky Problem of Culture." *Sociological Theory* 12(1):57–72.

———. 1996. *The Cultural Contradictions of Motherhood*. New Haven, CT: Yale University Press.

———. 2003. *Flat Broke with Children: Women in the Age of Welfare Reform*. New York: Oxford University Press.

Hedges, Chris. 2000. "Translating America for Parents and Family." *New York Times*, June 19.

Hochschild, Arlie Russell. 2012. *The Managed Heart: Commercialization of Human Feeling*. Berkeley: University of California Press.

Hochschild, Arlie, and Anne Machung. 1989. *The Second Shift: Working Families and the Revolution at Home*. New York: Avon.

Hoffmann, Diane E., and Anita J. Tarzian. 2001. "The Girl Who Cried Pain: A Bias against Women in the Treatment of Pain." *Journal of Law, Medicine & Ethics* 29(1):13–27.

Hondagneu-Sotelo, Pierrette. 2007. *Doméstica: Immigrant Workers Cleaning and Caring in the Shadows of Affluence*. Berkeley: University of California Press.

Hondagneu-Sotelo, Pierrette, and Michael Messner. 1999. "Gender Displays and Men's Power: The 'New Man' and the Mexican Immigrant Man." In *Gender through the Prism of Difference*, edited by Maxine Baca Zinn, Pierrette Hondagneu-Sotelo, and Michael A. Messner, 63–74. Boston: Allyn and Bacon.

Hong, Cathy Park. 2021. *Minor Feelings: An Asian American Reckoning*. New York: One World.

hooks, bell. 1984. *From Margin to Center.* Boston: South End Press.

Horvat, Erin McNamara, Elliot B. Weininger, and Annette Lareau. 2003. "From Social Ties to Social Capital: Class Differences in the Relations between Schools and Parent Networks." *American Educational Research Journal* 40(2):319–51.

Howell, Joseph. 1973. *Hard Living on Clay Street: Portraits of Blue-Collar Families.* Garden City, NY: Anchor.

Jacobson, Matthew Frye. 1999. *Whiteness of a Different Color.* Cambridge, MA: Harvard University Press.

James, Allison, and Alan Prout. 2015. *Constructing and Reconstructing Childhood: Contemporary Issues in the Sociological Study of Childhood.* London: Routledge.

Jones, Jennifer A. 2019. *The Browning of the New South.* Chicago: University of Chicago Press.

Jung, Moon-Kie. 2009. "The Racial Unconscious Of Assimilation Theory." *Du Bois Review: Social Science Research on Race* 6(2):375–95.

Kane, Emily W. 2012. *The Gender Trap: Parents and the Pitfalls of Raising Boys and Girls.* New York: NYU Press.

Kang, Miliann. 2010. *The Managed Hand: Race, Gender, and the Body in Beauty Service Work.* Berkeley: University of California Press.

Kanuha, Valli Kalei 1999. "The Social Process of Passing to Manage Stigma: Acts of Internalized Oppression or Acts of Resistance." *Journal of Sociology and Social Welfare* 26:27–46.

Kasinitz, Philip, Mary C. Waters, John H. Mollenkopf, and Jennifer Holdaway. 2008. *Inheriting the City: The Children of Immigrants Come of Age.* New York: Russell Sage Foundation

Katz, Vikki S. 2014. *Kids in the Middle: How Children of Immigrants Negotiate Community Interactions for Their Families.* New Brunswick, NJ: Rutgers University Press.

Keister, Lisa A., Jody Agius Vallejo, and Brian Aronson. 2016. "Chinese Immigrant Wealth: Heterogeneity in Adaptation." *PLOS One* 11(12):e0168043.

Kelley, Robin. 1993. "'We Are Not What We Seem': Rethinking Black Working-Class Opposition in the Jim Crow South." *The Journal of American History* 80(1):75–112.

Kett, Joseph F. 1977. *Rites of Passage: Adolescence in America, 1790 to the Present.* New York: Basic Books.

Kibria, Nazli. 1993. *Family Tightrope: The Changing Lives of Vietnamese Americans.* Princeton, NJ: Princeton University Press.

Kibria, Nazli. 2002. *Becoming Asian American: Second-Generation Chinese and Korean American Identities.* Baltimore, MD: Johns Hopkins University Press.

Kibria, Nazli, and Walter Suarez Becerra. 2020. "Deserving Immigrants and Good Advocate Mothers: Immigrant Mothers' Negotiations of Special Education Systems for Children with Disabilities." *Social Problems* 68(3):591–607.

Kim, Allen, and Karen Pyke. 2015. "Taming Tiger Dads: Hegemonic American Masculinity and South Korea's Father School." *Gender & Society* 29(4):509–33.

Kim, Claire Jean. 1999. "The Racial Triangulation of Asian Americans." *Politics & Society* 27(1):105–38.

Kim, Nadia Y. 2008a. "Critical Thoughts on Asian American Assimilation in the Whitening Literature." In *Racism in Post-Race America: New Theories, New Directions,* edited by Charles A. Gallagher, 53–66. Chapel Hill, NC: Social Forces Publishing.

———. 2008b. *Imperial Citizens: Koreans and Race from Seoul to LA.* Stanford, CA: Stanford University Press.

———. 2013. "Citizenship on the Margins: A Critique of Scholarship on Marginalized Women and Community Activism." *Sociology Compass* 7(6):459–70.

Kratochvil, Misha 2001. "Urban Tactics; Translating for Parents Means Growing Up Fast." *New York Times,* April 26.

Kupchik, Aaron. 2010. *Homeroom Security: School Discipline in an Age of Fear.* New York: New York University Press.

Kwon, Hyeyoung. 2014. "The Hidden Injury of Class in Korean-American Language Brokers' Lives." *Childhood* 21(1):56–71.

———. 2015. "Intersectionality in Interaction: Immigrant Youth Doing American from an Outsider-Within Position." *Social Problems* 62(4):623–41.

———. 2022. "Inclusion Work: Children of Immigrants Claiming Membership in Everday Life." *American Journal of Sociology* 127(6):1919–59.

Lamont, Michèle. 2009. *The Dignity of Working Men: Morality and the Boundaries of Race, Class, and Immigration.* Cambridge, MA: Harvard University Press.

Lamont, Michèle, and Nissim Mizrachi. 2012. "Ordinary People Doing Extraordinary Things: Responses to Stigmatization in Comparative Perspective." *Ethnic and Racial Studies* 35(3):365–81.

Lamont, Michèle, Graziella Moraes Silva, Jessica Welburn, Joshua Guetzkow, Nissim Mizrachi, Hanna Herzog, and Elisa Reis. 2016. *Getting Respect: Responding to Stigma and Discrimination in the United States, Brazil, and Israel.* Princeton, NJ: Princeton University Press.

Mora, Christina. G., and Dina Okamoto. 2020. "Boundary Articulation and Emergent Identities: Asian and Hispanic Panethnicity in Comparison 1970–1980." *Social Problems* 67(1):56–76.

Lara-Millán, Armando. 2014. "Public Emergency Room Overcrowding in the Era of Mass Imprisonment." *American Sociological Review* 79(5):866–87.

Lareau, Annette. 2011. *Unequal Childhoods: Class, Race, and Family Life.* Berkeley: University of California Press.

Lee, Jennifer. 2002. *Civility in the City: Blacks, Jews, and Koreans in urban America.* Cambridge, MA: Harvard University Press.

Lee, Jennifer, and Min Zhou. 2015. *The Asian American Achievement Paradox.* New York: Russell Sage Foundation.

Lee, Stacy J. 2015. *Unraveling the "Model Minority" Stereotype: Listening to Asian American Youth.* New York: Teachers College Press.

Lesko, Nancy. 2012. *Act Your Age!: A Cultural Construction of Adolescence.* London: Routledge.

Lew, Jamie. 2006. *Asian Americans in Class: Charting the Achievement Gap among Korean American Youth.* New York: Teachers College Press.

Lewis-McCoy, R. L'Heureux. 2014. *Inequality in the Promised Land: Race, Resources, and Suburban Schooling*. Stanford, CA: Stanford University Press.

Lewis, Amanda E, and John B Diamond. 2015. *Despite the Best Intentions: How Racial Inequality Thrives in Good Schools*. New York: Oxford University Press.

Lichter, Daniel T, Domenico Parisi, and Michael C Taquino. 2015. "Toward a New Macro-Segregation? Decomposing Segregationwithin and betweenMetropolitan Cities and Suburbs." *American Sociological Review* 80 (4):843–73.

Lincoln, Alisa. 2006. "Psychiatric Emergency Room Decision-Making, Social Control and the 'Undeserving Sick.'" *Sociology of Health & Illness* 28(1):54–75.

Lippi-Green, Rosina. 1997. *English with an Accent: Language, Ideology, and Discrimination in the United States*. New York: Routledge.

Lipsitz, George. 2006. *The Possessive Investment in Whiteness: How White People Profit from Identity Politics*. Philadelphia: Temple University Press.

Logan, John R., and Brian Stults. 2011. "The Persistence of Segregation in the Metropolis: New Findings from the 2010 Census." In *Census Brief Prepared for Project US2010*. New York: Russell Sage Foundation.

Lopez, Ian Haney. 2006. *White by Law: The Legal Construction of Race*. New York: New York University Press.

Lopez, Nancy. 2003. *Hopeful Girls, Troubled Boys: Race and Gender Disparity in Urban Education*. New York: Routledge.

López Turley, Ruth N., Matthew Desmond, and Sarah K Bruch. 2010. "Unanticipated Educational Consequences of a Positive Parent-Child Relationship." *Journal of Marriage and Family* 72(5):1377–90.

Lorde, Audre. 1984. *Sister Outsider*. Trumansburg, NY: Crossing Press.

Louie, Vivian S. 2004. *Compelled to Excel: Immigration, Education, and Opportunity among Chinese Americans*. Stanford, CA: Stanford University Press.

———. 2012. *Keeping the Immigrant Bargain: The Costs and Rewards of Success in America*. New York: Russell Sage Foundation.

Macdonald, Cameron Lynne. 2011. *Shadow Mothers: Nannies, Au Pairs, and the Micropolitics of Mothering*. Berkeley: University of California Press.

MacLeod, Jay. 1987. *Ain't No Makin' It: Aspirations and Attainment in a Low-Income Neighborhood*. Boulder, CO: Westview.

Malat, Jennifer, and Mary Ann Hamilton. 2006. "Preference for Same-Race Health Care Providers and Perceptions of Interpersonal Discrimination in Health Care." *Journal of Health and Social Behavior* 47:173–87.

Marshall, Thomas Humphrey. 1950. *Citizenship and Social Class*. Cambridge: Cambridge University Press.

Massey, Douglas S, Jorge Durand, and Nolan J Malone. 2002. *Beyond Smoke and Mirrors: Mexican Immigration in an Era of Economic Integration*. New York: Russell Sage Foundation.

Massey, Douglas S, Karen A Pren, and Jorge Durand. 2016. "Why Border Enforcement Backfired." *American Journal of Sociology* 121(5):1557–600.

Mears, Ashley. 2014. "Aesthetic Labor for the Sociologies of Work, Gender, and Beauty." *Sociology Compass* 8(12):1330–43.

Menjívar, Cecilia, and Leisy Abrego. 2012. "Legal Violence: Immigration Law and the Lives of Central American Immigrants." *American Journal of Sociology* 117(5):1380–421.

Menjívar, Cecilia, and Olivia Salcido. 2002. "Immigrant Women and Domestic Violence: Common Experiences in Different Countries." *Gender & Society* 16(6):898–920.

Meyer, John W. 1977. "The Effects of Education as an Institution." *American Journal of Sociology* 83(1):55–77.

Min, Pyong Gap. 1996. *Caught in the Middle: Korean Communities in New York and Los Angeles*. Berkeley: University of California Press.

Mintz, Steven. 2004. *Huck's Raft: A History of American Childhood*. Cambridge, MA: Harvard University Press.

Molina, Natalia. 2006. *Fit to be Citizens?: Public Health and Race in Los Angeles, 1879–1939*. Berkeley: University of California Press.

Morris, Edward W. 2012. *Learning the Hard Way: Masculinity, Place, and the Gender Gap in Education*. New Brunswick, NJ: Rutgers University Press.

Musto, Michela. 2014. "Athletes in the Pool, Girls and Boys on Deck: The Contextual Construction of Gender in Coed Youth Swimming." *Gender & Society* 28(3):359–80.

———. 2019. "Brilliant or Bad: The Gendered Social Construction of Exceptionalism in Early Adolescence." *American Sociological Review* 84(3):369–93.

Neely, Megan Tobias. 2020. "The Portfolio Ideal Worker: Insecurity and Inequality in the New Economy." *Qualitative Sociology*:1–26.

———. 2022. *Hedged Out: Inequality and Insecurity on Wall Street*. Berkeley: University of California Press.

Nissman, Cara. 2004. "Innocence Lost in Translation." *Salon*, August 4.

Oakes, Jeannie. 2005. *Keeping Track: How Schools Structure Inequality*. New Haven, CT: Yale University Press.

Ocampo, Anthony Christian. 2022. *Brown and Gay in LA: The Lives of Immigrant Sons*. New York: New York University Press.

Ochoa, Gilda L. 2013. *Academic Profiling: Latinos, Asian Americans, and the Achievement Gap*. Minneapolis: University of Minnesota Press.

Oliver, Melvin, and Thomas Shapiro. 2013. *Black Wealth, White Wealth: A New Perspective on Racial Inequality*. New York: Routledge.

Okamoto, Dina G. 2014. *Redefining Race: Asian American Panethnicity and Shifting Ethnic Boundaries*. New York: Russell Sage Foundation.

Omi, Michael, and Howard Winant. 2014. *Racial Formation in the United States*. New York: Routledge.

Ong, Aihwa. 2003. *Buddha is Hiding: Refugees, Citizenship, the New America*. Berkeley: University of California Press.

Ong-Dean, Colin. 2009. *Distinguishing Disability: Parents, Privilege, and Special Education*. Chicago: University of Chicago Press.

Orellana, Marjorie Faulstich. 2009. *Translating Childhoods: Immigrant Youth, Language, and Culture*. New Brunswick, NJ: Rutgers University Press.

Orellana, Marjorie Faulstich, Lisa Dorner, and Lucila Pulido. 2003. "Accessing Assets: Immigrant Youth's Work as Family Translators or Para-phrasers." *Social Problems* 50(4):505–24.

Ovink, Sarah M. 2018. "'They Always Call me an Investment: Gendered Familism and Latino/a Collge Pathways." *Gender & Society* 28(2): 265–88.

Oxfeld, Ellen. 1993. *Blood, Sweat, and Mahjong.* Ithaca, NY: Cornell University Press.

Paik, Leslie. 2021. *Trapped in a Maze: How Social Control Institutions Drive Family Poverty and Inequality.* Berkeley: University of California Press.

Park, Lisa Sun-Hee. 2005. *Consuming Citizenship: Children of Asian Immigrant Entrepreneurs.* Stanford, CA.: Stanford University Press.

———. 2008. "Continuing Significance of the Model Minority Myth: The Second Generation." *Social Justice* 35(2):134–44.

———. 2011. *Entitled to Nothing: the Struggle for Immigrant Health Care in the Age of Welfare Reform.* New York: New York University Press.

Park, Lisa Sun-Hee, and David N. Pellow. 2013. *The Slums of Aspen: Immigrants vs. the Environment in America's Eden.* New York: New York University Press.

Park, Robert 1950. *Race and Culture.* Glencoe, IL: Free Press.

Parreñas, Rhacel Salazar. 2015. *Servants of Globalization: Migration and Domestic Work.* Stanford, CA: Stanford University Press.

Pascoe, C. J. 2007. *Dude, You're a Fag Masculinity and Sexuality in High School.* Berkeley: University of California Press.

Peavy, Linda, and Ursula Smith. 1999. *Frontier Children.* Norman: University of Oklahoma Press.

Perry, Brea L., and Edward W. Morris. 2014. "Suspending Progress: Collateral Consequences of Exclusionary Punishment in Public Schools." *American Sociological Review* 79(6):1067–87.

Portes, Alejandro, and Rubén G. Rumbaut. 2001. *Legacies: The Story of the Immigrant Second Generation.* Berkeley: University of California Press.

Portes, Alejandro, and Min Zhou. 1993. "The New Second Generation: Segmented Assimilation and Its Variants among Post 1965 Immigrant Youth." *Annals of the American Academy of Political and Social Science* 530:74–96.

Posey-Maddox, Linn. 2014. *When Middle-Class Parents Choose Urban Schools: Class, Race, and the Challenge of Equity in Public Education.* Chicago: University of Chicago Press.

Powell, Brian, Bolzendahl Catherine, Geist Claudia, Steelman Lala Carr. 2010. *Counted Out: Same-Sex Relations and Americans' Definitions of Family.* New York: Russell Sage Foundation.

Pugh, Allison J. 2013. "What Good Are Interviews for Thinking about Culture? Demystifying Interpretive Analysis." *American Journal of Cultural Sociology* 1 (1): 42–68.

———. 2014. "The Theoretical Costs of Ignoring Childhood: Rethinking Independence, Insecurity, and Inequality." *Theory and Society* 43(1):71–89.

Pyke, Karen. 2000. "'The Normal American Family' as an Interpretive Structure of Family Life among Grown Children of Korean and Vietnamese Immigrants." *Journal of Marriage and Family* 62(1):240–55.

Ramirez, Hernan. 2011. "Masculinity in the Workplace: The Case of Mexican Immigrant Gardeners." *Men and Masculinities* 14(1):97–116.

Rawick, George P. 1972. *From Sundown to Sunup: The Making of the Black Community.* Westport, CT: Greenwood.

Ray, Ranita. 2017. *The Making of a Teenage Service Class: Poverty and Mobility in an American City.* Berkeley: University of California Press.

———. 2022. "School as a Hostile Institution: How Black and Immigrant Girls of Color Experience the Classroom." *Gender & Society* 36(1):88–111.

Ray, Victor. 2019. "A Theory of Racialized Organizations." *American Sociological Review* 84(1):26–53.

Reynolds Jennifer F, and Marjorie Faulstich Orellana. 2009. "New Immigrant Youth Interpreting in White Public Space." *American Anthropologist* 111(2):211–23.

Reese, Ellen. 2005. *Backlash against Welfare Mothers: Past and Present.* Berkeley: University of California Press.

Rendón, María G. 2019. *Stagnant Dreamers: How the Inner City Shapes the Integration of the Second Generation.* New York: Russell Sage Foundation.

Ridgeway, Cecilia L. 2011. *Framed by Gender: How Gender Inequality Persists in the Modern World.* New York: Oxford University Press.

Rios, Victor M. 2011. *Punished: Policing the Lives of Black and Latino Boys.* New York: New York University Press.

Robinson, Keith, and Angel L. Harris. 2014. *The Broken Compass: Parental Involvement with Children's Education.* Cambridge, MA: Harvard University Press.

Roediger, David R. 1991. *The Wages of Whiteness: Race and the Making of the American Working Class.* New York: Verso.

Romero, Mary. 2011. *The Maid's Daughter: Living Inside and Outside the American Dream.* New York: New York University Press.

Romney, Lee. 2003. "Translating a Problem into a Bill." *Los Angeles Times,* July 19.

Rorabaugh, William Joseph. 1988. *The Craft Apprentice: From Franklin to the Machine Age in America.* New York: Oxford University Press.

Roth, Julius A. 1972. "Some Contingencies of the Moral Evaluation and Control of Clientele: The Case of the Hospital Emergency Service." *American Journal of Sociology* 77(5):839–56.

Ruehs, Emily. 2016. "Adventures in El Norte: Masculinity and the Immigration of Unaccompanied Minors." *Men and Masculinities* 20(3):364–84.

Saito, Leland T. 1998. *Race and Politics: Asian Americans, Latinos, and Whites in a Los Angeles Suburb.* Urbana: University of Illinois Press.

———. 2009. *The Politics of Exclusion: The Failure of Race-Neutral Policies in Urban America.* Stanford, CA: Stanford University Press.

Sanchez, George J. 1997. "Face the Nation: Race, Immigration, and the Rise of Nativism in Late Twentieth Century America." *International Migration Review* 31(4):1009–30.

Saxton, Alexander. 1971. *The Indispensable Enemy: Labor and the Anti-Chinese Movement in California.* Berkeley: University of California Press.

Schippers, Mimi. 2002. *Rockin' Out of the Box: Gender Maneuvering in Alternative Hard Rock*. New Brunswick, NJ: Rutgers University Press.

Schnittker, Jason. 2004. "Education and the Changing Shape of the Income Gradient in Health." *Journal of Health and Social Behavior* 45(3):286–305.

Sennett, Richard, and Jonathan Cobb. 1972. *The Hidden Injuries of Class*. New York: Vintage Books.

Shedd, Carla. 2015. *Unequal City: Race, Schools, and Perceptions of Injustice*. New York: Russell Sage Foundation.

Smith, Dorothy E. 1993. "The Standard North American Family: SNAF as an Ideological Code." *Journal of Family Issues* 14(1):50–65.

Smith, Robert. 2006. *Mexican New York: Transnational Lives of New Immigrants*. Berkeley: University of California Press.

Solberg, Anne. 1997. "Changing Constructions of Age for Norwegian Children." In *Constructing and Reconstructing Childhood: Contemporary Issues in the Sociological Study of Childhood*, edited by Alan Prout Allison James, 126–44. London: Routledge Falmer.

Song, Miri. 1999. *Helping Out: Children's Labor in Ethnic Businesses*. Philadelphia: Temple University Press.

Spencer, Karen Lutfey, and Matthew Grace. 2016. "Social Foundations of Health Care Inequality and Treatment Bias." *Annual Review of Sociology* 42(1):101–20.

Spencer, Steven J., Claude M. Steele, and Diane M. Quinn. 1999. "Stereotype Threat and Women's Math Performance." *Journal of Experimental Social Psychology* 35(1):4–28.

Steele, Claude M. 1997. "A Threat in the Air: How Stereotypes Shape Intellectual Identity and Performance." *American Psychologist* 52(6):613.

Swartz, Teresa Toguchi. 2009. "Intergenerational Family Relations in Adulthood: Patterns, Variations, and Implications in the Contemporary United States." *Annual Review of Sociology* 35:191–212.

Swidler, Ann. 1986. "Culture in Action: Symbols and Strategies." *American Sociological Review* 51(2): 273–86.

Taft, Jessica. 2019 *The Kids Are in Charge: Activism and Power in Peru's Movement of Working Children*. New York: New York University Press.

Takaki, Ronald T. 1989. *Strangers from a Different Shore: A History of Asian Americans*. New York: Penguin Book.

Tamayo-Sarver, Joshua H., Susan W. Hinze, Rita K. Cydulka, and David W. Baker. 2003. "Racial and Ethnic Disparities in Emergency Department Analgesic Prescription." *American Journal of Public Health* 93(12):2067–73.

Thorne, Barrie. 1993. *Gender Play: Girls and Boys in School*. New Brunswick, NJ: Rutgers University Press.

———. 2009. "'Childhood': Changing and Dissonant Meanings." *International Journal of Learning and Media* 1(1):19–27.

Thornton Dill, Bonnie 1988. "Our Mothers' Grief: Racial Ethnic Women and the Maintenance of Families." *Journal of Family History* 13(4):415–31.

Tse, Lucy. 1995. "Language Brokering among Latino Adolescents: Prevalence, Attitudes, and School Performance." *Hispanic Journal of Behavioral Science* 17: 180–93.

Traustadottir, Rannveig. 1991. "Mothers Who Care: Gender, Disability, and Family Life." *Journal of Family Issues* 12(2):211–28.

Treitler, Vilna Bashi. 2015. "Social Agency and White Supremacy in Immigration Studies." *Sociology of Race and Ethnicity* 1(1):153–65.

Tuan, Mia. 1998. *Forever Foreigners or Honorary Whites?: The Asian Ethnic Experience Today.* New Brunswick, NJ: Rutgers University Press.

US Census Bureau. 2020. "American Factfinder." www.census.us.gov. (Replaced March 31, 2020, by data.census.gov.)

Valdés, Guadalupe. 2003. *Expanding Definitions of Giftedness: The case of Young Interpreters from Immigrant Communities.* Mahwah, NJ: Erlbaum.

Valdez, Zulema. 2011. *The New Entrepreneurs: How Race, Class, and Gender Shape American Enterprise.* Stanford, CA: Stanford University Press.

Van Natta, Meredith. 2023. *Medical Legal Violence: Health Care and Immigration Enforcement against Latinx Noncitizens.* New York: New York University Press.

Valenzuela, Abel, Jr. 1999. "Gender Roles and Settlement Activities among Children and Their Immigrant Families." *American Behavioral Scientist* 42(4):720–42.

Valenzuela, Angela. 1999. *Subtractive Schooling: U.S.-Mexican Youth and the Politics of Caring.* Albany: SUNY Press.

Vallejo, Jody. 2012. *Barrios to Burbs: The Making of the Mexican Middle Class.* Stanford, CA: Stanford University Press.

Van Hook, Jennifer, and Jennifer E Glick. 2007. "Immigration and Living Arrangements: Moving beyond Economic Need versus Acculturation." *Demography* 44(2):225–49.

Vasquez-Tokos, Jessica, and Kathryn Norton-Smith. 2017. "Talking Back to Controlling Images: Latinos' Changing Responses to Racism over the Life Course." *Ethnic and Racial Studies* 40(6):912–30.

Warikoo, Natasha, and Irene Bloemraad. 2018. "Economic Americanness and Defensive Inclusion: Social Location and Young Citizens' Conceptions of National Identity." *Journal of Ethnic and Migration Studies* 44(5):736–53.

Warner, William Lloyd, and Leo Srole. 1945. *The Social Systems of American Ethnic Groups.* New Haven, CT: Yale University Press.

Watkins-Hayes, Celeste. 2009. "Race-ing the Bootstrap Climb: Black and Latino Bureaucrats in Post-Reform Welfare Offices." *Social Problems* 56(2):285–310.

Werner, Anne, and Kirsti Malterud. 2003. "It Is Hard Work Behaving as a Credible Patient: Encounters between Women with Chronic Pain and Their Doctors." *Social Science & Medicine* 57(8):1409–19.

West, Candace, and Sarah Fenstermaker. 1995. "Doing Difference." *Gender & Society* 9(1):8–37.

West, Candace, and Don H. Zimmerman. 1987. "Doing Gender." *Gender & Society* 1(2):125–51.

Williams, Raymond. 1977. *Marxism and Literature.* New York: Oxford University Press.

Williamson, Joel. 1980. *New People: Miscegenation and Mulattoes in the United States.* New York: Free Press.

Willis, Paul 1977. *Learning to Labor: How Working Class Kids Get Working Class Jobs.* New York: Columbia University Press.

Wingfield, Adia Harvey. 2010. "Are Some Emotions Marked 'Whites Only'? Racialized Feeling Rules in Professional Workplaces." *Social Problems* 57(2):251–68.

———. 2019. *Flatlining Race, Work, and Health Care in the New Economy.* Berkeley: University of California Press.

Xu, Jun, and Jennifer C. Lee. 2013. "The Marginalized 'Model' Minority: An Empirical Examination of the Racial Triangulation of Asian Americans." *Social Forces* 91:1363–97.

Yukich, Grace. 2013. "Constructing the Model Immigrant: Movement Strategy and Immigrant Deservingness in the New Sanctuary Movement." *Social Problems* 60(3):302–20.

Zelizer, Viviana A. 1985. *Pricing the Priceless Child: The Changing Social Value of Children.* Princeton, NJ: Princeton University Press.

Zinn, Maxine Baca. 1989. "Family, Race, and Poverty in the Eighties." *Signs: Journal of Women in Culture and Society* 14(4):856–74.

INDEX

African American Vernacular English, 118–19

Alba, Richard, 196n11

American Dream, 25, 94–95, 141, 158, 184, 209n5

American identity, characteristics of, 48

American myth of national origins, 139

Americanness, as Whiteness, 114

Asian Americans: bilingualism assumptions regarding, 39; citizenship exclusions regarding, 197–98n20, 198n21; controlling images regarding, 14–15; cultural anchors of, 211n41; double bind of, 24; education expectations on, 101–2, 104–5; familismo of, 205–6n7; family strategies of, 200n32; fresh off the boat (FOB) stereotype for, 113; gathering responses from, 187–91; Immigration and Nationality Act of 1965 and, 201n49; as model minorities, 196n13; racialization of, 15, 207n30; racialized nativism of, 167; statistics regarding, 23; stereotypes of, 107, 113, 197–98n20; as teachers of color, 209n34; twoness of, 167. *See also* Korean Americans

assertiveness, 176

assimilation, 9, 48, 171, 195–96n10, 196n13

avoidance strategy, 111

belonging, 10–11. *See also* citizenship; social citizenship

bilingualism, 36–40, 45

Black Americans: African American Vernacular English and, 118–19; citizenship exclusions regarding, 197n20; controlling images and, 200n43; doing difference by, 207–8n2; double consciousness of, 16–17, 167; educational inequalities of, 131; emotions of, 207–8n2; family strategies of, 200n32; in labor force, 200n43; othermothers of, 200n32; passing as "American" Whites by, 119; poverty of, 198–99n22; racial profiling of, 117–18, 208n26; stereotypes of, 128; welfare programs and, 199n22

ARTICULATIONS STUDIES IN RACE, IMMIGRATION, AND CAPITALISM

EDITORS
Cedric de Leon
Pawan Dhingra

Change is afoot in sociology and related fields. Motivated by mounting social inequality and the latest groundbreaking research, a new generation of scholars is pushing for a more synthetic and empirically rigorous approach to race, immigration, and capitalism. This book series seeks work at the intersection of these three fields. The series is a space to push forward a positive research agenda that articulates immigration, race, and capitalism together as overlapping systems that are experienced in people's everyday lives. Such studies will allow us to offer more nuanced analyses on topics such as immigrant assimilation, the pervasiveness of white supremacy, and the governing economic structures that surround all forms of discrimination. With an emphasis on sociological and qualitative work, the series will also be interested in interdisciplinary work across the social sciences and humanities, with a range of methodological approaches.

The authorized representative in the EU for product safety and compliance is:
Mare Nostrum Group
B.V Doelen 72
4831 GR Breda
The Netherlands

www.ingramcontent.com/pod-product-compliance
Lightning Source LLC
Chambersburg PA
CBHW020852270326
41928CB00006B/670